Transnational Crime, Crime Control and Security

Titles include:

Vida Bajc
Security, Surveillance and the Olympic Games (*forthcoming*)

Jennifer Fleetwood
DRUG MULES
Women in the International Cocaine Trade

Sophie Body-Gendrot
GLOBALIZATION, FEAR AND INSECURITY
The Challenges for Cities North and South

Graham Ellison and Nathan Pino (*editors*)
GLOBALIZATION, POLICE REFORM AND DEVELOPMENT
Doing It the Western Way?

Alexander Kupatadze
Organized Crime, Political Transitions and State Formation in Post-Soviet Eurasia (*forthcoming*)

Jude McCulloch and Sharon Pickering (*editors*)
BORDERS AND TRANSNATIONAL CRIME
Pre-Crime, Mobility and Serious Harm in an Age of Globalization

Georgios Papanicolaou
TRANSNATIONAL POLICING AND SEX TRAFFICKING IN SOUTHEAST EUROPE
Policing the Imperialist Chain

Leanne Weber and Sharon Pickering (*editors*)
GLOBALIZATION AND BORDERS
Death at the Global Frontier

Linda Zhao
FINANCING ILLEGAL MIGRATION
Chinese Underground Banks and Human Smuggling in New York City

Transnational Crime, Crime Control and Security
Series Standing Order ISBN 978–0–23028945–1 hardback
978–0–23028946–8 paperback
(outside North America only)

You can receive future titles in this series as they are published by placing a standing order. Please contact your bookseller or, in case of difficulty, write to us at the address below with your name and address, the title of the series and one of the ISBNs quoted above.

Customer Services Department, Macmillan Distribution Ltd, Houndmills, Basingstoke, Hampshire RG21 6XS, England

Drug Mules

Women in the International Cocaine Trade

Jennifer Fleetwood
Lecturer in Criminology, University of Leicester, UK

palgrave
macmillan

First published 2014 by
PALGRAVE MACMILLAN

Palgrave Macmillan in the UK is an imprint of Macmillan Publishers Limited, registered in England, company number 785998, of Houndmills, Basingstoke, Hampshire RG21 6XS.

Palgrave Macmillan in the US is a division of St Martin's Press LLC, 175 Fifth Avenue, New York, NY 10010.

Palgrave Macmillan is the global academic imprint of the above companies and has companies and representatives throughout the world.

Palgrave® and Macmillan® are registered trademarks in the United States, the United Kingdom, Europe and other countries

ISBN: 978–1–137–27189–1

This book is printed on paper suitable for recycling and made from fully managed and sustained forest sources. Logging, pulping and manufacturing processes are expected to conform to the environmental regulations of the country of origin.

A catalogue record for this book is available from the British Library.

A catalog record for this book is available from the Library of Congress.

Contents

Acknowledgements

I am indebted to a number of institutions and individuals for providing me with either money or a room of my own while I was working on this book. I am exceptionally fortunate to have benefited from a very long, state-funded education, and I acknowledge the support of the ESRC in particular for funding the PhD on which this book is based (1+3 studentship PTA-030–2004–00460). The Programa de Estudios de la Ciudad, Facultad Latinoamericana de Ciencias Sociales (FLACSO), Quito, Ecuador generously hosted me for most of 2006. Professor Fernando Carrión, Jorge Nuñez, Paco Garcia, Andreina Torres, and Jenny Pontón welcomed me into the academic life of the department, shared their work, and offered all manner of support during fieldwork. Doctora Leticia Rojas at the Dirección Nacional de Rehabilitación Social, Ecuador, granted research access. John Jay College of Criminal Justice, City University of New York hosted me for three months while I was writing. In Quito, Sandra Edwards was a generous host, formidable intellect, and tireless advocate for women in prison. She was an inspiration to many young scholars and is sadly missed.

Thanks are also due to the following who commented on parts of the book at various stages in its development: supervisors Angus Bancroft and Jan Webb (University of Edinburgh) and Michele Burman (University of Glasgow); Richard Curtis and Jock Young (John Jay, CUNY); Sveinung Sandberg, Lois Presser, Ali Fraser, and Karin Andersson. Many thanks to colleagues at the University of Kent for many fruitful discussions: Keith Hayward, Roger Matthews, Phil Carney, Kate O'Brien, Caroline Chatwin, Johnny Ilan, and Nayeli Urquiza Haas.

Finally, research of this kind is never possible without the collaboration and enthusiasm of respondents. I was fortunate to have the backing of tireless, generous collaborators to whom I offer my most humble, most heartfelt thanks.

1
Introduction: Cartels and Cocaine Queens

Melissa Reid and Michaella Connolly made headline news in the UK when they were arrested for attempting to smuggle 11.5 kilos of cocaine out of Peru in August 2013. Aged just 19 and 21, footage of their arrest by Peruvian authorities quickly became the focus of a media furore. Initially, media sympathetically reported families' shocked reactions and neutrally relayed the young women's claims of having been forced to carry packages of drugs (McMahon and McMenamy 2013; Strange 2013). Some went further, describing them as having been threatened at gunpoint by a one-eyed gangster known as 'The Cockney' who was part of a 'cartel' (Bucktin 2013; Evans and Couzens 2013).

Although the initial press reaction drew on tropes of the drug mule as a victim, media reports soon became skeptical. Much was made of the girls' supposed party lifestyle, and most newspapers featured photographs of them partying in Ibiza (where they were working) gleaned from Facebook. Former Conservative MP Ann Widdecombe accused the 'silly girls' of 'behaving with more self indulgence than responsibility', like so many modern celebrities (ignoring the fact that neither woman appears to have much expendable income). Widdecombe gave no credence to their claims that they had been victimised (2013).[1] Though initially sympathetic, *The Belfast Telegraph* later published this vitriolic commentary:

> If all had gone to plan, she [Connolly] would be lounging on a yacht by now, sipping champagne... She knew what she was doing when she tried to board that flight in Peru. Was she thinking about the dangers of cocaine or the countless lives it has ruined? I doubt it... She is not a shy girl, as evidenced by photos that she has posted on Facebook... Everyone in the whole sordid coke supply chain makes

> a choice when they get involved. As so did Michaella Connolly when she got involved with something that will impact on her life and that of her family for a very long time. (Sweeney 2013)[2]

Whilst the extent of media coverage was of an unusually large scale, it drew on well-worn tropes about women's involvement in drug trafficking: the innocent victim, and the knowing deceiver (Schemenauer 2013). These are worth discussing in detail as they fundamentally shape popular, political, and academic 'imaginaries' about women in drug trafficking (Young 1996).

When drug mules first came to public attention in the early 1990s, women's participation was understood solely in terms of victimisation. In the United Kingdom and the United States, reports concentrated on black and ethnic minority women mules from 'Third World' countries. For example, *The New York Times* described a mother from Haiti who was 'terrorised by thugs into strapping a pound of cocaine to her' (Clines 1993). At the same time in the UK, *The Guardian* reported on the plight of foreign national mules, highlighting multiple aspects of women's victimisation:

> The burden of bringing up a family on a low income is often the motivation for the women to get involved. Before being arrested, many were unaware of the sentences they risked from four to 14 years. Some claimed they were duped into carrying bags through airports without knowing the contents. Others were clearly implicated by swallowing scores of condom packages of drugs, any of which would have been lethal if it split. (Carvel 1990; see also Gillan 2003)

Reports about young British teenagers in the 2000s reprise the theme of violent traffickers forcing women to transport drugs (Francis 2008; Ward 2008; Sturcke 2007). Discourse about drug mules as powerless victims corresponds with historically persistent discourses about female drug users as victims: naïve and exploited, victimised by both male dealers and drug addiction (Maher 1997; Anderson 2005). It also incorporates dualisms about nationhood and gender in which women are vulnerable and require protection from the (masculine) protective state against foreign men (Schemenauer 2012; Kohn 1992; Seddon 2008). Equally, the subtype of the female mule as victim fits neatly with the political and popular image of the drug trafficker as menacing, evil, and greedy (Green 1998; Reydburd 1994; Harper et al. 2000; Schemenauer 2012). Thus, the (female) drug mule as victim and (male) trafficker as exploiter have been conceptualised according to a gendered binary in which men are knowing and threatening and women are threatened and victimised. In short, there is a tendency to think of men as the brains of the business, and women as mere bodies bodies.

In addition to the victim discourse, women's involvement has been increasingly seen as 'equal' to men's. In 2010, *The Miami Herald* declared: 'Women break through glass ceiling of drug dealing underworld' in the headline of an article describing the arrest of two women who allegedly ran drug trafficking organisations (Reyes and Guillen 2010). Sandra Ávila Beltrán (nicknamed 'The Queen of the Pacific' by the press in her native Mexico) was described as a powerful player allegedly involved in laundering millions of dollars. Angela Sanclemente, a Colombian model, was allegedly the 'queen pin' of an international drug smuggling operation that employed female models as drug mules (CNN 2010). This article refers to them as 'cocaine queens' (see also Contreras 2007; Tuckman 2007) and attributes the apparent success of women in the cocaine trade to feminism.

Apparently the struggle for gender equality has been won not only in the legal world but also in the notoriously macho criminal underworld. Whilst on the one hand journalists claimed that women were as successful as men, they were also depicted as stereotypical femmes fatales (Jewkes 2009): 'sexy', 'stylish', and 'graced with both charm and beauty' (Contreras 2007; McKinley 2010). Drawing attention to their expensive tastes in fashion appears to be an attempt to denigrate their financial power and successes in the drug trade on the one hand, and on the other presents them as a caricature of the post-feminist consumer: 'empowered', selfish, and vain (Power 2009).

This post-feminist rhetoric has gained popular credence in the UK. Tony Thompson claims that Britain's 'girl gangsters are getting ready to fight their way to the top' (Thompson 2010). Citing a diverse array of examples, from all-girl gangs named 'Girls Over Men' to Angela Sanclemente's 'all-women gang that smuggles cocaine', Thompson's message is clear: women's participation in crime is the dark side of female liberation (ibid.). These same ideas underpin Sweeney and Widdecombe's descriptions of Reid and Connolly as selfish: motivated by champagne and yachts (Sweeney 2013; Widdicombe 2013).

The idea that feminism is to blame for female offending is not new (Adler 1976; Chesney-Lind and Irwin 2008; van Wormer 2009), but it is a relatively recent development when it comes to explaining women's involvement in organised crime and drug trafficking, which have long been considered a 'man's world' (Adler 1993; Zhang et al.

2007). Nonetheless, this notion has clearly gained popular attention. Emancipation discourse appears to directly contradict long-standing victimisation discourse, yet they are both underpinned by binary notions of gender. Victimisation discourses tends to depict women as passive vessels for traffic; emancipation discourse still positions women as bodies by linking women's success in trafficking to their sexuality (Schemenauer 2012). Further, as 'vamps' and gender deviants, such discourses also serve to render them equally punishable (Fleetwood 2011; Schemenauer 2012). These discourses are not only significant in shaping popular conceptions of women drug traffickers, but are also echoed by policy makers, sentencers, and criminal justice professionals (Schemenauer 2012; Fleetwood 2011). Media discourse is particularly important given that organised crime is extremely hidden. According to Dick Hobbs 'As science fiction has been so influential in shaping our visions of alternative worlds and distant galaxies, so crime fiction, television and film mould our perspectives of the serious end of the crime spectrum' (Hobbs 1995: 1; Hobbs 2013; del Olmo 1993).

This book examines the reality beyond these gendered stereotypes and in particular seeks to unpack the relationship between gender, agency, and victimisation in the context of the international cocaine trade. As the news articles at the start of the chapter indicate, questions of women's agency and victimisation are popularly and politically salient. The same questions are also at the heart of international drug policy reform (Fleetwood and Haas 2011; UNCND 2009, 2011). Furthermore, questions about victimisation/agency and women's offending connect with contemporary debates in feminist criminology. They play a central role in research and theory on women's violence (Batchelor 2005; Chesney-Lind and Irwin 2008), drug dealing (Denton 2001; Dunlap et al. 1994; Grundetjern and Sandberg 2012; Maher 1997), and prostitution (Phoenix 2000; Agustín 2007; Matthews 1997; Benson and Matthews 1995) as well as other non-acquisitive deviant behaviour such as gang involvement (Batchelor 2011; Joe and Chesney-Lind 1995; Laidler and Hunt 2001; Morgan and Joe 1996; Miller 2001; Brotherton 1996; Young 2009). Nevertheless, these issues have not yet been examined in relation to women's participation in the international drug trade.

Recently, feminist criminologists have drawn attention to global dimensions of inequality, and the need for transnational feminist approaches (Sudbury 2004, 2005a; Reynolds, 2008; Cain 2000; Cain and Howe 2008; Renzetti 2013; Radford and Tsutsumi 2004). This book therefore seeks to extend questions about victimisation, agency, and women's offending in transnational crime by examining women's participation in drug trafficking.

Drawing on ethnographic fieldwork spanning five years, this book forefronts women's narratives to better understand their experiences as both agents and victims in the international cocaine trade. It aims to make women 'sociologically visible' (Stanley and Wise 1993) in an area where women's participation is routinely downplayed, misunderstood, and misrepresented. This book explores how and why women become involved in trafficking, and whether their participation can be understood as the result of poverty, social structural disadvantage and victimisation, or agency and choice.

This book also explores the processes surrounding trafficking drugs to consider how (or indeed if) women are disadvantaged by their gender. It focuses on the smallest scale of gender: human interaction. Doing so is necessary to be able to 'see' gender, coercion, and agency. This is not to discount the significance of large- scale social structures and geopolitics; however, as Chapter 2 demonstrates, research at this 'scale' has been problematic in accounting for the possibility of women's agency. In contrast, this book explores how individuals make sense of their worlds through narrative, and how coercion and threat come into being through social interaction.

The rest of this chapter offers a snapshot of the scale of women's participation in the international cocaine trade, before explaining why and how fieldwork was undertaken in prisons in Ecuador. This chapter concludes with a summary of the main argument and content of each chapter.

Women's participation in the international cocaine trade

Women's involvement in trafficking as mules was first noted over 30 years ago (Cloyd 1982), and there are noted examples of women undertaking leading roles for nearly 100 years (Campbell 2008; Kohn 1992; Seddon 2008). The hidden nature of the drug trade makes statistical measurement very difficult. Nonetheless, quantitative data show that although the majority of people arrested for drug trafficking are men, women comprise a significant minority. Most recently, in 2011, the United Nations Commission on Narcotic Drugs attempted to measure the scale of women's participation globally and concluded:

> Women represent about 20 per cent of drug traffickers arrested worldwide.... Whilst there is evidence of an increasing number of

drug-related crimes worldwide, the data suggest that involvement of women and girls in drug trafficking has not increased disproportionately in comparison with that of men.

Compiling such a figure is inevitably fraught with methodological problems (Fleetwood and Haas 2011; Thoumi 2005); nonetheless, this figure is close to national studies which consistently report that 20 to 30 per cent of those arrested for the importation/exportation of drugs are women (Albrecht 1996; Bjerk and Mason 2011; Dorn et al. 2008; Harper et al. 2000; Green et al. 1994; Huling 1995; Lawrence and Williams 2006; Sentencing Council 2011a; Unlu and Ekici 2012; Unlu and Evcin 2011).[3] Women's involvement is perhaps higher than might be expected given that, in general, women are much less likely to be involved in crime than their male counterparts, and tend to commit less serious crimes (Burman 2004; Gelsthorpe 2004). For example, women represent just 10 per cent of those sentenced for offences related to drug supply in England and Wales (Ministry of Justice 2012, table 1.3a).

Arrest data may under- or over-represent women (Anderson 2005). Ellie Schemenauer's research found that customs agents in the US were influenced by popular discourses about drug mules that stereotype women as victims and vamps (2012). Some women may be more likely to be arrested than others due to racial bias in profiling (Ruggiero and South 1995: 116; also Green et al. 1994: 480; Lawrence and Williams 2006; Newsome 2003). Interestingly, medical/forensic data paint a similar picture. The majority of 'body packers' seen in hospitals are male (Heinemann et al. 1998; Traub et al. 2003), although Traub et al. also note increasing demographic diversification to include pregnant women and children (2003: 2519).

Thus, all data show that the crime of carrying drugs across borders for others cannot be considered particularly 'female'. Whilst arrest data gives a useful snapshot of the scale of women's involvement, it does not indicate what women were doing when they were arrested (Harper et al. 2000; Fleetwood and Haas 2011). Whilst it seems unlikely that many of them were 'cocaine queens', it is not possible to assume that all were mules either.. Since 'drug trafficking' is ambiguously defined, arrest data will include offences such as include possession, use, growing, selling, or transport of drugs (Gottwald 2006).

Perhaps confusingly, a variety of terms have been employed by researchers to describe those arrested with drugs at international borders, such as 'drug importer' (Green et al. 1994) and 'courier' (see for example Harper et al. 2000). These terms have mainly been used to report the findings of quantitative research reflecting the legal ambiguity of trafficking and drug offences. These data probably include independent entrepreneurs and people carrying drugs for their own consumption, as well as people carrying drugs for someone else (Green 1998). Qualitative researchers have used terms like 'swallowers', 'body packers', or *boleros*, referring to the method used to smuggle cocaine (Zaitch 2002). This adds detail about the method employed, but not their role. Caulkins et al. usefully distinguish between 'self-employed couriers' and 'courier-employees' on the basis of interview data from respondents (2009).

The term 'mule' has been used to refer specifically to those employed by others to carry drugs across borders (Campbell 2008; EMCCDA 2012; Metaal and Edwards 2009; Sevigny and Caulkins 2004), however the term has derogatory connotations which are acknowledge by lawyers (such as the Working Group of the Criminal Bar Association of England and Wales 2011: 3, fn 4), professionals and academics working in this area (Harris 2011). Given that the term 'drug mule' brings with it assumptions regarding the gender, nationality, and agency of the drug carrier, many academics and campaigners in this area have used the word 'courier' as a suitable replacement (Green 1996, 1998; UNCND 2009). Whilst acknowledging that the term 'mule' has problematic connotations, the word 'courier' arguably lacks methodological clarity since the term has been used to describe drug importers broadly (for example in studies describing arrest data), rather than solely those who carry for others (mules).

I use the term 'mule' throughout this book. Firstly, it marks out a methodological and conceptual distinction: a mule is someone who carries drugs across international borders *for someone else*. This is a specific role in the cocaine trade and differs greatly from self-employed couriers (Fleetwood 2011). Secondly, respondents used the term mule (including mules, and those who had recruited, employed, and managed mules). Thirdly, I disagree that the word 'courier' is necessarily less problematic. It suggests similarities with the work of legal couriers who escort important documentation or goods internationally, a job which is ironically much in decline as a result of the proliferation of the kinds of information technology that are thought to fuel the increase in illicit traffic (Findlay 1999). 'Courier' also suggests business discourse that I problematise in the next chapter.

Despite popular notions that the number of women involved in trafficking is increasing, the reality is rather more complex. Data from the United Nations (above) carefully conclude that women's involvement 'has not increased disproportionately in comparison with that of men' (UNCND 2011), yet there is a lack of historical data to enable a meaningful analysis, as gender is not routinely recorded in seizure data (Fleetwood and Haas 2011). What is clear is that prison populations evidence a steady increase in the number of women in prison for 'drug trafficking offences' since the 1980s. This has been noted in the US and Canada (Bush-Baskette 2000, 2004; Chesney-Lind 2002; Lawrence and Williams 2006; Reynolds 2008; Sudbury 2002) and is especially apparent in Latin America. Drug offenders comprise the majority of female prisoners in Argentina (87%) (Corda 2011: 17), Peru (67%) (Soberón 2011: 79), and Costa Rica (64%) (Palma Campos 2011). Although this is especially high in Latin America, (Giacomello 2013b) it is arguably a global trend (Sudbury 2005a; Iakobishvili 2012; Bewley-Taylor et al. 2009).

In England and Wales in 2005, 1 in 5 women in prison were foreign nationals, of whom 80 per cent of were sentenced for drug trafficking offences (Joseph 2006: 156). Drug offenders comprised 35 per cent of the women's prison population in 2005, a much higher portion than in men's prisons (Joseph 2006: 146). Women imprisoned for drug offences were also disproportionately likely to be of an ethnic minority (ibid.). Foreign national women are also disproportionately represented, suggesting that many are arrested for international drug trafficking. 40 per cent of foreign national women in prison are sentenced for drug offences (Ministry of Justice 2012, table 21.1). This is a much higher rate than foreign national men (22%), British men (18%) or women (28%) (Ministry of Justice 2012, table 1.6). These high figures also reflect the harsh punishments faced by women and the use of 'mandatory minimums' in particular (Raeder 1993; Oliss 1994; Gaskins 2004; Chesney-Lind 2002).

Despite the complexities in measuring women's involvement in the international drug trade, it is clear that the number of women arrested for drug trafficking offences worldwide has long been significant (Huling 1996), and now represents a substantial aspect of women's criminalisation. The drivers behind this trend are complex, and reflect geopolitical dynamisms including the war on drugs, the rise of global capitalism, and the globalisation of gendered and raced inequalities (Diaz-Cotto 2005; Gaskins 2004; Sudbury 2005a, 2005b; Joseph 2006; Reynolds 2008).

Trends in women's imprisonment in Ecuador

The situation in prisons in Ecuador in the early 2000s reflected international trends. During fieldwork (2002–2007), drug offenders comprised 70–80 per cent of the prison population in the women's prison in Quito, Ecuador (Gallardo and Nuñez 2006; Edwards 2011). This was greater than the men's prison in Quito, where the figure was around 58 per cent (Gallardo and Nuñez 2006). Overall, 23 per cent of the female prison population were foreign nationals, of which the overwhelming majority (90%) were drug offenders (Edwards 2011:56). These figures are not solely a reflection of the scale of women's participation in drug trafficking, but are strongly related to drug war politics in the region, and especially harsh punishments (Bergman and Azaola 2007; Pontón and Torres 2007; Edwards 2003; Edwards 2011). Since the early 1990s, Ecuador has had some of the longest sentences for drug trafficking in the entire continent, including the US (Edwards 2003). In 2003, Congress raised the mandatory minimum sentence to twelve years (ibid.).[4]

In the early 2000s, international politics agreements encouraged a 'logic of quantification' (Edwards 2003) whereby arrests of drug traffickers were required to meet internationally set targets. In 2005 the United States and Ecuador 'signed a bilateral agreement which stipulated that for an investment of $15.7 million in the security of the country, they [the US] demanded a 12 per cent increase in the capturing and processing of narco-traffickers and a 10 per cent increase in the capture of drugs in relation to the year 2004' (Pontón and Torres 2007: 64, my translation).[5]

This agreement explicitly targeted and criminalised not only drugs, but people, too. Whilst operations targeting large-scale operations (such as increasing surveillance in shipping containers) were also underway (UNOCD 2009), such efforts inevitably yield lower numbers of arrests compared to the investment involved. In the context of the bilateral treaty, drug mules, street dealers, and even users were arrested and imprisoned – even though drug use was decriminalised in 1998 (Pontón and Torres 2007: 63, fn 19; Edwards 2003).

As such, the Ecuadorian prison estate was arguably the product of a transnational exportation of anti-drug politics and policies (Norton-Hawk 2010). This presented an opportunity and challenge for research. Local academics at the Latin American Faculty of Social Sciences (FLACSO) documented these changes as part of their project 'Prison in Ecuador: daily life, power relations and public policies'[6] conducted by the Urban Studies program (Camacho 2007; Carrión 2007; Flores Aguirre 2007; Herrera 2005; Nuñez 2006a, 2006b, 2007; Pontón 2008; Pontón and Torres 2007; Torres 2006, 2008).

Getting into prison: a biographical account

Neither stereotype (manipulated mule or cocaine queen) adequately describes the women that I met while undertaking research for this book.

I first visited prisons in Ecuador in 2002. Like many backpackers (I was in Quito learning Spanish), I visited one of the many foreign nationals imprisoned for drug trafficking. Getting in was surprisingly straightforward: all that was needed was formal identification (such as a passport) and the name of the prisoner to be visited.[7] I was not prepared for the poor conditions in which inmates lived, or for inmates' enthusiasm for showing me around and telling me about themselves and about how they came to be in prison.

This chance encounter turned into a series of fieldwork 're-visits' over a five-year period (Burawoy 2000). No formal institutional ethical review procedures were in place, and I undertook a quick piece of exploratory research into women in the drug trade for my undergraduate dissertation. At the time, it seemed like 'this was a piece of research just waiting to be done' (Winlow 2001: 12). The majority of data on which this book is based were collected during one period of fieldwork lasting sixteen months (in 2005–2006), during which I spent about four days a week in prison. During fieldwork, I joined a team of researchers at the Latin American Faculty of Social Sciences, (FLACSO), who negotiated the extensive access to prison necessary for undertaking ethnographic fieldwork.

Although working in a closed institution shaped this research in significant ways (described in more detail in Chapter 3), the ethnographic methods employed had much in common with ethnography on the 'outside' (for example Maher 1997; Skeggs 1994, 1995). With the encouragement of a small number of foreigners who acted as gatekeepers, I hung out, got to know people, and immersed myself in the daily goings on in the women's prison and two men's prisons. This on-going commitment to being present enabled me to undertake participant observation and eventually, after many months gaining trust, interviews. I sought to encourage participants 'to explore purposefully, with the researcher the meanings they place on events in their worlds' (Heyl 2001: 369).

For example, I interviewed one respondent, Paula, several times throughout the course of her imprisonment: when she first arrived, during her imprisonment, and after, when she was on parole. This allowed her to reflect on how she interpreted her experiences differently in relation to her current experiences and issues (more on this in Chapter 3). Where possible, this research was 'respondent directive' (Smith and Wincup 2000: 342). I formally interviewed 31 people imprisoned for drug trafficking offences: a mixture of women and men, mules, middlemen, recruiters and investors, and had informal conversations with many more.

Building and maintaining a presence in the field was time consuming; entering the lives of respondents and having them enter mine was at times exhausting.[8] Although it was tempting to 'get in, get the information and get out...there are no shortcuts to or through women's [or men's] lives. Ethnography is a messy business and nowhere more so than when it seeks to traverse race, class and cultural boundaries' (Maher 1997: 232–233). In addition, this research is informed by narrative analysis and so could be described as a 'narrative ethnography' (Gubrium and Holstein 2008).

Researching drug trafficking in prison: problems and possibilities

It has long been assumed that genuine qualitative research about crime and criminals cannot be done with an imprisoned population: as a group they are not representative and as individuals they lie (Polsky 1985). This is an important criticism that must be addressed. The first justification for researching drug trafficking from prison is that there is a lack of a viable alternative. Given that drug trafficking does not take place in a fixed geographical location but is a loose network spanning continents (Dorn et al. 1992: 201), observing trafficking first-hand is neither especially practical nor safe.[9] Previous ethnographies on drug trafficking have been conducted at a distance from the transnational movement of drugs (Adler 1993; Zaitch 2002).

Patricia Adler's *Wheeling and Dealing* is based on ethnographic participant observation with a group of drug importers and wholesalers in Southern California in the late 1970s (1993). In this instance (and in Zaitch's research), trafficking overlapped with subculture: there was a palpable, geographically embedded social phenomenon to be studied. Although Adler's research says much about drug trafficking subculture, her account relies heavily on respondents' descriptions and explanations about trafficking. She also comments that drug trafficking took up very little of the drug traffickers' time, which made it difficult to observe (ibid.).

Zaitch's ethnographic research involved prolonged immersion with Colombian immigrants in the Netherlands, and two long visits to Colombia (2002). This kind of long-term cultural immersion is demanding and produces rich, detailed data. Like Adler, he relied on respondents' accounts of trafficking rather than observations. This was especially the case for boleros (mules who swallow 'balls' of cocaine). He also noted that mules tended not to be directly involved with trafficking groups, but were often recruited specifically because they did not have a criminal record, were well-travelled, employed, and had a passport (2002). Similarly, drug mules who participated in my research were not usually connected with subcultures or social groups relating to trafficking and may not have necessarily been reached through ethnographic immersion with traffickers.

Lastly, although most traffickers do not get caught, some do (sometimes more than once). Interviewing arrested traffickers produced data that could not have been obtained otherwise. For example, it was only when they were arrested that mules discovered that they were carrying different drugs or larger quantities than they had agreed.

Prisons may actually be a good site from which to research drug trafficking. Given that trafficking appears to be happen everywhere and nowhere, doing research is not simply a case of 'getting out of our offices onto the street' (Chambliss 1979; Hobbs 1995: 3). Prison is a tried and tested locale for locating traffickers and the majority of research on drug traffickers (and mules) has been conducted in prison (Caulkins et al. 2009; Dorado 2005; Sudbury 2005b; Huling 1996; Pearson and Hobbs 2003; Reuter and Haaga 1989; del Olmo 1986; Matrix Knowledge Group 2007; Desroches 2005; Decker and Chapman 2008). Furthermore, during fieldwork it became clear that prisons are part of the networks and flows of drug trafficking, rather than simply standing apart from it. Imprisonment did not stop those in the middle or upper levels from continuing to be involved in traffic. It was also a place from which traffickers could extend their expertise and web of contacts. As such, prison can be considered a 'hub' at which transnational drug trafficking networks/flows converge (Urry 2000). This was especially the case in Ecuadorian prisons since they hosted a particularly high concentration of traffickers (as described above). This was partly due to its geographic location: although cocaine is not produced in Ecuador, it was a strategic transit route for drugs to all over the globe (Rivera 2005). Prisons in Quito hosted traffickers from all over South America, North America, all corners of Europe, the Middle East, and Southeast Asia. This broad variety of international populations hints at the significance of Ecuador in international trafficking routes and networks. It also offers a unique opportunity to study the international drug trade from many national viewpoints.

'Wasn't it dangerous? How did you get them to speak to you?'

I am often asked: 'How did you get them to speak to you? Wasn't it dangerous?' (see also Jacobs 2006: 157), a question all the more salient because of being female, white, Scottish, and quite young, at least when the research began (See also Piacentini 2004). I was often asked what a nice girl like me was doing in prison (by both academics and prisoners!). Such concerns are largely fuelled by popular stereotypes that all good researchers have a duty to interrogate (Sluka 1995). The subject of risk to the researcher is rarely discussed in the methodology textbooks, or even by researchers themselves (Lee 1995; Sluka 1995).[10] Unfortunately, there is not the space to discuss in detail, but in brief, I found that ethnography demands understanding local concerns and practices and so is invaluable for judging situations and keeping safe in the field (Williams et al. 1992: 344).

Although prison was a dangerous place for inmates, visitors were almost always welcomed, and women had a privileged status. Although conducting ethnography in the men's prison (as a solo woman) might seem particularly risky, I was not the only one to do so. Margarita Camacho, an artist and anthropologist, undertook an ethnography of transvestites (2007). As women and as interested friends, writers, and witnesses to the brutal conditions of imprisonment, we were perhaps treated with a reverence that other visitors were not.[11]

Most research on trafficking/traffickers in prison relies on intermediaries such as prison guards, directors, and psychologists (Decker and Chapman 2008; Desroches 2005, 2007; Dorn et al. 1992; Reuter and Haaga 1989). In contrast, I had the kind of 'full and unaccompanied access' that is rare in prison research (Crewe 2006: 349) which enabled me to 'hang out' extensively and negotiate interviews with respondents directly and sensitively. In the main, respondents participated in research enthusiastically, and although I cannot say exactly why, I suspect that the amount of time I was involved in the prisons allowed me to gain trust.

Furthermore, the position of the researcher can be a privileged one: 'where others fear or ignore them or want to lock them up, you're trying to tell their story' (Jacobs 2006: 160). The isolation of prison could be overwhelming for respondents at times. More than one inmate commented that imprisonment was like being buried alive. Wacquant describes prisons in the United States as 'humungous human storehouses': 'a safe for men buried alive far away from societies' eyes, ears and minds' (2002: 373). Birkbeck notes that imprisonment in Latin America is distinct and is better considered as internment (2011).

For many men and women in prison (and foreign nationals in particular), I was the only woman who visited them during their imprisonment. In both prisons, I was a distraction from the boredom and monotony, a listening ear and confidante, a reminder of home and someone to be relied on in an emergency. One female respondent commented: 'You've got to be visited; you've got to be seen and heard.' Some inmates had no interest in me personally and little to gain through being seen talking to an 'outsider'. Some studiously avoided me, or bluntly said they were not interested in 'nosy kids', but in the main, respondents welcomed me with unexpected generosity of time and spirit. They gave me endless cups of tea and coffee, stole cigarettes, and shared their gossip, stories, and hopes for the future. Some respondents organised meetings with prison directors to allow me to take in a tape recorder, and even hosted a visit from my supervisor, Dr Angus Bancroft. They were quick to tell me when I got things wrong or right, for which I remain extremely grateful.

Research wasn't always straightforward but was not as difficult or as dangerous as might have been expected. Indeed: 'most difficulties that one meets and solves in doing field research on criminals are simply the difficulties one meets and solves doing field research' (Polsky 1985: 119).

Chapter outline

The central argument of this book is that women's involvement in the international cocaine trade cannot be adequately understood through the lens of either victimhood or volition. Chapter 2 reviews previous research and demonstrates that common conceptualisations of the drug trade draw on problematic binaries of structure and agency that are also profoundly gendered. In other words, men's participation has been generally assumed to be rational and intentional, whereas women's has been understood through the lens of exploitation and victimisation. Although this is not the first piece of research to examine women in the drug trade, it is the first to critically explore the role of gender and victimisation. This book draws on narrative theory to understand structure/agency in women's offending. A short outline of its usefulness for understanding structure/agency can be found at the end of Chapter 2.

Due to the transnational, hidden nature of the international drug trade, the only practical way to access women's experiences (and to understand the work done by mules more generally) is through individuals' narratives. Interpreting them is complex, however. Chapter 3 draws on ethnographic participation and observations in prison to explore the circumstances under which women constructed narratives about their involvement in drug trafficking. It shows that women negotiated complex demands for them to both give an account, and to stay silent. Some kinds of discourses and speakers received popular support, whilst others did not. Chapter 3 also describes the methods employed in eliciting and probing respondents' accounts.

Chapter 5 draws on narrative theory to explore women's motives for offending. Interpreting their narratives *as narrative* offers the opportunity to understand the connection between individual meaning-making through narrative and participation in crime. Women's narratives centred on poverty, money, mothering, and relationships; however, other themes were also present including escape, opportunity, and excitement. In contrast to prior research, this chapter explores the role of both objective, material circumstances and women's subject positions in relation to dominant discourses about women/gender.

Chapter 4 addresses a gap in the existing research: how women are connected to the international drug trade. This chapter approaches the drug trade as a phenomenon comprised of social relationships between people (rather than an illegal enterprise comprised of business connections), and explores the gendered nature of trafficking connections and contacts, revealing that women's and men's pathways into mule work are distinct and gendered. Nonetheless, the relationship between gender, power, and exploitation is more complex than previous research has suggested.

The second half focuses on the role of gender in the workings of the international cocaine trade, focussing on processes surrounding mules. Chapters 6, 7, and 8 examine the work undertaken by mules of both genders, along with interviews with recruiters and managers. Contextualising women's experience within wider practices of the drug trade makes it possible to disentangle gender and agency/victimisation. The work of the mule is characterised by a lack of opportunities for decision-making, or control over one's actions. International travel (or rather, being outside of one's usual social milieu) served to make mules more isolated and more vulnerable. Mules had so little control over their labour that in fact gender had much less significance than might have been expected. Indeed, the most effective resource for gaining control was social capital, which women were more likely to have since they were connected through boyfriends or close friends.

This book shows that women play an important role in the international cocaine trade and have much to say about it. The drug trade is gendered, yet the importance of gender plays out in a variety of ways vis-à-vis agency. Popular imaginaries of the trade which rely on gendered binaries of men/women, agent/victim are not borne out in empirical research. Most women's narratives about becoming involved revealed a mixture of compulsion, obligation, and willing. Employing narrative approaches reveals that women's choices were not solely limited by material social structures (poverty, single parenthood, etc.), but also by women's sense of self *as women*. In other words, being parents, girlfriends, wives, and daughters shaped their narratives for involvement. Thus social structures play out in women's material circumstances, and also in their on-going narrative sense of self, which was structured by cultural stories about what women ought to do and be like. Thus, narrative theory offers new tools for thinking about how women's offending is a response to, and engagement with both material and ideological inequalities.

Furthermore, agency was contingent upon emerging situations. As women travelled as mules, they found themselves in increasingly constrained circumstances. Indeed, once mules left home, they were virtually compelled to carry drugs. Thus, women who began as agents could find themselves in circumstances with very little choice or control over their actions. This was not only the case for women, but also for men. Thus, drug mules can neither be considered as agents or victims in any absolute way. Rather it is the case that the role of carrying drugs across international borders (or mule-work, for short) is one characterised by lack of control or choice. Having stepped into that role, it was nearly impossible to step out again. The central argument of this book is therefore that agency and victimisation are context-specific and contingent, rather than absolute.

2
Imagining Drug Trafficking: Mafias, Markets, Mules

Introduction

Twenty years ago, Venezuelan criminologist Rosa del Olmo noted that 'discourses corresponding to specific economic and political interests have masked the true nature and dynamic of the drug issue by casting it in semi-mythical terms' (1993: 1). Indeed, 'trafficking can be portrayed in a variety of ways, depending on the techniques and interests of those accredited to speak on the subject: the enforcement agencies, media, politicians and sometimes, criminologists' (Dorn et al. 1992: 201).

Following attacks on the World Trade Centre on the 11 September 2001, the link between drug trafficking, organised crime, and terrorism emerged as an important new research agenda (Levi 2007; Wright 2006). At the time of writing (in 2013), the most recent report on organised crime highlighted the financial cost to the UK, adding fraud and money laundering to the list (Her Majesty's Government 2011); perhaps no coincidence at a time when the deficit and government cuts are consistently in the headlines. Clearly, the intensity and nature of the threat posed by drug trafficking can be played up or down, or skewed according to current political climates and/or budget restraints (Dorn et al. 1992). Political priorities shape research directly through agenda setting (Home Office 2011; Her Majesty's Government 2011) and funding, but also indirectly by shaping how the drug trade is conceptualised. Attempts to quantify the trade are no less problematic. Francisco Thoumi notes that quantitative research too often plays the 'numbers game': summing up the value of the international cocaine trade in figures (often a single figure) to concretely confirm its size and importance (Thoumi 2002, 2005).

Describing the international cocaine trade, the subject of this research, is therefore fraught with difficulty. With this in mind, I only need to re-state here what is undisputable: the cocaine trade is significant in size, range, and effects. All of the world's cocaine is produced in Latin America. Coca is grown in Colombia, Bolivia and Peru (EMCCDA 2010; Fukumi 2008; Gootenberg 1999; UNODC 2012; Zaitch 2002, 2003). Most is processed at its source; however, some is made into cocaine in neighbouring countries such as Ecuador, Venezuela, and Brazil (Youngers and Rosin 2005; UNODC 2012). Most cocaine is exported from the continent to the US and Western/Central Europe, sometimes via transit countries in the Caribbean and West Africa (UNODC 2012; Zaitch 2003), although this is subject to change from year to year. Cocaine can now be found in most industrialised nations and in many developing ones (UNODC 2008, 2012; Zaitch 2003). Although the majority is transported in large shipments, a small percentage (around 15 per cent) will be transported via air by mules and couriers. Despite global efforts to curb trafficking in cocaine, all available data suggests that the international cocaine remains buoyant (Barham et al. 2003; Coomber 2006; UNODC 2012). Furthermore, a small amount of heroin is also produced in Colombia and Mexico, mostly destined for the US (Bagley and Walker 1994; Bagley 2012; UNODC 2012).

Explaining why the international cocaine trade is shaped as it is is beyond the scope of this book. Colonial histories, economic neoliberal globalisation, relative strength of states, and international migration all play a role in shaping the trade (although cause and effect are blurry) (Bagley 2012; Bancroft 2009; Kleemans and van de Bunt 1999; Klein 2008; Madsen 2009; Marez 2004; Zaitch 2002), as does demand (Costa 2008).[1] Equally, researchers have drawn attention to the significance of prohibition (Klein 2008). According to Findlay, 'without criminalisation, the profit motive behind drug trafficking would not be insured'; without prohibition there is no illicit drug trade and there are no traffickers (1999: 103).

This chapter traces the recent history of drug war discourse and shows that trafficking has been conceptualised according to a gendered 'binary logic of representation' (Young 1996) that renders women's participation unintentional and passive. The international drug trade has been conceptualised in two main ways: firstly as a 'war' waged on a foreign enemy, and secondly as an illicit business/enterprise. Both discourses bring with them assumptions about what is (and is not) worth knowing about drug trafficking. These assumptions have shaped the kinds of research undertaken and have contributed to a lack of attention to gender and women's participation in drug trafficking. This chapter therefore offers a 'feminist critique' of research about drug trafficking (Heidensohn 1968; Smart 1977, 1979).[2]

The second half of this chapter examines the small body of research on women's participation in international drug trafficking and considers the dominant explanations for women's involvement in trafficking as mules. Whilst this research has made important advances, I argue that it has tended to reinforce gendered dualisms in the way that trafficking has been conceptualised. Finally, I propose that narrative analysis may offer a way to move forward.

The war on drugs: creating a 'suitable enemy'

The international drug trade emerged in the early 1970s in its current form (Zaitch 2002; Bancroft 2009), following the 1961 United Nations Convention on Drugs and paralleling technological changes, which have increased mobility of people and goods around the globe (Urry 2003; Beck 1999). Contemporary notions of the 'drug trafficker' were crystallised in their current form in the 1980s when Reagan declared 'war' on drugs (Coomber 2006; Green 1998; del Olmo 1996; Zaitch 2002). He defined the threat posed by cocaine as 'an urgent matter of national security' (del Olmo 1996: 33), and so the 'war' was directed both discursively and literally against an 'external enemy' or 'alien threat' (Agozino 2000; Hobbs 1998, 2001; Fukumi 2008). This premise shaped (and continues to shape) political anti-drug discourse in the US (del Olmo 1996: 36), the UK, and beyond (Sudbury 2002: 65). The French blame the Russians; the British blame everyone from 'the threat in the East' to the Jamaicans, Chinese, Colombians, Turks, and Italians (Hobbs 1998: 407–408; 2013).[3]

Green contends that 'blaming ethnic minorities is central to western strategies of drug control' (1998: 16–17). This is not confined to Western Europe and North America but is replicated around the world. In Argentina, the influx of heroin was attributed to Turkish immigrants (Rossi 2007) as it is in Germany (Albrecht 1996). In the Philippines (and Southeast Asia), 'Ethnic Chinese' are blamed for methamphetamine and West Africans for cocaine (Martel 2013). In Ecuador, drug problems are often attributed to neighbouring Colombia (Rivera 2005).

Reaganite drug war discourse linked drug trafficking with other forms of 'foreign' organised crime, and in particular with foreign mafias (Russian and American), the Italian Cosa Nostra, Chinese triads, and Colombian cartels (Green 1998: 17; see also Reydburd 1994; Boyd 2007). Associating drug trafficking with organised crime borrows notions about organised crime as top-down, unified, secretive, and threatening (Woodiwiss and Hobbs 2009), even though drug trafficking is arguably not in fact particularly well organised (Dorn et al. 2005; Reuter 1983; Kenney 2007). This kind of discourse also associated drug traffickers with the notion of the ruthless, hyper-masculine Mafioso boss:

> One of the linguistic legacies of the 1980s was the transformation of the 'drug trafficker' into an ideological cue, a shorthand reference encompassing the menace, evil, greed, depravity and corruption (moral financial and political) required to ease the passage of repressive anti-drug legislation and policies. (Green 1998: 78)

Since the legitimacy of the war on drugs depended on the construction of a 'suitable enemy' (Christie 1994), portraying traffickers in this way legitimised (morally and practically) a response to the threat of drugs that was similarly armed, militarised, centralised, and secretive (Dorn et al. 1992). The characterisation of the drug trafficker as foreign, armed and organised, has prevailed partly due to political power and 'discursive usefulness' (Findlay 1999: 50). Desroches notes that depicting drug trafficking as 'organised crime' in this way 'has long been popular with journalists, law enforcement, some academics and has been endorsed by several governmental investigations and enquiries' (2005: 35).

Although recently there has been a renewed move to make users responsible for the drug trade (Costa 2008), the stereotype of the drug trafficker as 'Mr Big' can still be found in government documents. For example, a recent press release about new sentencing guidelines for drug offences draws on discourses about 'drug barons' (Sentencing Council 2011b).

Women in the war on drugs

> When a woman commits a crime and does it with a man, we focus our attention on the man because we think he was the instigator... Perhaps this is due to a patriarchal vision that keeps us from seeing women in a role we consider purely male... I am not aware of any studies of criminal women in Argentina. Crime is a man's game. We leave you [women] the role of victim. (Federal Judge in Argentina, cited by Rossi 2007: 163)

Women's presence in the drug trade has been conceptualised according to a 'binary logic of representation. Oppositional terms (man/woman, white/black, rational/irrational, mind/body) and so on are constructed in a system of value which makes one visible and the other invisible.'

(Young 1996: 1) While drug trade participants had been seen as serious, rational criminals, conversely women's participation was accommodated within the same discourses by framing it as the exact opposite: insignificant, futile, and even unintentional.

Although the target of the drug war was implicitly male, a significant number of women have been imprisoned for drug trafficking offences globally. Researchers have described this as an unintended consequence of anti-drug policies. Dorn is typical: 'one of the *by products* of the anti-trafficker push of the 1980's has been the number of women *caught up* in the drug enforcement effort' (Dorn et al. 1992: 189, my emphasis). Women have various been referred to as 'prisoners of war' (Huling 1995), or 'collateral damage' (Norton-Hawk 2010). This tendency seems to be based on an assumption that women are not the proper targets of crime control because (within this binary logic) they cannot be real criminals. Similarly, women's involvement in the drug trade has often been depicted in passive terms. For example Dean et al. start their book *Policing Illegal Business Entrepreneurs* with accounts of three women imprisoned after unknowingly carrying drugs (2010). They are young, Swedish, decent, and middle class; one is even a theology student. Their passive involvement in trafficking is employed to demonstrate drug traffickers' ruthlessness:

> The great tragedy is that *ensnared victims* like these young women can be anyone's daughters. They could be a politician's daughter, a police officer's daughter, or a grocer's daughter. Organized criminals don't care who they use or abuse to make profits. (Dean et al. 2010: 3, my emphasis)

Similarly:

> Women are increasingly *drawn into* the narcotics trade as smugglers. It has been found that a great deal of the smuggling in central Asia is done by women who are forced or paid to do so. It has also become a common strategy to sacrifice female traffickers carrying small amounts of narcotics to get larger shipments though. If women are drawn into the narcotics business, either as users or traffickers, the consequences will be devastating for their family structures, and children. (Swanstrom 2007: 12, my emphasis)

Women's involvement is thus employed to shore up dominant discourses about the barbarity of foreign, male traffickers. In the first, the ruthless 'foreign' trafficker is pitched against an idealised vision of middle class, domestic, national femininity: young women are *ensnared victims*. The implication is therefore that fighting foreign traffickers is necessary to protect women and the nation (see also Schemenauer 2012). This kind of discourse echoes early twentieth century concerns about the vulnerability of young women to foreign opium smokers and drug pushers (Kohn 1992; Seddon 2008). In the second, the consequences of 'Asian' women's involvement are also considered in local, rather than global, terms as damage to family and community. In both, women's involvement is depicted as not 'real' trafficking. In the first, women carry drugs unknowingly; in the second, they are set up to be arrested while the 'real' smuggling goes on. In both examples above, women's involvement is described in brief, with little empirical evidence presented to support these claims.

Overall, research on drug trafficking tends to pay little attention to women. At the same time, a separate stream of research has developed focussing on drug mules, and in particular on Jamaican, West African, and Latin-American women imprisoned in the US, the UK, and Spain (Dorado 2005; Heaven 1996; Sudbury 2005b; Prison Reform Trust and Hibiscus/FPWP 2012; Marshall and Moreton 2011). This stream of research has been partly driven by charitable concerns about rapidly rising numbers of women imprisoned far from home. For example, Tracy Huling's early research was the result of an invitation from chaplains working in Rikers Island, New York, (Huling 1995, 1996). Whilst raising awareness about the profile of women imprisoned abroad face was and continues to be necessary, research in this vein has tended to reproduce dominant gender/agency binaries. Despite the fact that most drug mules are men (see the previous chapter), research on mules tends to focus exclusively on women. Furthermore, researchers also tend to describe women in terms of their poverty and victimisation. For example, Huling describes female mules as doubly victimised: 'once by the drug dealer and again by the law ... it is obvious that the poor and unfortunate women of Jamaica have become yet another cheap and expendable labour in the deal' (1996: 57).[4]

By appealing to dominant gender ideology, women's involvement in drug trafficking can be discursively transformed from deviant to 'inoffensive' (Torres 2008). Women's involvement in the drug trade has been effectively 'subtyped' (Harper et al. 2000: 105). Sub-typing maintains the stereotype of the dominant group (the trafficker) by dissociating deviant cases (vulnerable women) (ibid). This can be seen in the way that the stereotype of the poor Jamaican woman who swallows capsules of cocaine under circumstances of duress has become standard fare in the press (Boseley and Radford 1992; Carvel 1990; Gillan 2003). It is also invoked in academic writing, as the examples above suggest. At worst, the subordination of women as mules is understood as an inevitable effect of gendered inequality: 'overall, the position of women in the drug underworld does not differ from the position of women in general: blocked in criminal careers as they are in legal ones.' (Ruggiero and South 1995:141) In short, 'the politically sedative myth of women's compliance and harmlessness can be conveniently preserved' (Allen 1998: 63). Doing so inadvertently reinforces the myth of trafficker as exploiter.

Women's participation in the international drug trade has become synonymous with drug mules and vice versa. This gender/agency binary tends to obscure that which does not fit neatly, such as women in any capacity entailing agency, or men who have been exploited. Qualitative research on drug mules has paid little attention to men as mules, and has generally described women mules from the global south (see for example Dorado 2005; Huling 1996; del Olmo 1986; Sudbury 2005b). Whilst it is true that women are present in drug trafficking arrest statistics in greater numbers than is typically the case for female offenders (Green et al. 1994), the overwhelming majority of those arrested at international borders with illegal drugs are men (Green et al. 1994; Albrecht 1996; Sentencing Council 2011a; UNCND 2011).

An important exception is Penny Green's research, which presents an interesting case study of men and women from Nigeria arrested for trafficking in the UK (1991). Her later research (1998) also looks at men and women mules, as well as professional traffickers. Although her research is not about gender and victimisation, she presents a number of interesting case studies that do not fit common assumptions about gender and agency. Most recently, Howard Campbell's research on women in the international drug trade in Juarez/El Paso is the first research to demonstrate that women can and do occupy positions of power in the drug trade, albeit rarely (2008).

Drug trafficking as illegal enterprise

> Drug trafficking is no longer considered only as a 'criminal activity' but rather as a 'commodity trade conducted by trans-national consortiums' that are able to operate successfully only by interacting with and blending into already established legitimate markets. Moreover, the drug business is compared to a modern multinational corporation

> with the necessary ingredients to conduct successful international enterprise, such as global reach and a creative, flexible organisational structure (del Olmo 1996: 42).

The 1990s saw a shift in the dominant discourse about drug trafficking towards seeing it as a business, especially in politics (del Olmo 1996). McIllwain argues that this change reflects the influence of economics on the study of organised crime from the 1980s onwards (2000), but arguably this also relates to the influence of neoliberal doxa on crime control (Wacquant 1999; Newburn 2002; Fleetwood 2011). The metaphor of the market is a common one in contemporary research. Drug crime is seen as a form of 'enterprise' (Edwards and Gill 2002; Desroches 2007) and as 'business' (Wright 2006; Dean et al. 2010; Smith 1994). Although Wright makes clear that legitimate and illegitimate businesses differ, his analysis nonetheless explores trafficking using the terminology of legitimate business such as 'enterprise', 'transaction costs', 'profitability', and so on (2006: 60). Readers may well respond that the drug trade simply *is* a market. There are indeed buyers and sellers, and prices may fluctuate in response to supply and demand (see, for example, Wilson and Stevens 2008). Yet what exactly a 'market' is, is not clear and the use of the term does not necessarily add conceptual clarity (Murji 2007; Ritter 2006). Furthermore, the fact that the drug trade was previously understood not as a market but as a security threat, hints at the social construction of the phenomenon. Indeed, these two approaches are not mutually exclusive. Fukumi's analysis demonstrates that US policy framed drug trafficking as a matter of 'national security' and potential harms included damage to the economy, moral values, and regional security, while the EU framed the issue as a social security threat, focussing instead on the potential spread of infectious diseases and violence (2008). These distinctions are subtle but play a vital role in legitimating divergent policy reactions.

There is no denying that the metaphor of the market is a useful one. Rather than simply assuming that traffickers are necessarily ruthless, it draws attention to the fact that drug traffickers may make reasonable, rational assessments about risk and profit (these are evident in interviews with traffickers in Chapters 6–8 of this book). It also draws attention to the significance of demand in driving production. Nonetheless, it brings with it a set of assumptions about what the 'problem' is, framing valid research questions as: 'how it works, the routes and methods used to supply the market, the size of the market itself, how the trade reacts to interventions and who the key players are' (Browne et al. 2003; see also Dean et al. 2010; Matrix Knowledge Group 2007; Home Office 2011).

These types of questions justify approaching the drug trade as if it is not comprised of people but of a series of automatic processes. One effect of this is to marginalise questions about gender and exploitation.

The metaphor of the market is also connected with a general tendency away from empirical research on/with/about traffickers. For example, the effects of intervention can be monitored indirectly through indicators such as price and purity, making research with traffickers redundant (UNODC 2012). Secondary sources such as phone taps (Natarajan 1998, 2000), trafficker autobiographies (Morselli 2001), or psychological deduction (Bovenkerk 2000) are used instead. Such innovation is arguably necessary since researching the international cocaine trade is fraught with difficulties: 'by their very nature – clandestine, illegal and highly demonized – drug markets and those that inhabit them are relatively hard to access and comparatively difficult to research' (Coomber 2007:1). Arguably, 'lack of evidence is simply down to the illicit and by nature, elusive context in which the activity takes place' (Browne et al. 2003: 326). Whilst this may be the case, perhaps this has become a self-fulfilling prophecy since few researchers have tried. Furthermore, data gleaned from secondary sources may say more about crime control than about criminal behaviours (Von Lampe 2011).

As a result of conceiving international drug trafficking as dangerous, then as a market, research with drug traffickers has been largely limited to arrested/imprisoned populations (Caulkins et al. 2009; Decker and Chapman 2008; Desroches 2005; Matrix Knowledge Group 2007; Pearson and Hobbs 2003; Reuter and Haaga 1989; Sevigny and Caulkins 2004). This research typically relies on one-off interviews with imprisoned traffickers in which the interviewer elicits information about the nature and functioning of the drug trafficking industry during a period of up to four hours (most recently Matrix Knowledge Group 2007; Caulkins et al. 2009). Traffickers are treated as experts about 'the market' from their privileged position at the top (see, for example, Desroches 2005; Decker and Chapman 2008).

Women in the 'market'

The 'drug trafficking as enterprise' paradigm has a tendency to exclude gender. Terms such as 'drug traffickers', 'offenders', and 'respondents' present an apparently gender-neutral account, but close attention to methodological notes reveals that women are mostly absent from the rare research that involves speaking to traffickers. Reuter and Haaga cite 'logistical reasons' since 'women make up only 7 per cent of drug offenders in federal prisons' (1989: 24). Desroches searched for high-level female traffickers to take part in his research but found none. His searches of the case files of the Royal Canadian Mounted Police revealed no evidence of women's participation (personal communication). Decker and Chapman only interviewed men, although their own data demonstrates that women comprise 8 per cent of high-level drug smugglers in federal prison (2008: 184, Appendix 2).

This is not bad research, per se. There may be good practical or ideological reasons for researching only one gender. However, the rationale is rarely made explicit, and the absence of women is rarely noted.[5] Despite the apparent neutrality of the economic approach, 'an enterprise model of crime as economy more often than not concedes to popular mythologies about organised crime and the threat it poses' (Findlay 1999: 223). By side-lining gender, stereotypes of evil trafficker/exploited mule are left unquestioned.

Research premised on the metaphor of the market is underpinned by the assumption that (male) traffickers run their illegal business according to rational principles (Cornish and Clarke 1986). Desroches makes these assumptions explicit:

> Rational choice theory is applicable to an understanding of drug trafficking since it considers the dealer's perspective in order to understand motives, modus operandi and decision-making. Offenders are viewed as instrumentally rational actors who choose specific behaviours that will maximise benefits while minimising costs. Crime is chosen as a rational means that offenders believe will be the most effective way to achieve their goals. The expected utility model in economics... views offenders as no different from other citizens who select among behavioural options and maintains that individuals behave 'as if' they are aware of all possible outcomes and their probabilities, potential costs and possible benefits. Would-be offenders use this information to choose rationally between various actions and voluntarily and purposefully choose crime if the expected utility outweighs possible losses. (2005: 11)

Like the metaphor of the market, rational choice theory may bring important aspects of the drug trade to light, however it is not gender-neutral. The concept of 'rationality' and the 'rational actor' have been generally employed in ways that marginalise the significance of emotion and care for others, for example (Okin 1979; Ferber and Nelson 1993; England 1989; Davies 2003; Gilligan 1982; Norrie 1986).[6] The application of rational choice theory has also been problematic. I have already argued that there has been a tendency to understand women's participation as unintentional, and as such there have been few attempts to use rational choice theory to understand women's participation in trafficking as mules. The use of rational choice theory in research on trafficking arguably perpetuates the gender/agency binary. This is especially the case where rational choice perspectives are employed in research exclusively on men. In sum, then, the 'trafficking as market' discourse frames drug trafficking in a way that privileges men's involvement and the kind of knowledge that men (as rational businessmen) would possess. This includes an implicit, gendered hierarchy about who the real traffickers are, and therefore who the real 'knowers' are (Harding 1987).

Research on women's involvement in the international cocaine trade

Women are undeniably present wherever coca/cocaine is farmed, processed, exported, imported, stored, and sold. Women make up the majority of those employed as *pisadoras* (people who tread coca leaves during early stages of processing) and coca leaf vendors in the markets of Bolivia (del Olmo 1993: 40). Women are involved in selling cocaine and crack everywhere: the streets of St. Louis, Missouri (Jacobs and Miller 1998), New York (Dunlap et al. 1994; Bourgois 2003; Maher 1997) England (Fleetwood 2014); Chile (Aliaga 2001), Australia (Denton 2001), and Argentina (Rossi 2007).

Men who traffic drugs do not do so in a vacuum: Adler's research into high-level drug smugglers in California in the late 1970s found women as 'dope chicks' and trophy wives: 'Universally beautiful and scantily clad, they served as prestigious escorts, so that dealers could show them off to the other members of the community' (1993: 91). In Argentina, women may exercise power indirectly 'as wives, sisters, cousins, in-laws, wives of friends, friends and lovers of men involved in organised crime...They occupy positions thanks to their loyalty or pull the strings backstage.' (Rossi 2007: 165–166) In Curaçao, Marion Van San encountered women acting as facilitators, stashing drugs and weapons for their partners (2011). Historically, women have successfully (albeit rarely) occupied key roles in the international cocaine trade. Most famously, 'La Nacha' allegedly controlled heroin supply in Juarez from the 1930s to the 1970s, and Griselda Blanco (aka The Miami Godmother) imported cocaine from Colombia to the US in the 1970s (Campbell 2009). If the press are to be believed, then Sandra Avila

Beltran and Angela Sanclemente are the latest in a long line of women at the top of trafficking. Yet, although women are present, the nature of their participation is not known.

There are two main theories about women's involvement in the international drug trade. First, the 'feminisation of poverty' thesis explains women's involvement primarily in terms of their victimisation. This parallels the construction of the (male) drug trafficker as an archetypal villain and the (female) mule as the model victim. The second theory explains women's participation as the result of women's emancipation and greater participation in public life. This explanation is underpinned by the conceptualisation of the drug trade as a market. Both perspectives are underpinned by problematic conceptualisations of gender/agency.

Feminisation of poverty

> Among the couriers there is one group that in my opinion always has to be seen as victim. They are the women. The backward position of women in the third world makes it impossible for them to refuse the exploitation, pressure or even blackmail they are confronted with. (John van Putten, corrections officer, cited by Huling 1995: 60)

The feminisation of poverty[7] is an enduring explanation for women's involvement in drug trafficking in print journalism (Boseley and Radford 1992; Gillan 2003; Jeavans 2005; BBC 2003; Clines 1993) and film (Marston 2005). It also dominates academic research. The first sociological account of women mules (from Venezuela) found that a large percentage of women imprisoned for 'drug trafficking' offences[8] were single (67.6%), described their occupation as 'housewife' (53%), and were arrested in their homes (48%) (del Olmo 1986: 170/173). She concluded that a combination of economic globalisation and local economic crisis created conditions led to the 'development and consolidation of the drug industry on the American continent during the 1980s, a decade that forced broad sectors of the population to devote themselves to the production, exportation, maintenance, and logistical support of drugs and the drug trade' (del Olmo 1993: 8). At a local level, 'participation in other aspects of the drug trade is closely linked to rural and urban unemployment and the rise and acceptance of the "informal economy" as a way to cushion the effects of the economic crisis' (1993: 9). Furthermore, 'economic hardship, which affects women more severely than it does men in times of crisis and unemployment, pushes them towards illegal activities which provide greater employment...Due to their dependent and subordinate condition in society, they are usually assigned to perform the most difficult and risky tasks' (1986: 164), and receive 'pittances for their work' (del Olmo 1986: 167). Her analysis relies on structural explanations for women's offending. The figure of the trafficker-exploiter lingers in the background.

Subsequent research has supported this orthodox explanation. Quantitative analyses report that a significant portion of women imprisoned for trafficking internationally are single mothers (Dorado 2005; Green 1991; Huling 1995; Harper et al. 2000). Dorado's study of female Colombian mules imprisoned in Europe found that 85 per cent were single parents who had the sole responsibility of care for their children and often also for parents (2005: 314). She concludes that women are propelled into drug trafficking out of 'economic desperation' (Dorado 1996: 35/2005). Similarly, Julia Oparah (nee Sudbury) interviewed 24 Jamaican women imprisoned in Canada, England, and the US for trafficking offences:

> The women I interviewed became involved in the trans-national drug trade through three paths: economic need, threats and coercion and deception. Faced with poverty and often without a second income to support the family, many women make the choice to risk carrying drugs, sometimes believing it will be a one-off. (2002: 67; see also 2005b)

Like del Olmo and Dorado, Sudbury concludes that 'it is this erosion of women's economic security under neoliberal globalization that drives many to participate in criminalized drug networks' (2005b: 174). In addition, she highlights that poverty is not only feminised, but also racialised (2002).

Sudbury is the first to highlight the problems of seeing women as *either* victims or agents:

> It is tempting to separate these women into two groups, the innocent victims of intimidation and deception and the willing participants of crime. [...] However, this dualistic portrayal limits our ability to analyse the reasons why women are willing to risk their lives and liberty by swallowing condoms filled with heroin or carrying criminalized drugs in their luggage. (2005b: 172)

Two decades have passed since del Olmo's research, but gendered inequality and poverty remain the dominant explanation for women's involvement in drug trafficking (see also Bailey 2013; Reynolds 2008; Martel 2013; Giacomello 2013a). Subsequent research confirms this hypothesis, suggesting that it is a valid and valuable explanation for women's involvement in the trade. Yet, the 'feminisation of poverty' thesis is not an adequate explanation for women's involvement in the international drug trade.

Poverty is widely recognised as an important factor in offending generally, but especially women's offending. In general, women in prison continue to be drawn from deprived backgrounds (Gelsthorpe and Morris 2002), and their offending is characterised by economically motivated offences such as theft and handling of stolen goods (Carlen 1988; Davies 2003; Burman 2004; McIvor and Burman 2011), fraud (Cook 1997), drug dealing (Denton 2001; Maher 1997), and prostitution (Phoenix 2000). Yet, Gelsthorpe notes that attempts to theorise women's offending have been fraught with problems (2004). In addition to poverty, women in prison persistently have experience of foster care as children, histories of domestic or sexual abuse, and drug and alcohol abuse issues however, the connection between these vulnerabilities and offending is not clear, and they can be best understood as 'indirect pathways to crime' (Gelsthorpe 2004). Furthermore, explanations that rely on social structures such as gendered poverty cannot explain why some poor women offend and others do not. Pat Carlen's research on women shoplifters in England found that although many of her respondents were living in poverty at some time during their offending careers, many claimed they offended because of a desire for excitement, rather than economic need (1988: 72).

The way in which poverty influences women's offending is not clear. In some accounts, the feminisation of poverty renders women vulnerable to exploitation by male drug dealers (Bailey 2013), or women become involved as a route to financial survival in times of crisis (Sudbury 2002). Poverty and deprivation are relative to local and historical circumstances (Townsend 1979; Young 1999), so focusing on 'survival' leaves little space to appreciate offending that may be both rational and economically motivated by 'a vision of prosperity and the attraction and pull of material possessions' (Davies 2003). This is well established in mainstream feminist criminology (Heidensohn 2006: 2) and is particularly apparent in research on women's involvement in drug dealing (Dunlap et al. 1994; Denton and O'Malley 1999; Denton 2001). So, although the 'economic' may be an important motivating factor in women mules' involvement, economic motivations beyond survival are yet to be explored.

The 'feminisation of poverty' arguably relies on conventional terms of female gender: women appear primarily as mothers motivated by caring responsibilities. As a result, it cannot account for women who are not carers. This is important given that around a third of women imprisoned in Ecuador did not have children (Pontón and Torres 2007). Furthermore, Mohanty offers an important postcolonial critique of the ways in which 'woman' has been used in research:

> A homogeneous notion of the oppression of women as a group is assumed, which, in turn, produces the image of an 'average third world woman'. This average third world woman leads an essentially truncated life based on her feminine gender (read: sexually constrained) and being 'third world' (read: ignorant, poor, uneducated, tradition-bound, domestic, family-oriented, victimized, etc.). (1991: 337; Mohanty 2003; see also Cain 2000; Oakley 1996)

In order to avoid this trap, women's subjective interpretations of gender and poverty must be foregrounded to make space for understanding how exactly poverty might provide positive draws for offending as well as understanding the particularities of women's experiences according to gender, ethnicity, class, and nation (Henne and Troshynski 2013).

Not all research focuses on poverty. Torres' research suggests that participating in trafficking was a rational trade-off by her respondents for love (Torres 2008) suggesting there may be draws beyond money. Indeed, an ethnographic study of the 'zona cafetera' commissioned by the Colombian government revealed that some men became involved in drug trafficking in response to financial hardship and to be able to fulfil the role of the male provider. Some, however, were motivated by the desire to gain status, particularly through consumer goods (DNE 2002). This hints at the fact that gender is not static, but is enacted in response to situated norms and values, chiming with situated action theories of crime (inter alia Messerschmidt 1993, 1995, 1997; Miller 2002).

Finally, explanations premised on social structural deprivations (or 'poverty') tend toward macro scale analyses, leaving little space to appreciate the ways in which women may act in agential ways even in circumstances of poverty and desperation. As a result: 'women are cast as submissive objects, serving as mere automata for the reproduction of determining structures. Constituted by and through their status as victims they are devoid of choice, responsibility or accountability; fragments of social debris floundering in a theoretical tide of victimage' (Maher 1997: 1).

The drug trade as employer

Conceptualising the drug trade as a market suggests particular ways of thinking about women's participation: firstly, that drug markets have provided new opportunities for women (as markets, rather than macho cartels); or secondly, that women are 'breaking the glass ceiling' of organised crime in the same way they have in legal markets. These kinds of explanations attribute women's involvement to choice rather than social structure. Aside from the fact that this appears to be based on a simplistic and confused understanding of the process of emancipation (Smart 1979), these conclusions are rarely subject to empirical research.

The idea that women's involvement in crime parallels their 'emancipation' owes much to Freda Adler, whose claim that women's emancipation leads to crime (1976)[9] has been subject to considerable critique and counter-analysis (Smart 1979; Box and Hale 1983; Batchelor 2005, 2011). Nonetheless, the stereotype of the 'new female criminal' (Maher 1997) endures, especially in relation to the drug trade. In the US, Fagan argued that women's increased presence in the street-level drug trade resulted from both women's emancipation from their domestic role and the simultaneous rapid expansion of cocaine and crack cocaine markets (1994). Bourgois similarly contends that 'greater female involvement in crack reflects in a rather straightforward manner the growing emancipation of women throughout all aspects of inner city life, culture and economy' (1989: 643). However he also acknowledges that women's presence in the crack market may result in victimisation rather than emancipation: 'The underlying process of emancipation that has enabled women to demand equal opportunities in street culture and to carve out an expanded niche for themselves in the underground economy has led to a greater deprecation of women as sex objects.' (1989: 645) Writing about women in the street-level cocaine market, Maher contends that 'the desire to demonstrate that women are active subjects often degenerates into accounts which can be misread as evidence of women having control and power equivalent to that of men' (1997: 198). Drawing on extensive ethnographic research on women in a Brooklyn crack market, she contends instead that 'the drug economy neither creates nor produces distinguishing statuses of sex/gender and race/ethnicity but rather seeks to reproduce them to individual, organizational and economic advantage.' (1997: 203; see also Measham 2002).

Structural change has been posited as an explanation for women's involvement in drug trafficking, and indeed in organised crime more generally. International drug trafficking organisations have arguably experienced structural change from hierarchical criminal organisations to smaller, more flexible groups, according to Reuter (1983; Reuter and Haaga 1989). Further empirical research has confirmed his claims (Decker and Chapman 2008; Desroches 2005; Dorn et al. 1992; Paoli 2001, 2002a, 2002b; Ruggiero and South 1995; Kenney 2007; Zaitch 2002).[10] The move towards smaller, less hierarchical impermanent groups may facilitate women's involvement.

This change may also intersect with globalisation. According to Fiandaca, 'the development of illegal markets, connected in part to socio-economic evolution and globalization offers greater opportunities to women as well.' (Fiandaca 2007a: 4) Furthermore, she argues that women's 'growing entrance into the criminal world constitutes a reaction against discrimination, an instrument (though arguable) of emancipation from the perspective of gender equality' (Fiandaca 2007a: 4). She makes this claim on the basis of chapters published in the edited collection *Women in the Mafia* that includes a variety of international contributions from Japan, Argentina, the US, Russia, and Brazil (Fiandaca 2007a; Fiandaca 2007b; Allum 2007; Rossi 2007; Siebert 2007). These contributions overwhelmingly rely on secondary sources – court transcriptions, phone taps, newspaper accounts, and so on. Again, although this data reveals that women are indeed present, the nature of their involvement remains unclear.

The idea that women's involvement in the international drug trade can be attributed to women's 'emancipation' has mainly appeared in the press (see Chapter 1), with some exceptions. Campbell's ethnographic research on women on the US/Mexican border concludes that greater mobility and freedoms for women plays some role in women's participation, yet he describes the drug trade as male- dominated and patriarchal, and notes more continuity than change vis-à-vis drug market structure: 'Women in drug smuggling are thus victims of patriarchal class/race/gender structures but also active agents for their own emancipation (although, in some cases, oppressors of others)' (Campbell 2008: 259). His research usefully draws out the diversity in women's experiences: there is a great deal of difference between working class women who are mules and those women at the top.

For Dick Hobbs, organised crime has undergone significant structural and cultural changes, creating new opportunities for women in the illegal economy:

> Although they remain rarities within this characteristically masculine culture, the drug trade in particular offers opportunities for women

> that were unimaginable within the male dominated enclaves of safe breaking, extortion and armed robbery. Particularly where industrial processes and their attendant relations have become redundant...women are increasingly likely to become involved in illegal trading. (2013: 153)

In his latest book *Lush Life,* Hobbs offers a case study of Yvonne Miller, a cannabis seller in 'Dogtown', East London. He describes her involvement as a logical choice:

> She functions as the main source of income for the entire family, keeping the kids well dressed, three homes clean and well furnished and creating a silo of self respect, discipline, and well being in a landscape of fragmentation and uncertainty that features a scarcity of overly successful men and a dearth of job opportunities for women beyond the fast food and office-cleaning sectors.' (2013: 155)

Despite being a business entrepreneur, Yvonne's main concerns and responsibilities (family and home) suggest more continuity than change in women's role. Furthermore, Hobbs' observation reminds that available legitimate employment opportunities are extremely limited (2013). For Hobbs, the old orthodoxies of organised crime have been broken down and replaced by market logics; the drug trade is an 'equal opportunities employer' (2013). Hobbs' ethnographic research is invaluable: no academic in the UK (or beyond) has done as much to document organised crime, and certainly no one is better placed to understand historical changes. Yet, I cannot wholeheartedly agree; it seems more probable that 'equal' opportunities are limited to specific places and times (Fleetwood 2014).

Emancipated women or victims of poverty?

The question of whether women's offending result from (or even results in) victimisation or emancipation dominates the literature; however existing research answers it only in part. With specific regard to drug trafficking, data has been rather limited in scope, tending to focus on women's motives, rather than processes within trafficking. In other words, existing research has little to say about the role of gender in how drug trafficking is organised. Furthermore, research has developed along a set of gendered binary categories (male/female, trafficker/mule, agent/victim, victimiser/victimised, powerful/powerless and rational/natural) that effectively limit the kinds of questions prioritised in research. On the one hand, studies of drug trafficking have learnt from men about the 'business' of drug trafficking. On the other, studies of drug mules have tended to study women. The result is that research has not been able to separate the situation of mules in general, and women's particular experiences of victimisation. Thus, structure and agency have been seen as 'ontological binary positions' (Maher 1997: 200). Maher proposes working in the 'space between the twin discourses of victimization and volition that inform current understandings of women's [...] law breaking. While this space must be large enough to include the constraints of sexism, racism and poverty that structure women's lives, it cannot be so big as to overwhelm the active, creative and often contradictory choices, adaptations and resistances that constitute women's agencies.' (Maher 1997:201).

Moving beyond dualisms

This short section sets out the theoretical approach adopted here to bridge the problematic dualisms outlined above. My approach is underpinned by the symbolic interactionist tenet that people 'act towards things on the basis of the meanings that things have for them' (Blumer 1969: 2).[11] Forefronting subjective interpretations and evaluations offers a way of avoiding the problems of structural explanations, which tend to leave little space for agency. My approach draws on McNay's reconceptualisation of Bourdieu's habitus and Presser and Sandberg's development of narrative analysis in criminology. As well as offering ways of thinking about structure and agency beyond dualisms, they are also appropriate for tackling the challenge of researching transnational global phenomena, and drug trafficking in particular.

Global scales

Drug trafficking represents a particular kind of social arrangement. It is comprised of associations between people that are temporary and globally dispersed (Dorn et al. 1992: 201; Hobbs 2001). It is also characterised by movement: money flows across continents, as do quantities of drugs and people carrying them. The drug trade is not located in one place (geographically or socially) and stretches across time zones (Dorn et al. 2005: 22), yet it is ubiquitous in almost all corners of the globe. As Findlay puts it so memorably: 'crime is no longer hidden in dark alleys, spooky interrogation rooms or gloomy prison cells. It is up for sale in the networks and is there at the dinner table.' (Findlay 1999: 48 see also UNODC 2008, 2012) Conceptualising the 'global' is theoretically and methodologically complex (Appadurai 2009).

According to Aas, 'As an adjective, the global [in criminology] has been associated with the telling of "big stories" and the use of big words, such as justice, markets, neoliberalism and human rights' (2012: 9). This is also the case in sociology (Connell 2007; De Sousa Santos 2008). These large scales of analysis are ill suited for understanding individual action. There is no doubt that economic neoliberalism is reshaping the contexts in which women make their lives (Sudbury 2005b); however, something more is needed to understand why some women, living through particular circumstances of structural inequality connected to processes of globalisation, become involved in trafficking.

The global scale tends to 'zoom out', producing a context free, global social science 'from above' (Burawoy 2008), resulting in epistemological ethnocentrism, or 'reading from the metropole' (Connell 2007). This is particularly problematic when it comes to interpreting the experiences of women's lives (hooks 1984). Mohanty notes that western theorists tend to overemphasise women's victimisation (1991). On the other hand, 'The danger is that the western observer, imbued with an ideology which associates the feminine with passivity, is so astonished at finding individual women elsewhere to be self possessed that she or he confuses individual agency with Western notions of equality and freedom.' (Oakley 1996: 211) This is not only the case with gender, but also age and poverty (Cain 2000). To avoid misreading women's experiences, it is important to listen to women's own accounts (Sudbury 2005b), and specifically their subjective interpretations.

Rather than a transnational illegal business, or mafia, trafficking is viewed here as the result of social connections and interactions (more in Chapter 4). Writing as a proponent of symbolic interactionism, Plummer uses the term 'social worlds' to encompass various arrangements of human interaction in a globalised world: 'face to face, large scale and global, criss-crossing the world and bringing together a diverse range of enterprises that go well beyond any notion of subculture or community' (Plummer 2000). Two scales of the global feature in this book: First, the 'sub-national' is understood as a site of globalisation (the globalised local) (Sassen 2007: 7). Chapter 3 examines prisons in Ecuador, which have been re-shaped by geopolitics in the form of the war on drugs. In particular, this chapter examines how global processes in the form of the war on drugs have shaped prisons, as well as notions of women's criminality. The second scale of globalisation is the 'trans-local', 'locally scaled practices and conditions articulated with global dynamics' (Sassen 2007: 7; also Brotherton and Barrios 2011). This refers to social processes that become transnational due to the influence of globalisation. Here, the international drug trade is understood as a set of social interactions that take place in the context of transnational travel (explored in more detail in Chapter 4).

Women's offending and structure/agency

Prior studies on offending have relied upon geographic locales to help understand social structure (for example, 'neighbourhood', or in studies of trafficking, 'nation') (Sudbury 2005b; Green 1991). By contrast, respondents in this research came from geographically and socially diverse backgrounds. For example, one respondent was a black woman who grew up under apartheid in South Africa and another was a single parent born in the US to Puerto Rican parents. Gendered (and raced) forms of oppression played out in these women's lives, yet their experiences are in no way the same (Henne and Troshynski 2013).[12] Such international diversity presents a fresh challenge for thinking about structure and agency, an already notoriously tricky problem (Phoenix 2000; Matthews 2009).[13]

Most studies of structure/agency and women's offending have been premised on realist epistemologies (Daly and Maher 1998: 7), and so constraints on women's lives have largely figured as material limits for action (and poverty in particular). Agency retains an 'elusive albeit resonant vagueness' associated with a variety of things including 'selfhood, motivation, will, purposefulness, intentionality, choice, initiative, freedom and creativity' (Emirbayer and Mische 1998: 962). In studies of female offending, this has usually meant demonstrating women's capacity for action and participation in offending, despite material inequalities (and sometimes because of them) (for example Batchelor 2009; Denton 2001; Denton and O'Malley 1999; Maher 1997; Jacobs and Miller 1998; Miller 2001).

Although criminology has tended to focus on material factors, the influence of postmodernism can be found in empirical research focussed on the discursive construction of women offenders, for example Carol Smart's research on legal discourse in constructing 'women' in court (Smart 1989; Daly and Maher 1998).[14] Daly and Maher describe these two approaches as 'real women' and 'women of discourse' (1998: 4). According to Comack, this has led to a theoretical impasse, and she advocates an approach combining the two:

> This is not to revert to an empiricist stance, nor does it by necessity impose a dualism between 'thought' and 'experience'. Rather, it suggests that women's standpoint(s) will be very much informed by

> their social context (what happens in their day-to-day lives), their histories (what has happened to them in the past) and their culture (modes of thought available to them). (1999: 294)

Possibilities for combining material and discursive approaches can be drawn from feminist debates in sociology that encounter a similar impasse between material (Fraser 1995) and discursive (Butler 1990) facets of gender.[15] McNay argues:

> Even if it were possible to settle the question of whether it is the economy or culture that remains determining in the last instance, this would tell us little about why individuals act in some circumstances rather than others and why it is some individuals rather than others who act in some circumstances. In other words, agency cannot be deduced from abstract social structures. (2004: 178)

Overcoming this impasse entails examining questions of gender and agency in social interaction (following Bourdieu 1990; McNay 2004; M. Jackson 2002; S. Jackson 2001). Whilst gender is comprised of material hierarchies of gender (Connell 1987, 2002; Walby 2009), it is also negotiated at the level of meaning in everyday social practice (S. Jackson 2001: 289).

Narrative criminology and structure/agency

Narrative criminology offers a way to take into account both material realities and culture, through discourses: 'Stories thematize the points of connection between personal and collective experience, desire and effort. The point at which individual agency is configured, phenomenologically, as group will and vice versa is limned in stories' (Presser 2009: 178–179).[16] Narrative criminologists work with a constitutive view of narrative: that is, narratives shape our experiences; reality is narratively constituted (Presser 2009; Presser and Sandberg, forthcoming). Thus, for narrative criminologists, there is no distinction between 'experience' and 'narrative' since there is no experience prior to narrative.

Narratives are not freely chosen, however. In constructing personal narratives, individuals adopt, adapt, and borrow from available discourses. Discourses are culturally and historically specific (Plummer 2000; S. Jackson 1998), and may belong to particular social settings (Wright Mills 1940) or institutions (Foucault 1972). Furthermore, an individual's social structural position will also make some kinds of discourses available (S. Jackson 1998; Somers 1994). The concept of habitus is useful for thinking through the ways that social positioning and experience make available particular kinds of discourses and rule out others (Sandberg and Pederson 2009).[17]

Habitus is part of Bourdieu's conceptual 'toolkit' for understanding social practice (1990). It is shaped by social structure (through experience), and in turn perpetuates social structures; it is a generative structure that shapes how people encounter, interpret, and act on their social worlds (Bourdieu 1990). Rather than seeing social structure as acting upon individuals, Bourdieu imagines social structures as embodied, durable, and portable. Bourdieu's theory is mainly concerned with pre-reflexive, embodied action (le sens pratique). Nonetheless, he also emphasises that the habitus is a set of 'internalized structures, common schemes of *perception, conception* and action which are the precondition of all objectification and apperception' (1990: 60, my emphasis). Thus, le sens pratique is not solely embodied (the way that one walks, talks, and acts), but also structures how a person experiences and interprets their social world. As a generative structure, the habitus shapes how one experiences the social world as someone who is classed, raced, gendered, and so on, by evaluating the possibilities for action, and probabilities of outcomes, which are differentiated along class, race, and gender lines. Possibilities for action are 'infinite yet strictly limited' (1990:55) as the habitus acts in such a way that 'the most improbable practices are therefore excluded, as unthinkable, by a kind of immediate submission to order that inclines agents to make a virtue out of necessity, that is, to refuse what is anyway denied, and to will the inevitable' (1990: 54).

Bourdieu does not rule out the possibility of strategic evaluation, yet his theory has been critiqued for a lack of attention to it, and subsequent social theorists have sought to re-work Bourdieu's theory to take it into account (Bohman 1997). Of particular relevance is Lois McNay's reconceptualisation of habitus, which centres gender and agency (2004). For McNay, individuals negotiate gender (as both materially and culturally constituted) in everyday social practice through the habitus (2004)[18]. In other words social structures do not act directly upon individuals, but are mediated by the individual's agency (as the capacity for evaluation and reflection) (2004: 178). As such, 'action and struggle are motivated by perception and representation not just by abstract social structures and economic forces' (McNay 2004: 184). Furthermore, language is central to an individual's reflections and evaluations; however, this process is a double one: people are always already positioned *by* social structures that shape the possible interpretations and projections of future action, through discourse (McNay 2004; S. Jackson 2001; Sandberg 2010).

At the same time this process can nonetheless be creative since 'even shared meanings are subject to constant interpretation and reinterpretation, often in ways that contest current identities and practice' (Bohman 1997: 176). Bohman calls this reflection through language 'practical reflexivity' (1997: 180).

Individuals produce, and are produced by, these discursive frameworks as the 'imagined protagonist' in an evolving story (Presser 2009). The 'self' (or discursive subject position) is enacted in relation to available discourses. McNay explains that 'unlike the post-structural account of constraint in terms of an external determining force, the notion of narrative suggests that constraint is also self-imposed. Individuals act in certain ways because it would violate their sense of being to do otherwise' (1999: 318). Discourses make available, or rule out particular subject positions: 'the creation of subject-positions is not a free or voluntaristic process – it is produced through accessing available and material and discursive resources' (Byrne 2003: 37).

With regard to gender in particular, stories about womanhood are transmitted and sustained through dominant discourses, institutions, and individual practice. These 'public stories' form discourses about gender that are lived through private interpretations and re-tellings (S. Jackson 1998). Although gender is always co-constituted by a myriad of other social structures (Burgess-Proctor 2006; Daly 1997), the stories that can be told about female gender are not limitless. There can be creativity, but only within limits: 'because certain kinds of "gender identities" fail to conform to these norms of cultural intelligibility they appear as developmental failures or logical impossibilities from within that domain' (Butler 1990:17).

Arguably, gender has a special status here in that 'it is difficult, if not impossible, to have a socially meaningful existence outside of the norms of gender' (McNay 1999: 322; also Butler 1990). Furthermore, female gender identities have a 'deep historical resonance and durability' (McNay 1999: 323). Stability of gender narratives is not simply the result of powerful imposition through patriarchal institutions, but also due to perpetuation by individuals who adapt such discourses into individual narratives (McNay 1999).

Narrative is employed in two ways in this book. The first is as 'talk as action' (Sandberg 2010: 455, 2011). This perspective is informed by ethnomethodology, and examines storytelling as socially situated action. In other words, 'stories are assembled and told to someone, somewhere, at some time, with a variety of consequences for those concerned' (Gubrium and Holstein 2008: 247). In criminology, this involves understanding how people account for their offending. Little attention has been paid to female deviance, and so I also draw on social interactionist perspectives that understand gender as 'done' through interaction according to local notions of masculinity and femininity (contingent on other social structures) (Connell 1993; West and Zimmerman 1987; West and Festernmaker 1995). West and Zimmerman's influence also leads to feminist linguistics – to see gender as 'done' through talk, rather than preceding it (Weatherall 2002).

Second, narrative is considered as a guide to action (Presser 2009; Sandberg 2010). This builds on the observation that experience is narratively constructed, and that people act on the basis of the self as 'the protagonist of an involving story' (Presser 2009: 184; inter alia Gergen and Gergen 1988; Somers 1994; Holstein and Gubrium 2000). Narratives may guide offending behaviours, and some kinds of narrative may be 'criminogenic' (or a precursor to offending) (Presser 2009). For example, drawing on Katz, Presser notes that crime may be used to enact particular kinds of masculine self-narratives (Katz 1988; see also Agnew 2006). In *Been a Heavy Life*, Presser draws on James Messerschmidt's concept of 'doing crime' (1997) in order to accomplish masculine identity (2008). This theory is problematic in relation to women, since 'crime is almost always stigmatised for females' (Steffensmeier and Allen 1996: 476; Lloyd 1995). This raises questions about how women may 'accomplish' female gender through talking about, or doing, crime.

Conclusion

Narrative analysis offers ways to take into account gender and structure/agency in a novel way. Firstly, it offers a way to think about how both discursive and material aspects of gender shape female offending. This is important given that prior research on drug mules has focussed mainly on material aspects. Secondly, narrative offers a way to bridge structure/agency dichotomies.

Agency is understood here in two ways. The first aspect of agency is evaluation and reflection (McNay 2004; Emirbayer and Mische 1998). This process is a narrative one: evaluations are made through discourses (which structure knowledge). This involves a creative appropriation of available narratives whilst at the same time creativity is structured by the habitus. This socially structured capacity for evaluation and reflection through language is summed up in the concept of 'practical reflexivity' (Bohman 1997). Social structure also figures here as material limits on action, the objective, material circumstances that are 'at one remove' from respondents' experiences (Bourdieu 1990). Taking into account macro structures is necessary to contextualise subjective interpretations and evaluations. Finally, narrative offers possibilities for exploring local and global connections since individual's biographies reflect personal history in respondents' habitus but narratives must engage with the 'there' and 'then' to be socially meaningful.

This book approaches globalisation and crime from 'below', interpreted loosely.[19] It explores trafficking from the perspective of participants in the underbelly of globalisation (Findlay 1999). Participants (prisoners in Ecuador) can also be imagined as punished under global regimes of crime control in the form of the war on drugs. 'Below' is also gendered: globally, women are more likely to be employed in the illegal economy (Ray 2007: 168), or employed at the peripheries of the drug trade, occupying the most mobile, marginal role of the drug mule. Finally, 'below' refers to the scale of this research: rather than reaching for the large scales of globalisation and trafficking involving geopolitics, neoliberalism, and global scale inequalities (see Green 1998; Sudbury 2005b), this book explores the smallest frame: human interaction. Bracketing off these large scales makes space to focus on how individuals recognise, evaluate, and act upon possibilities for involvement in crime on a global scale.

3
What Do Women Talk about When they Talk about Trafficking?

Paula was the first drug mule I interviewed. Like me, she had travelled to Ecuador to take advantage of relatively inexpensive Spanish classes during the long summer break from university. We were both in our early twenties at the time (2002): I was halfway through my undergraduate degree, and she was two years into an eight-year sentence for trafficking cocaine. Crouched on stools in the tiny cell she shared with two other women, she explained to me that on the last day of her trip to Ecuador, her boyfriend called from Europe and asked if she could carry something home for him, which he described as 'like small medicines'. She explained her reasons for agreeing to swallow around a kilo of thumb-sized packages (or 'capsules') of cocaine:

> My boyfriend needed help clearing a bad debt. At the time it seemed like a good idea... Everything happened very fast, and it wasn't like actually planned by me, OK, it was planned by other people, but it wasn't so much planned by me. It was a fast decision for sure.'
>
> I wondered if she blamed her boyfriend. 'No,' she replied. 'I've made peace with myself.'

She described herself unambiguously as a decision-maker. At the time she was wearing an engagement ring sent by her boyfriend. She remained committed to him and described looking forward to sharing a future with him after prison.

Five years later (in 2007), we sat down to do a final interview, this time in a café in Quito's old town. Paula was on parole; I had recently finished a year of ethnographic research in the women's prison for my PhD. We snacked on *humitas*[1] and chatted over coffee like old friends. Although

I had finished fieldwork, we did one last interview. She started the interview by offering a remarkably similar account to her original explanation, describing how she agreed to swallow capsules of cocaine to help her boyfriend clear some bad debts.[2] Interestingly, she doesn't say that her first explanation was mistaken, or offer a corrected explanation and in fact, she reflected on the functionality of her original explanation for her involvement (to save her boyfriend). She also described the long process of leaving him, and finding a new self, through God, while she was in prison. In doing so, she connects her 'self' who trafficked drugs then (girlfriend) and now, as someone who had found God while she was in prison:

> [At time of our first interview] I was talking to him [on the phone], and I was with him for two years when I was arrested, and our relationship kind of kept me going. It helped me…I guess to deal with why I did it. Why would I do it [swallow cocaine] for something that had no purpose? But the purpose was still there: we're still together, he's alive. So, that's what I can see [now], after many years, that…it gave me strength, it helped me not to be scared or totally secluded and [gave me] a reason to keep going.
>
> We [Paula and boyfriend] were in touch for two years until…It was a pretty major breakdown for me…I kept on hearing stuff from some friends [at home], like he was actually in [another country] on a fake passport and all that… [They] would tell me, 'We've seen him with this girl, and she's pregnant, and they hang out a lot' and you know…I would just block it out. I thought they're just saying that because they don't want us to be together. But still, the doubt was there. And also the Lord started working on my heart and made me stronger to accept that I can live without this guy. So, I made a commitment to live for God, and it really helped strengthen me, but I was still with my boyfriend alongside.

Shortly after the first time we met, Paula was interviewed by an Interpol officer (after she was sentenced, and while she was still engaged to her boyfriend). Although Paula did not speak to the officer about her boyfriend directly, she was keen to assist in arresting the people who she thought had threatened her boyfriend. She recalls speaking to him afterwards on the phone, and he was furious that she had spoken to Interpol agents:

> He was like, 'Why would you even talk to them? You don't have to!' and I was like, 'But I want for these people to be caught, and you will be safer,' and it sounded simple and all that.

Shortly afterwards, Paula was poisoned and was in a coma for three days. Paula thought she had probably been poisoned by a fellow inmate as retaliation for meeting with the Interpol officer. This event triggered a major break in her narrative:

> The day I woke up at the hospital and realised I was poisoned, I was just like: enough of it! And I guess I was strong enough to make it without [my boyfriend] and really, at this point, God became totally number one for me, so I just decided to live for Him.

Whereas Paula had previously been convinced that she had been protecting her boyfriend, these events problematised that narrative, making it an unstable basis on which to establish a self. Although she never said it directly, her narrative suggests that he may have had something to do with her being poisoned, although she never knew for certain who had poisoned her, or why.

Paula received considerable support from a missionary group, and they facilitated her parole.[3] Thus, her current, lucky circumstance as one of the few foreign national women on parole offers a strong basis for a narrative centred on faith in God. Furthermore, Paula's account is crafted for me, as a social researcher: Paula reflects upon the complexities of constructing a narrative and incorporates them into the narrative. It also draws on our commonalities, being of similar ages and backgrounds and is therefore a co-constructed narrative (Presser 2005, 2008).

Paula's narrative may not be typical, but it says much about the complex process of talking about trafficking and the significance of gender, not only in doing crime but also in telling about it. Paula's account was not only a record of events, but was also functional: believing that she was protecting her boyfriend helped her make sense of her involvement in crime and face an eight-year sentence. Her account was subject to revisions and changed subtly in response to her surroundings and circumstances. The meaning of her involvement is far from settled and is subject to revisions and reinterpretations in relation to going concerns. This changeability (or rather multiplicity) poses difficult questions: which account is more accurate? Her original interview would be more clearly remembered, but arguably her later account was better informed. Both accounts are carefully crafted toward the listener, her current circumstances, and identity.

Despite the apparent malleability of Paula's narrative, the events that it describe change surprisingly little: she continues to see herself as a decision-maker even after serious doubts arose about her boyfriend's involvement. Furthermore, Paula's experience incorporates elements of both individual choice and compulsion: she *could* have chosen otherwise, yet she made her decision in constrained circumstances in which her boyfriend seemed to be at serious risk of violence.[4] Notably, Paula's account does not fit neatly into dominant political and academic accounts of drug mules (seen in the last two chapters) premised on binaries of victim/agent (see previous chapter).

This chapter contextualises Paula's (and other respondents') accounts within the narrative setting of the women's prison in Quito, Ecuador. It considers why, when, and how women gave an account of their involvement in trafficking. In other words, it explores women's 'narrative practice' (the imperatives for constructing accounts about trafficking) and the discourses in practice (the kinds of discourses which were available and institutionally supported) (Holstein and Gubrium 2000). This is important given that discourses make available particular subject positions vis-à-vis victim or agent (McNay 2000; Sandberg and Pederson 2009). Narrative analysis offers theoretical and methodological tools to take the *narrativity* of Paula's account into consideration and so better unpack questions of gender, structure, and agency by seeing these as not solely acting upon women (compelling them to traffic) but as the product of women's evaluations and interpretations. Doing so enables an appreciation of Paula's (and other respondents') agency and creativity as storytellers.

Situating narratives: gender, crime and imprisonment

This section offers a description of the politics surrounding women's imprisonment in Ecuador, and offers a description of El Inca. Ethnographic immersion in the daily life of El Inca revealed that women's accounts not only reflected individual life experiences and biographies, but were also a response to material realities, institutional demands, and global geopolitics. These shaped when women could spoke, what it meant to speak (or stay silent), as well as the ways in which women's accounts were shaped according to local webs of meaning and the kinds of female gender and subject positions (victim or agent) which were commonly available and supported. At the end of this chapter, I return to Paula's narrative before briefly outlining my narrative methodology.

Misrecognition, femininity, and protest selves

El Inca (the women's prison in Quito) was profoundly shaped by drug war politics at the time of fieldwork. In 2002, Ecuador signed a bilateral agreement with the US in which the US requested a 10 per cent increase in the number of people arrested for drugs offences, and a 12 per cent increase in the quantity of drugs seized, in return for an investment in Ecuadorian security infrastructure (Pontón and Torres 2007). Between 2002–2009, the portion of women imprisoned for drugs offences rose from around 60 per cent to around 80 per cent, outpacing equivalent changes in the men's prison (Edwards 2011: 55). In the capital city, Quito, three quarters of women in prison were serving sentences for drug offences, compared to a third of men (Dirección Nacional de Rehabilitación Social 2005). Overall 10 per cent of those serving sentences for drug crime were women (Pontón and Torres 2007: 66). 23 per cent of the female prison population were foreign nationals, of which the vast majority were drug offenders (Edwards 2011: 56).

All drug offenders (users, dealers, and traffickers) were sentenced under the same law (Ley de Sustancias Estupefacientes y Psicotrópicas, Ley 108), which initially included a mandatory minimum of ten years (Edwards 2003). Sentences between 8–12 years were common. These were the highest on the continent for drug offences and were on a par with those for serious, violent offences such as murder (Edwards 2003). Furthermore, Law 108 was incompatible with the Ecuadorian constitution at that time (Edwards 2003, 2011).[5] Although previously prisoners had been released automatically at the midpoint of their sentence, this was abolished in 2002, effectively doubling sentences overnight (DNRS 2005; cited by Pontón and Torres 2007; Edwards 2003). Besides this, some inmates waited up to three years to be sentenced (Flores Aguirre 2007),[6] an unconstitutionally long wait, largely the result of courts being overloaded with drug cases (Edwards 2003). As a result, only 31 per cent of inmates had their sentence confirmed (Gallardo and Nuñez 2006).[7]

All of the above factors led to a dramatic rise in the prison population, but particularly in the women's prisons in Quito and Guayaquil, due to their proximity to international airports. Although the women's prison in Quito was designed to hold 384 women (Pontón 2008) by the end of fieldwork in 2006 it held around 700 women. Small rooms designed for one to two women were shared by three to four (and sometimes their children, too). Subsequently, there was a shortage of almost everything, including beds, food, space, meaningful activity, and medical treatment (Torres 2008; Pontón 2005, 2008; Fleetwood and Torres 2011). Human rights abuses were a routine feature of daily life in prison. The Standard Minimum Rules for the Treatment of Prisoners set out by the United Nations were not met (United Nations 1955).[8] Daily life was characterised by a lack of privacy and security. During fieldwork, one female inmate was reputedly beaten up by guards, who then left her handcuffed in the yard for others to see. This resulted in a mass protest by inmates. The prison was also unsafe for staff. A female guard was shot and killed after leaving the prison, allegedly assassinated by drug traffickers (El Comercio 2006), further eroding the little sense of security that women had. Furthermore, women suffered additionally due to the androcentric nature of the prison, reflected in architecture, regime, and management (Pontón 2008; Chesney-Lind and Pollock 1994). For example, women were afforded less privacy than their male counterparts, as male guards could access their corridors. Women were also required to slop out, whereas men had access to toilets during the night.

Prisoners (in both women's and men's prisons) were acutely aware that their incarceration had much to do with the transnational transfer of the US's war on drugs (Corva 2008; Youngers and Rosin 2005). I was frequently told that the US paid a bonus of $10,000 to police officers for each 'drug trafficker' arrested. Regardless of whether or not this had a basis in fact (and no concrete evidence of this claim was ever found), this reveals much about how inmates understood the geopolitics behind their incarceration, and the dire circumstances under which they served their sentence. Prisoners in Ecuador campaigned against judicial and constitutional injustices, human rights abuses, overcrowding, and inhumane living conditions in prison.[9] Protests, including public campaigns, strikes, and taking visitors hostage, were coordinated nationally by a network of inmates' committees (a democratically elected assembly of inmate representatives). Although protests took place simultaneously nationwide, each prison planned and managed protests according to local priorities.

Prisoners in El Inca played an active role in national protests about unjustly long sentences and desperate prison conditions. Narrative identity was an important resource for protest, and the drug mule was adopted as emblematic at a collective level: both by the committee of inmates and by women themselves in front of visitors to the prison. Prisons in in Ecuador were open three days a week to visitors who entered directly into prison rather than a discrete visiting area. Most visitors were friends and family of inmates, but visitors also included legal professionals, members of non-governmental organisations, including Christian and feminist organisations (Mujeres de Frente 2006), volunteers (affiliated to organisations as well as independently), journalists, researchers, and even a small number of tourists (Baker 2009).

Visitors were often told 'everyone here is a mule' (Torres 2008). Typical mule narratives justified women's involvement in trafficking through poverty and emphasised lack of choice. For example,

> I had to pay my rent in a week or the marshal was gonna come 'n padlock my door. I had nowhere to go. My mother was being evicted, too, so I, if I was gonna go live with my mum, she was gonna get kicked out also so ... everybody would be in the doghouse. (Amanda)[10]

Interestingly, prison guards and administrative staff reiterated the same discourse:

> You will see for a fact that the majority of the population in this centre are here for drug trafficking. The majority of them are mules, people that have been *used* to carry the drugs and perhaps they did this because at that time they were *forced* to do that work out of economic necessity. It is simply a person with a need who they [traffickers] offer the world. (Torres 2008: 89, interview with an administrator, my translation and emphasis)

Both accounts highlight the gendered nature of poverty: specifically women's role as primary carers for children and head of household. The discourse emphasises the moral connectedness of the woman in relation to her family (Gilligan 1982) and appeals to normative ideals about maternal sacrifice. Although women were also motivated by the wish to provide for parents, grandparents, and siblings, the most commonly circulated stories centred on motherhood, perhaps due to its centrality to normative femininity, especially in the Ecuadorian context (Pontón 2008; Bosworth 1999: 148). These kinds of discourses also render women's participation passive and 'inoffensive' (Torres 2008: 113). Interestingly this discourse echoes the 'feminisation of poverty' thesis commonly found in academic and popular accounts (see Chapter 2). Yet only 27.5 per cent of women in El Inca self-identified as a mule and less than half of inmates (40%) were mothers (FLACSO-DNRS 2005 cited by Torres 2008).[11] Collective identification with the drug mule did not reflect an objective kind of truth, but rather a collective adoption of an effectual identity necessary for protest.

Several other kinds of standard narratives drew on the same gendered discourses. These included women who were unknowingly 'set up' by men who asked them to post a parcel, or carry a package containing drugs, or women who had been arrested with boyfriends who they were not aware were carrying drugs. Stories about women who are set up by men/boyfriends were quite commonly iterated, despite the fact that only a handful of women personally claimed this experience. When speaking to visitors, women often said things like: 'None of us are really traffickers; there is one woman here who was arrested with 5 kilos her boyfriend had put in her suitcase without her knowing'. Despite the fact that these kinds of account were not believed in the courts, (where possession of drugs was evidence of guilt), this narrative was rarely questioned in prison. These accounts were therefore not necessarily meaningful outside the context in which they were created.

Less commonly, women's involvement in drug trafficking was explained through discourses of romantic love (see Torres 2008). Indeed, the story of the woman led astray and taken advantage of is a recognisable cultural script (Fraser 2005). This discourse differed from the above in that the woman *did* know she (or her boyfriend) was carrying drugs. This narrative appealed to natural and universal facets of femininity (since heterosexual love is 'timeless'). Interestingly, this narrative offered both passive and active subject positions: women could be 'caught up in the moment' or could be active players in ensuring the future of the relationship. Nonetheless, the stories that were most 'heard' were those in which women were not culpable and therefore not blameworthy.

The collective adoption of the drug mule as a symbolic figure is worth reflecting on. The kinds of stories that were widely circulated tended to be characterised by passive (or unintentional) involvement in drug trafficking. This strategic adoption of victimhood can be interpreted as a collective form of (gendered) 'repair work' (Goffman 1968). It was also an attempt to counter misrecognition, which 'is to be denied the status of full partner in social interaction and prevented from participating as a peer in social life – not as a consequence of distributive inequality...but rather as a consequence of institutionalised patterns of evaluation that constitute one as comparatively unworthy of respect or esteem' (Fraser 1995: 280).

Women in El Inca were subject to various 'misrecognitions'. The law treated them as drug traffickers (even those who were arrested for possession or dealing) and long sentences designated them as particularly dangerous or serious offenders. The title of drug trafficker (or even drug dealer) was experienced as highly shameful and stigmatising. This stigma was doubly felt since women had not only transgressed the law, but also transgressed gender norms (Lloyd 1995). Sara (who is one of the few women who claimed not to know she was carrying drugs in her suitcase) describes how she felt when she was arrested for trafficking:

> I was getting angry cause they [police] kept calling me a *mula* [mule], and I was getting very upset about it. I was getting really, really upset about that. They weren't thinking the type of person I was, you know, the job, the lifestyle I had, and then someone catch me in a foreign country with drugs, that was shameful, you know I felt very embarrassed. Very... very.

The resulting misrecognition compounded their inability to campaign effectively against the injustices they suffered as a result of the war on drugs. As criminals (and therefore gender deviants), their protests would simply not be heard, so their public protest relied upon the construction of a non-deviant identity. Because femininity is a cultural imperative (Skeggs 2001: 299), women could not construct a non-deviant identity without countering their gendered deviance. The kind of femininity that women collectively undertook drew on cultural scripts about gender centred on extremely traditional 'feminine' characteristics, for example caring for children and romantic love. As Skeggs notes, 'when you have restricted access to small amounts of capitals, femininity may be better than nothing at all.' (ibid) However, strategically adopting victim status may not have been that successful as even victim identities carry stigma (Goffman 1968), and the value of femininity is limited (Skeggs 2004). Interestingly, claiming victimhood is not an exclusively female strategy. In his research on black drug dealers in Norway, Sandberg found that men also adopt 'victim' subject positions, especially in relation to official authorities and envoys of the welfare state (2009).

Considerable effort was invested in maintaining this collective narrative. The committee organised day-to-day life in the prison, including mandating everyday conduct in prison. On visit days, everyone had to be properly dressed (no pyjamas, no flip flops), for example. They also organised the annual 'Queen of the prison' pageant, which was attended by local dignitaries, friends, and family and was covered by local newspapers. These were key events for public representation and protest about their incarceration. In addition to catwalks, dresses, and dancing, women spoke out about the pains of imprisonment, emphasising their gendered, caring responsibilities and the minor nature of their offending. These public accountings were self-conscious performances of the kind of female gender that adhered to normative discourses – a public appeal for both entitlement to human rights, prison reform, and, fundamentally, for participation in public debate. Establishing themselves as respectable was not solely a matter of talking the talk, but was backed up by an embodied performance of (hyper) femininity.

The committee also attempted to shape the kinds of narratives that I collected. About halfway through fieldwork, the committee tried to block my research access. I was called into a meeting by the prison director (the equivalent of a governor in an English prison) and two women from the committee. The women said that there had been 'complaints' about my research,[12] and the director declared that a tape recorder was a security risk. He agreed that I could continue my fieldwork as long as he could listen to any interviews undertaken. Having worked peacefully for seven months, this came as a surprise. Just prior to this, I had begun hanging out in the oldest pavilion, which housed the least 'respectable' women (lesbians, drug users, and serious criminals). By contrast, women on the committee tended to be educated and middle class. This incident made clear that some women were not considered entitled to represent the collective. It was also notable that the formal control came from inmates themselves, rather than the director.

Although this chapter focuses on women's narratives, it is worth noting how different they were to those in the men's prison. Identity played almost no role in men's protests. Instead, human rights, the unfairness of the prison system, and the pains of imprisonment (Sykes 2007) took centre stage. Protests employed theological imagery to highlight these pains; for example, inmates staged crucifixions (Garces 2010).[13] Although having a 'loose tongue' was frowned upon, at the level of corridor talk, anecdotes about trafficking feats were iterated nonetheless. This contrast was stark: narratives in the men's prison emphasised autonomy; women's emphasised victimisation and relationships. These narrative constructions say more about how women and men are supposed to be, than about what they actually did (West and Zimmerman 1987). In fact, interviews with women and men in prison revealed that many more men were mules than would have been anticipated on the basis of corridor talk. Furthermore, interviews with men and women involved in trafficking revealed significant similarities between men and women who worked as mules (see Chapters 6, 7, and 8).

Crime networks and the code of silence

Although public narratives emphasised that women were mere mules and not 'real' drug traffickers, crime networks were a powerful (if hidden) presence in prison that prohibited some women from speaking about trafficking. Speaking to outsiders could have very real consequences, judging by Paula's experience of being poisoned, described earlier in this chapter. This silence, or 'absent presence', was an important aspect of discourse (Hallsworth and Young 2008). Conversely, being seen to speak about one's experience publically was a way of enacting a particular kind of identity; 'There's a code of privacy, because if you're so high up they'll kill you [for talking]. But what am I? A drug mule – nobody cares about me.' (Caroline)

Thus, for Caroline and Paula, being seen to do an interview was a way of publically demonstrating that they were not like 'others' who were involved in serious crime networks:

> We're more open to talk to people who we don't know about what happened. But they did it [trafficking] many times, and it's kind of dangerous for them; they're mixing with these people still (Paula).[14]

By doing an interview publically, Paula claimed a particular subject position for herself: as the lowly, non-criminal mule. Note also that Paula observes the taboo against talking about trafficking directly, talking about 'it', rather than trafficking.

Some women chose to do interviews in public view: for example, in the shared patio or kitchen. In contrast, I interviewed three women who had considerable experience in the trade: one worked in partnership with her boyfriend for several years, and it was widely known that she was a 'real' trafficker. Our interviews were conducted in secret under the guise of other activities. Two women privately told me they had recruited or minded drug mules[15] but publically claimed to be a drug mule. They had little to gain from publically admitting being involved in trafficking in any willing capacity.

'Audit selves'

Although the code of silence discouraged women from speaking about trafficking, the prison required women to give an account of themselves to various functionaries in the prison, including social workers and psychologists. An account is a 'linguistic device employed whenever an action is subjected to valuative enquiry' (Scott and Lyman 1968: 46). Accounts are therefore a particular type of narrative. Here, women's accounts mainly functioned to explain their involvement in the drug trade and manage perceptions of deviance in front of prison staff.

Shortly after arriving in prison, women met a psychologist. Amanda explains:

> We have to speak to the psychologist, and he has to determine, like, I guess try to get into our minds on what kind of people we are, where we come from, what kind of background, character, personality, everything in one.

Inmates' accounts formed the basis of psychologists' assessments, rather than any formal classification such as remand/sentenced, time served, or offence. This had implications for accommodation. Women could be placed in one of the three buildings. The newest pavilion was inhabited by educated, middle class women (including many foreign nationals). The oldest pavilion housed poor and Afro-Ecuadorian women who were seen to be troublesome or violent. Thus it seemed women's accounts, as well as their class and ethnicity, shaped how they were categorised. Placement in prison had a lasting effect on how women were perceived by prison officials, and impacted the kinds of resources they could expect to receive. Since resources were in short supply, access was limited to the most 'deserving'.

Stanley refers to self-narratives produced through organisational encounters as 'audit selves', which she claims are 'constrained or compelled by organisational purposes and functions' (2000: 49).[16] The women's prison was one such institution (see also Fox 1999; Guo 2012). As with 'protest' narratives, most women drew upon normative scripts of gender as a way of denying deviance; however 'audit narratives' also highlighted remorse (see Guo 2012). Pontón examined how disciplinary power operated on and was resisted by women in El Inca (2008). She notes that the Catholic Church traditionally had responsibility for delinquent women (up until 1982), and religious doctrine continued to shape ideas about women's rehabilitation. Specifically, the reformed woman was supposed to be 'docile, demure, submissive and selfless' (Pontón 2008: 320, my translation).

Stanley notes that 'audit' selves are not solely performative: 'People may feel or may actually be constrained to perform the characteristics of the audit selves with which they are associated because of the surveillance consequences involved' (2000: 54). Here, women iterated audit narratives even when officials were not present. For example, weekly pavilion meetings began with a group prayer thanking God for his help to keep them on the right path. Before speaking, women greeted the group with *buenos días, familia* (Good day, family), a phrase imbued with gendered undertones. These meetings also included poems, prayer, and speeches, often tracing journeys to recovery. These public performances of audit narratives reproduced discursive formats connected to the prison in spaces not under the purview of guards, psychologists, or any other institutional surveillance.

Feminine ideals centred on docility, submission, and demureness were imbued with class and race prejudices. Not all women could successfully enact this type of self-presentation. Being one of the 'girls from the back' (the oldest pavilion) brought with it a great deal of stigma, even from other women in the prison. Women in the oldest pavilions were deeply ambivalent about the requirement to perform this kind of femininity, much like Skeggs' working class, English respondents who found middle class femininities ill-fitting (1997). The requirement to appear demure was unrealistic given that many women had been homeless before prison and expected to be afterwards. Women in this part of the prison rarely gave accounts about their involvement in crime and were rarely invested in constructing self-narratives in relation to institutional discourses about femininity (see also Skeggs 2004). Their inability (or unwillingness) to give remorseful accounts worsened their poverty in prison, as they were the least able to access health care or other scarce resources.

Yet, although institutional power shaped women's daily lives in important ways, it was not a 'total institution' (Pontón 2008). Indeed, those women who were seen to be the most troublesome experienced the least intervention. In response to stigmatisation, they developed counter-discourses about what it really meant to be decent and feminine while serving a prison sentence. They assembled alternative forms of respectability based on being 'up front' and looking out for one another. This included any number of favours, such as sharing tobacco, drugs, food, babysitting, and clothes.

Marta was a foreign national who lived in the oldest pavilion with her girlfriend. She smoked crack, so she was barred from being housed elsewhere. She describes life in the oldest pavilion, drawing together discourses about gender and class to construct femininity differently:

> 'Oh, the girls from the back are gonna come, be careful!' [Have you] ever heard that in the new pavilions?! (laughs) The girls here, if you don't mess with them, they don't mess with you... When there's a fight, there's a fight, and it's called a fight. It's a good fight, you know... and they're happy again ten minutes later. But a lot of the women here are street women. They all sell their drugs outside, they're always on the roads late, and the roads outside on Quito aren't very safe, aren't very nice, so they're all roughnecks, you know. But they're really down to earth, you know, you can talk to some of them and they'll give you such... what's the word in English... good advice... I'm forgetting my English, dude... Yeah, they'll give you some amazing advice that you'd never think they'll be able to give you. Like people think these are the stupid people but no, man... and when you find a friend, you really find a friend, you know.

Whilst research has explored the inmate code in men's prison, there is a lack of similar research on women's prisons (McGuire 2011). Nonetheless, Marta draws on aspects of 'street' code, such as being street smart, standing up for yourself, and taking care of (criminal) business. Interestingly, this discourse was only adopted by a small section of the prison population that was not invested in constructing 'audit selves' according to dominant discourses.

Conversely, men in prison were not required to iterate narratives about themselves to gain access to resources. Rather than psychologists, entry into pavilions were organised by the committee, who managed an informal market in which cells were bought and sold (although cell owners were required to share their cell). Thus, the institutional requirement placed on women to give an account of themselves reflects wider social norms about gender and deviance. Whilst men's offending did not require an explanation, women's apparent deviance was doubly problematic and required much greater involvement in their day-to-day life, included the involvement of psychologists (Carlen 1983). Thus, being required to give an account of oneself reflected not only institutional power, but gender power, too.

Dealing with imprisonment

Lastly, narrative was a way of re-establishing a meaningful sense of self. Maruna et al. (2006) note that imprisonment can produce a crisis of self-narrative, and examine how (male) prisoners used narrative to make sense of imprisonment. Similarly, anthropologist Michael Jackson understands storytelling as a 'vital human strategy for sustaining agency in the face of disempowering circumstances' (M. Jackson 2002: 14). Respondents frequently spoke of experiencing 'disorientation' when they were arrested. This was especially the case for those women who had previously defined themselves through being mothers and doing motherhood (see also Fleetwood and Torres 2011). The sudden disappearance of the key resources for constructing a self was keenly felt. Constructing a meaningful self was especially difficult in the context of imprisonment, compounded by the stigma of being a drug offender. The experience of imprisonment was depersonalising.

Amanda struggled to express her experience of arriving in prison, reflecting her feelings of disorientation at that time:

> Explaining to you what happened to me and how I dealt with it the first couple of weeks I was here, it's like…it's hard to explain sometimes, Sometimes, I get like…when people get writer's block, I, I can't explain

> because it's...it's like a harsh...the way they treat people here, it's...it's like you're being totally wiped off the face of the earth, it's like you're not here, you're not in the world, it's like you don't exist anymore especially if you're from a foreign country, such as myself, 'n the...like your embassy comes to visit, and they don't actually pay no mind to you, and they just come and just give you vitamins and magazines?

Amanda felt deeply depersonalised by her embassy, who were not interested in who she was or what she was experiencing. She found being given magazines deeply insulting.

Being unable to care for children often resulted in feelings of guilt and anger (Clark 1995), especially since stigma connected to the drug trade had a concrete impact on families. Sara's husband lost his job after her arrest was reported in the local papers, for example. Families also bore the financial brunt of legal proceedings and even paid for the flight home, in most cases. Relationships with boyfriends often fell apart after imprisonment. The collapse of these relationships was keenly felt. Tisha was arrested with drugs hidden in her suitcase by her boyfriend. He stayed in contact for a few months after Tisha's arrest, but then disconnected his number. She remembers the time shortly after being arrested:

> All these charges are starting to come...All the accusations, and they're painting this picture, and they're talking these words about 'author' and all, and I'm starting to learn what they're talking about, and they're telling me 12 years...I had not time to even mend a broken heart.[17]

In the face of such judgement and confusion, narratives were a key way to maintain agency (S. Jackson 1998; M. Jackson 2002), especially given the unlikelihood of being able to enact material change in their lives.

Narrators need listeners: women gave 'testimonials' at church services, confessions at Narcotics Anonymous, and had informal conversations in the corridors or bedrooms with volunteers. They also had conversations and interviews with me (see the end of this chapter). These settings provided different discourses and formats for making sense of one's experience. In addition to discourses about family and love mentioned above, religion offered an important way for the women to make sense of imprisonment and their involvement in crime (Maruna et al. 2006). For example, it was common to hear the phrase, 'I am not guilty, but I must have done something for God to have me here' (see also Torres 2008: 124). Tisha incorporates this into her personal narrative:

> I don't know why I'm here, but for whatever reason... I've been using that time to talk as much as I can, to explain, to show, to give proof of something and make a difference. I'm here in prison, but there's something inside me driving me to do that. I don't know. Well, I know where the energy comes from, but I'm tapped into it, and I'm digging it!

The format of religious testimonials enables the narrator to separate the deviant act from the self and claim moral authority (Maruna 2001; Maruna et al. 2006). It also enabled women to reframe their experiences in a completely different way to the account of offending demanded by the courts or prison. For example, women often began the story before becoming involved in trafficking, at a moment when they felt that their faith in God had faltered:

> I did stop seeking [God] for some time, and that's when I made choices that... [There were] so many obstacles in my way to come here. In hindsight, I can see the 'do not go' signs, but I was determined, not realising there was a trap. Even when I wasn't seeking [God], the forces were working on my behalf. (Tisha)

Such accounts did not end with arrest, but instead with their return to recognising the power of God in their lives. The subject position offered by this kind of discourse is notable. God plays an all-powerful role: he could put the narrators into prison or take them out. Nonetheless, the narrators have agency insofar as they could work hard on their faith. Importantly, shifting the goalposts from an appeal to legal innocence to an appeal for divine forgiveness took place in the context of a legal and criminal justice system that was overwhelmingly corrupt and un-listening. As noted above, women found the experience of prison (and their dealings with embassy and other officials) deeply depersonalising. In contrast, many described their relationship with God as deeply personal, comforting and empowering. Furthermore, Christian belief was often the basis for making connections with others, and building support networks inside and outside the prison with missionaries.

Not narrating oneself

Caroline was arrested with her boyfriend just before she was due to travel to the airport. She was a teenager at the time, and had originally travelled to Ecuador as part of a language exchange. Whilst she was keen to do an interview and talk about her experiences publically (see above), her account rejects typical explanations for women's involvement in trafficking. She also avoids constructing a non-criminal sense of self whilst also detaching herself from her involvement in trafficking:

> Our plan was to get married. [My boyfriend and I] came back [from my home country], met the wrong people, a group of Colombians, and I swallowed almost a kilo of heroin. It didn't seem real to me. It didn't seem like I was really going to do it until it was too late to back out. [...] I think it was because I didn't actually think I was going to go through with it, and it was kind of like the risky thing going on, it was really something I had never imagined and kind of exciting and interesting.

Caroline's narrative did not draw on the usual narratives of poverty or love (indeed she denied that these were an important part of her experience). Despite holding strong religious convictions, she does not draw on these to 'explain' her imprisonment. Despite her lack of motive, Caroline resists describing her involvement as passive, saying,

> For me it was a long series of bad decisions that led to this decision 'cause I don't think you're just going to wake up one day and say 'I'm going to carry 2 kilos. I'm going to swallow capsules.' It's not like that.

There is a sense that her experiences do not fit neatly with available discursive structures, making them difficult to voice (Byrne 2006). Caroline hints at the draws of excitement and risk (Katz 1988), but this possible account is not one that is particularly convincing, given her current surroundings. Caroline spoke of the difficulty in explaining to her family:

> I didn't want to tell them [family] at first, but at that point I was in a hospital, and there was a chance I could die because the capsules [of heroin] were in my system for six days, and so I said, OK, I told my embassy, 'go and tell my family', and I couldn't talk to them. I didn't have the courage to talk to them. For a long time, I just wrote letters, and finally I did call. They never asked me why I did it...They never asked me, and I'm glad that they didn't ask because I didn't really have an answer.

Caroline occupied a privileged position in prison. She was bilingual, highly educated and well liked. She received support from her family, her boyfriend (who was also in prison), and a local missionary group. She studied long distance and was a model student, consistently getting excellent grades. As such, she was able to draw on a variety of capitals (cultural, social and economic) (Bourdieu 1986, 1990) to enable her to present herself as respectable.

A handful of women were able to resist institutional demand to construct a self-narrative. They were typically arrested with their boyfriends and received financial support from their partners or families, enabling them to avoid institutional demands to give an explanation. They were able to buy a variety of necessities in the prison, including food and clothes, and so were much less reliant on the prison system for support.

Paula's narrative revisited

It is easy to imagine that had Paula not been arrested, she would simply have returned to university and continued to un-reflexively employ the same, unquestioned self-narrative: as a student, girlfriend, and backpacker. Being a drug mule would probably not have had a particularly important role in her narrative, if at all. By the time I first interviewed Paula (when she had been in prison for just under 2 years), she had constructed accounts of herself for the prison, courts, her parents, missionaries, and other prisoners. As a prisoner and convicted 'drug trafficker', she had little choice but to bridge the gap between actual and expected behaviour, and as the above shows, this was done through narrative (Scott and Lyman 1968). Further, as a woman in prison, she had little choice but to 'do' gender (Skeggs 1997), which she enacted in and through narrative (Weatherall 2002). These gender performances and narratives are oriented to the situation in which they are produced. Her narrative is undoubtedly a product of imprisonment, but that is not all it is.

Paula's narrative (like most women in prison) did not neatly reproduce any of the dominant discourses in prison, but was a creative appropriation of several in response to emergent circumstances. Although institutional discourses supported passive subject positions (as did the committee of inmates), Paula consistently avoided these ways of interpreting her experience. Narrating herself as a girlfriend (and then fiancée) allowed a sense of agency in disempowering circumstances. Nonetheless, even despite significant life changes (engagement, coma, split from her fiancé, finding God, getting out of prison on parole), her account of why she became involved changed surprisingly little.

In addition to responding to the 'here and now' of prison (and then release on parole), her narrative is also shaped by ingrained dispositions of gender, class, and nation; in other words, it was shaped by her habitus (Bourdieu 1977, 1990; Maton 2008). Her narrative is the result of experiences of trafficking, her biography, and life experience (habitus), drawing on available discourses, and responding to material requirements and imperatives. Thus, a close analysis of Paula's narrative sheds light on the complex processes involved in giving an account of oneself as a woman, prisoner, and participant in the international cocaine trade.

What do women talk about when they talk about trafficking?

It is recognised that prisoners use narrative to make sense of imprisonment (Maruna at al. 2006), to construct themselves as moral agents (Ugelvik 2012), or that prisoners' narratives are organised by 'going concerns', or institutional requirements to present oneself as reformed (Fox 1999; Guo 2012; McKendy 2006). This chapter further details the ways in which prisoners negotiate multiple, competing narrative demands, drawing on ethnographic observation and participation to explore talk as a kind of social action. Gubrium and Holstein refer to this as 'narrative practice' (2008). They see 'the storytelling process as both actively constructed and locally constrained' (Gubrium and Holstein 1998: 164). They elaborate:

> Self stories come from somewhere, relate to larger stories, are shaped by other stories, and are affirmed and challenged through time by yet different and transformed narratives. Stories are relentlessly drawn through the gamut of contingent interests that bear on their particular content and shape. Narrative ethnography provides an encompassing sensitivity to the fluid contingencies, in this case the challenges, of narrative production. (Gubrium and Holstein 2008: 254)

Women's narratives about involvement in the drug trade were not just records of events but were a response to, and engagement with, micro and macro level politics: the war on drugs and the prison regime. They were also a creative response to, and appropriation of, global and local discourses about crime and gender. The adoption of subject positions such as the drug mule as victim draws on political and popular discourses about trafficking that are premised on gendered binaries of structure/agency (see Chapter 2). Individual's habitus made available different discourses according to gender, nation, class and race/ethnicity. In other words, speakers 'rely on ways of self-presenting and thinking that they have learned and used elsewhere' (Sandberg 2010: 455). Some women's habitus fit neatly with those discourses demanded by the institution, but others did not, especially those who were lesbian, drug users, or serious criminals. Some women were experienced narrators, or in Bourdieuian terms, had greater cultural capital, enabling them to successfully navigate institutional demands to give account. In this way, respondents' narratives entailed 'practical reflexivity' (Bohman 1997; McNay 2004): creativity within limits proscribed by their habitus, and the social context in which they gave their accounts.

Since gender is arguably the most significant social structure at play here, it is worthy of special consideration. Gender did not solely constrain women's narratives, but rather women drew upon discourses about gender to construct their narratives in comprehensible ways. Although gender has a special status, in that it is a cultural imperative (Skeggs 2001; McNay 1999; Butler 1990), women could 'do' gender in a variety of ways. Feminist linguists draw on West and Zimmerman's concept of 'doing gender' to draw attention to the fact that gender does not precede talk, but is 'done' in it (Weatherall 2002). Thus, women's narratives were situated, narrative accomplishments of female gender. Although passive, demure kinds of femininity were supported by prison, a myriad of reinterpretations were possible. Miller notes that 'recognizing gender as situated action allows for recognition of agency, but does so in a way thoroughly grounded in the contexts of structural inequalities such as those of gender, sexuality, race, class and age' (2002: 434).

Miller is concerned with how women 'do' gender though action; this chapter shows they also 'do' gender through talk. According to McNay, 'highlighting the active role played by the subject in the construction of a coherent identity allows a more nuanced concept of agency to emerge' (2000: 73). Ethnographic immersion in El Inca reveals the agency involved in collectively claiming victimhood through the figurehead of the drug mule. It also reveals that their narrative was the result of institutional imperatives, and was constrained by available discourses and narrative formats. Thus, agency/structure here operates upon individuals, but at the same time, women actively engaged with these limited possibilities for meaning-making.

These narratives are historic and belong to a particular set of geopolitical circumstances. Until 2008, no one could have foreseen the rapid and remarkable changes that have since occurred in drug policy in Latin America (Soberón 2013; Pontón 2013). Political leaders across South

America have become increasingly vocal in their opposition to the US-led war on drugs in the region, and there now exists a strong counter-discourse emphasising decriminalisation and framing drugs as a health, rather than a criminal, issue (Youngers 2013; Carrión 2013; Jelsma 2010). In 2009 (after fieldwork), the Ecuadorian government issued a nation-wide pardon (*indulto*) for convicted drug offenders who had served a year in prison and had been sentenced for offences relating to quantities of less than two kilos (Metaal and Edwards 2009). I visited El Inca for the last time in 2010 and saw the profound impact of the pardon. The vast majority of respondents had been pardoned, and prison overcrowding had been vastly reduced. There were only a small number of foreigners, all in prison for drug trafficking offences. They reported being sentenced very quickly (several months after arrest). Sentences were on a par with those before the pardon.

At the time of writing, the Ecuadorian penal code is under review. Sentences for drug offences have undergone major revision, including formal provisions for decriminalising possession of small quantities of drugs for use.[18] International trafficking and sale will not be distinguished as separate offences; however, the new law will distinguish between 'scales' of trafficking (minimal, medium, high, and grand) (Article 222, Asamblea Nacional de la República del Ecuador 2013). The table setting out these thresholds has not been confirmed. By all accounts, the effects of the pardon have been short lived, and El Inca is overcrowded with drug offenders once again (El Comercio 2013; Bravo 2013).

Finally, ethnographic immersion reveals not only those discourses that are encouraged and supported, but also absences and silences which are an important element of discourse: 'The make up of discourse ... has to be pieced together, with things both said and unsaid, with required and forbidden speech' (Foucault 1981, cited by Hallsworth and Young 2008: 133). Here, discussing actual participation in the drug trade was virtually taboo (Torres 2008). Interviews (including Paula's) tended to skim over descriptions of actually swallowing or carrying drugs. As will be seen in later chapters, few women's narratives actually included descriptions of doing trafficking (focussing instead on their motivations). They also tended not to talk about drugs concretely. Euphemisms include: 'capsules', 'the stuff', 'merchandise', 'it', 'that shit', etc. (see also Torres 2008: 21). Furthermore, respondents struggled for a word to sum up the work of being a mule. Many use the euphemism of travelling (rather than trafficking). Some women simply did not talk about their involvement in trafficking (or crime) at all. This lack of narrative was significant. On the one hand, it may reflect a lack of available discourses, which allowed active, purposeful involvement in crime. On the other, it may have been the case that women simply had nothing to gain by giving accounts of themselves as active agents: either publically or privately.

Co-constructing narratives about trafficking

With careful probing, prompting, and reflection, I aimed to understand not *if* women were victims or agents, but rather how victimisation and agency were enacted/accomplished by women, and done to them by others. Doing so meant careful attention to the value of narrative, and my role in co-constructing it. In brief, my narrative methodology entailed the following:

Listening to everything

Narrative analysis, like feminist methodologies, situates women as subjects rather than objects of knowledge (Gelsthorpe 1990; see also McNay 2000; Cosslett et al. 2000; Harding 1987; Comack 1999). Doing so in practice meant giving respondents control over conversations and interview, especially given the institutional demands on women to give account, and the climate of judgement and gossip amongst women (which was a form of both social cohesion and control). My first principle was to listen to everything respondents wanted to tell me, or talk about. During fieldwork from August 2005 to December 2006, I visited prisons about four times a week (three days in the women's prison; one in men's prisons). I usually arrived at 10 am and stayed in prison until 4 pm (according to the conditions of my work pass). I made myself available as a listener (not only to women, but also to men). Entire weeks were spent hanging out, chatting and listening to anyone who wanted to take advantage of my presence. Despite spending around 20 hours a week in prison, my time was constantly in demand. We chatted about loads of things, but especially family, cellmates, gossip, money worries, legal problems, relationships, news from home, and reminiscences of better times. Many commented that they really enjoyed speaking to someone from the outside, as it gave them the chance to feel normal for a while. Although respondents knew that I was writing a book about women, prison, and trafficking, I made a point of not asking for an interview about trafficking during the first four months of fieldwork.

Listening to everything was connected to local dynamics of power (Presser 2005, 2010). The isolation resulting from imprisonment could be overwhelming. As one inmate said with conviction: 'You've got to be visited; you've got to be seen and heard.' Here, where speaking was often an act of resistance, listening could be an act of solidarity (Harding 1987; Scheper-Hughes 1995). It was especially important for potential respondents to see that I was not merely interested in them as objects of study. This meant being earnestly engaged and non-judgemental. Most of the time, this was not difficult, but occasionally it could be (Fleetwood 2009).

As important as it was to listen, it was important that my research also respect silences. This meant probing accounts gently, cognisant that they were a means for survival and would be with respondents far longer than I could be. It also meant upholding all confidences (not just research-related ones). I was often tested: women would talk about others and say, 'They will have told you about that, I'm sure', asking me to confirm what I knew or didn't. They sometimes asked direct questions about who had undertaken an interview. My response was usually, 'Ask her yourself!' This was especially important, as some of the people I interviewed were couples. Lastly, women sometimes gave me details of their 'story' which were very important but they insisted could not go into print. These confidences have been upheld. In most cases, such details were fortunately more significant for respondents than for the analysis that follows.

Creating opportunities for different kinds of narratives

Reciprocity extended to my narrative practice. This was inevitably an imperfect process, and I am not claiming that reciprocity was achieved, but that it was an important principle that shaped how I approached the research (Oakley 1981; Skeggs 1995).[19] As insider/outsider, I occupied a special place in the narrative landscape of prison. I had access to outside style, forms, and topics of discussion. Sharing anecdotes, jokes, news, and my own experiences helped to construct an inter-subjective space that I hoped would allow respondents to explore their experiences in different ways. This research had the potential to expose respondents to judgements and perceptions of stigmatisation as 'criminal women'. Many women simply wanted to forget about the past and move on (see also Torres 2008: 21). Others found talking about their involvement in drug trafficking painful and emotional. Interviews were regularly postponed when respondents were in pain, ill, or down, having received bad news about home or their legal process.[20]

In an attempt to counter stigma and open up space for talking about deviance, I talked about my own (Burman et al. 2001). Rather than taking the form of confessions, I tried to structure them in diverse ways, most commonly light-hearted, humorous anecdotes. I chose this format to avoid appearing too penitent or reformed (and therefore different to institutional discourses). I also shared secrets, extending my trust. If I had a tape recorder, I would switch it off to show that respondents could, too. This was a useful way of separating what was 'on record' and what was not.

Probing and prompting

Ethnographic interviewing offers possibilities 'to explore purposefully, with the researcher the meanings they place on events in their worlds' (Heyl 2001: 369). Interviews usually began with a sole open-ended question: 'Tell me how you got here.' This usually elicited a narrative the respondent had told before and was comfortable with. Sometime these were very short; some lasted for as long as an hour. Respondents started and finished where it was important to them and were free to highlight aspects of their experience that they saw as the most important. Torres notes that initially she found it difficult to find women who would talk to her about drug trafficking, noting that, at first, women volunteered to 'tell their story' but didn't want to be interviewed (questioned or interrogated) about their experience (2008). Torres' experience hints at the fragile nature of women's public narratives of being a drug mule. Some respondents were not comfortable with giving a long narrative (usually those whose command of English or Spanish was not so confident). One respondent said it would be better if I just asked her lots of questions. In sum, interviews were designed to encourage respondents to take control, but I tried to do so in a way that did not place any additional burden on them (Maher 1997: 231).

Where possible, I interviewed respondents more than once, encouraging them to retell or reflect on aspects of their story in different ways and to go 'off script'. Sometimes this could be fun – an opportunity to talk about the good experiences they may not have voiced publicly – but sometimes this could be upsetting. Some had unhappy memories of coercion and threats of violence related to trafficking. Furthermore, since for many women trafficking represented an escape, talking about life before could also be difficult. Often respondents got upset during interviews: although I always offered to postpone the interview, everyone said that they wanted to continue. Even though it was upsetting, many said that it was good and important to tell their story. Whenever I asked women to reflect or retell aspects of their stories, I sought to position them as interpreters of their own experiences.

Reflective interviews were also an important tool for addressing silences. In most cases, this concerned actually doing trafficking.

Probing interviews explored what women and men did as mules (and occasionally as recruiters or minders). This was important to understand how victimisation was accomplished and agency enacted. This data forms the bulk of Chapters 8 and 9. Prior to interviews with me, few had actually spoken about these aspects of their experience, and they commented that it was interesting to do so. Some things about their experiences puzzled respondents (for example, why their contact asked them to change hotels), and this created opportunities for reflecting on what they knew at the time as well as possible interpretations or explanations. As a researcher, I was uniquely positioned to know more about how trafficking worked, as I was able to query aspects of trafficking with those in organising positions.

Summary of data

In addition to ethnographic observations, I conducted around 80 interviews (which were distinguished from ethnographic chats by the use of notebook or a recorder). Although this project focussed on women (especially as mules), I also interviewed men to contextualise their experiences, and so unpack gendered exploitation from general exploitative practices. It also helped to understand the ways in which prison talk was gendered. I interviewed 18 women, all of whom had worked as a mule at some stage. Some had also undertaken other roles (minder, recruiter), and some had been a mule more than once. I interviewed most mules several times (and some up to five times). I also interviewed 17 men, of whom 11 had once worked as a mule. Most had also undertaken other roles, such as recruiting and managing mules. A small number described themselves as investors and bosses.

Not all interviews were done in a narrative style (Reissman 1993, 2008); however most interviews with drug mules were. I had permission to take a tape recorder into the women's prison, but I was advised by respondents in the men's prison that using a recorder was likely to be met with suspicion, in particular that I was working for the police (Lee 1995). I did take a recorder into one of the men's prisons on one occasion, but in this instance, the men involved accompanied me to the director's office to gain special permission. Most of the time, I relied on taking notes that I wrote up soon afterwards and then destroyed.[21]

Finally, a note on language: doing research in a second language is complex but is nonetheless possible. Due to the globalised nature of the research setting, many languages were spoken, including English (Hoefinger 2013). I speak Spanish more or less fluently. Interviews were conducted in Spanish and English. In some cases, these were respondents' first languages, but many spoke English as a second language. Learning prison slang from respondents disrupted potential power imbalances by placing respondents as teacher and me as student. Issues of translation created opportunities to explore ambiguities and better understand meaning, rather than relying on 'taken for granted' assumptions. For example, when a mule said she felt *glücklich* about travelling to Ecuador, we struggled to translate it into Spanish or English, but in the process were able to explore how she felt and why. Or when Bobby said his female mafia boss was *muy mandóna* (meaning bossy, literally, 'she who gives a lot of orders'), this prompted a discussion about the role of his boss's gender in how she ran business, as Bobby gave me examples of her being a *mandóna* and the difference between being a *mandón* and *mandóna*.

4
Who are the 'Traffickers'?

The last chapter showed that women rejected labels such as 'drug trafficker' and denied any serious involvement in the drug trade (at least publically). The converse was true in the men's prison. Men tended to talk up their involvement in drug business (see also Decker and Chapman 2008). Lorenzo often implied he was connected to the mafia. After about 6 months, I approached him about an interview. 'Who, me...?', he replied in mock flattery. Two of his good friends sat in the cell with us: probably more curious about watching an 'interview' than about Lorenzo's history.[1] Despite his bluster, Lorenzo worked alone: 'I didn't have a mafia. I didn't have contacts. [This way] you don't owe anything, and no one owes you.'[2]

Lorenzo's involvement in trafficking is far from the mafia myth. When Lorenzo was in his twenties, an acquaintance from a short jail spell invited him on a trip to South America. Lorenzo jumped at the opportunity. Lorenzo saw it as a free holiday, guessing the trip would involve something vaguely illegal, but he wasn't sure what. Indeed, he did not know he would be a mule until shortly before he returned home. On the last day, they made capsules of cocaine together, swallowed them, and flew back to Europe. Lorenzo was given half of the capsules he had swallowed as payment. Following this, he made several trips a year on his own, buying around a kilo of cocaine, which he smuggled in thumb-sized, latex-covered capsules that he made himself as his friend had shown him. As someone who regularly used cocaine, he had little trouble finding buyers.

Caulkins at al. would refer to Lorenzo as a 'self-employed courier' (2009) and Zaitch as an 'independent trafficker'.[3] Either way, he was certainly no *mafioso,* or 'Mr. Big', even though he was happy to let others to think he might be. In this respect, Lorenzo was typical of many of the self-employed traffickers that I encountered in the men's prison. Indeed, like previous researchers, I failed to find anyone who bore much resemblance to the trafficker popularised by political, drug war discourse (Chapter 2).[4] Researchers have long challenged stereotypes of so-called 'Mr Bigs' and *carteleros*: 'There is no person, no mafia organising the market overall. Rather a large number of small organisations operate fully autonomous of one another in a manner that may be best described as unorganised.' (Dorn et al. 1992: 202).

This was echoed by Bobby, who described working in a 'cartelito':

> The large cartels that there were before the Medellín cartel, the Cali cartel, they have disappeared. After they disappeared, the small cartels were left – they're families: the Ochoa, Varela, Montoya. They're small families that control specific zones of the country and which have their businesses. Sometimes they collaborate, but it usually ends in conflict.

Whilst it is impossible to rule out the possibility that organised, cartel-type groups coexist with smaller, flexible, less permanent collaborations (Levi 2007: 785; Wright 2006), most research reports that drug trafficking is organised through informal connections between people (friendship, kinship, and ethnic networks in particular) rather than hierarchical, formal crime groups. These connections form the basis for temporary criminal collaborations, rather than purposive, organised collaborations (Adler 1993; Decker and Chapman 2008; Desroches 2007; Dorn et al. 1992; Dorn et al. 2005; Hobbs 2013; Kenney 2007; Levi 2007; Paoli 2005; Pearson and Hobbs 2001, 2003; Reuter and Haaga 1989; Wright 2006; Zaitch 2002).[5] Most recently, the Matrix Knowledge Group found that three-quarters of respondents became involved in drug trafficking through 'friends and family' or through a friend involved in the business (2007: 24).[6]

Gender has rarely been considered as a significant aspect of trafficking networks, with few exceptions. Adler's ethnography of traffickers in California found that trafficking was a 'man's world' where men preferred to do business with men but women occasionally became involved, for example when their husband got arrested. Most recently, Van San's ethnographic research in Curaçao found that traffickers' girlfriends and wives undertook domestic-based tasks in line with local expectations about women's role (including stashing drugs and money, or selling small quantities of drugs) (2011). She also argues that women encourage men's participation in crime, especially as mothers.

Like Adler, Van San's research reveals that the kinds of role available to women are structured by local norms and values.[7] In sum then, sociological approaches reveal that trafficking is organised according to social networks and connections between people; however, the role of gender remains underexplored.

Whilst sociological approaches have challenged myths of cartels and mafiosos, these often lurks in the background of research on drug mules. Tracy Huling mainly describes women involved following threats from boyfriends, neighbours, or in one instance, a neighbourhood priest (1995). Oparah (née Sudbury) finds that women were '"compelled to crime" by a combination of gender violence, global inequities and a paucity of alternatives' (Sudbury 2005b: 181, 2002: 68), drawing on Beth Richie's claim that black women may be 'compelled into crime' by abusive partners and triple discrimination (1996). Most recently, Dorado reports that some Colombian women were groomed by men who gave them presents and romanced them to gain their trust (2005). This appears to draw on a common idea that traffickers search out women 'because they are likely to have clean records, create less suspicion and can conceal drugs more easily' (Steffensmeier 1983: 1025). Press accounts have claimed that young women are 'groomed' by traffickers (Francis 2008; Ward 2008). For example, the BBC reported on a Trinidadian woman befriended by a local loan shark who then forced her to work as a mule to repay her debt (Jeavans 2005). Nevertheless, Dorado also notes that some women became involved through others who were successful mules, indicating a more purposive involvement than research has previously suggested (2005). Penny Green found that some young women were pressured into trafficking by 'powerful men in their lives' such as landlords and loan sharks (Green 1998: 98). This research usefully draws attention to the fact that social connections and networks may be gendered, and there may be gendered inequalities at play. However, reliance on trafficker myths leaves questions about why women might make agential decisions to involve themselves in trafficking unexamined.

This chapter explores who the 'traffickers' were in women's accounts. It confronts two prevailing assumptions: firstly, that women are mostly involved unwillingly, as a result of coercion, threats, and deception from powerful men/traffickers, and secondly, that traffickers purposefully seek to recruit women, either because they are vulnerable to exploitation due to poverty, or because they are less likely to be detected. The second half of this chapter explores the 'traffickers' in women's accounts and demonstrates that rather than being sought out by traffickers, most women became involved through incidental social relationships, including boyfriends and friends who were involved. These relationships had important implications for how women interpreted the opportunity to become involved in trafficking. This chapter also draws on interviews with male mules and traffickers in order to better understand the social relationships between mules and their 'contacts'. The term 'contact' here follows respondents' use of the term and simply describes the person who was mules' first contact in the drug trade.

Involvement by force: coercion, threats, and deception

Given that all available research on drug mules reports coercion (especially Caulkins et al. 2009; Green 1998; Sudbury 2002; Huling 1995), it is perhaps not surprising that I encountered people who were involved unwillingly. Nonetheless, this was not the main route into trafficking for women, nor was it the case that solely women were subject to coercion and threats. It is nonetheless worthwhile understanding how coercion works.

Marina was in her mid-twenties when her ex-partner kidnapped their daughter and threatened Marina with an ultimatum:

> He told me you will travel for me to Ecuador, and you bring me that shit [cocaine] so that you will get your daughter back. If [you do] not, you will never see her alive.

Marina contacted the police and social services, but since her ex-partner was a legal guardian, no assistance was available. Marina was very scared; when she was pregnant, he beat her badly, and she lost her daughter's twin:

> I was so confused [about what to do] because I never [did] something like that, to travel with drugs. I didn't know what to do because I am also against this, especially cocaine and all that. [Marina explained that her partner became extremely violent towards her when he had been using cocaine] but somehow my only desire was to get my baby back. So at last I said yes, because I was really worried. [...] I can expect anything from him: when he is saying he wanted to kill her, I will believe it. For real.

Marina's experience echoes those previously reported in that she was compelled to traffic by gendered violence in the context of a historically abusive relationship (Sudbury 2002; also Huling 1995). Marina's narrative describes a conflict between two possible paths of action connected to her sense of self, which guides her perceptions and actions (Presser 2009; McNay 1999). On the one hand, she describes herself as someone 'against this, especially cocaine' but also as a mother who desperately wants to get her 'baby back'. Her identity as a mother is clearly deeply and emotionally held and so wins out. Thus, Marina's compliance was shaped by her identity as a mother, which she positively embraces. At the same time, it is also clear that Marina's ex-partner used this to coerce her.

Men also experienced coercion and threats. Howard worked in the music business in the 1970s and 80s and toured with Latin bands in Colombia. Twenty years later, Howard was visiting Ecuador when the brother of an old colleague and friend got back in touch, asked if he would carry some packages to North America, and offered him $8,000 to do so. Howard was approached several times; each time he refused, the wage increased. Howard had no interest in getting involved, describing himself as an ex-addict who had successfully rebuilt his life. For Howard, involvement with drugs would be incongruous:

> I mean $10,000, $20,000...no. I could use the money, yes, I could absolutely use the money. But what am I risking? You know. Anything and everything I re-attained. I'm not talking about material goods. [...] What did I have to gain? $20,000? [...] Here, that's what? Two years, four years of work, and you're talking about a six-hour trip. To them, it's the gold, it's the ark, it's the golden pot. To me it's not, it wasn't.

After Howard refused to get involved, his friend appeared suddenly and told Howard the 'material' was on its way. Howard was furious, they fought, and shortly after, Howard's wife received threatening phone calls saying there would be 'problems' if Howard didn't comply. When the drugs arrived, Howard's friend had a 9mm pistol tucked into the waist of his trousers. Although no explicit verbal threat was made to Howard, the threat was plausible due to the presence of a pistol and threats to his wife, backed up with Howard's first-hand knowledge of the drug industry:

> [In the 70s and 80s] we would have to perform at the cartel headquarters, and I would see all the Tommy guns and machine guns and AK-47s, and everybody armed to the teeth. [...] So...that was my mind-set. That's who I think they are.

Even though it violated his self-narrative as an ex-addict, Howard could not bear to consider *not* taking any available action to protect his wife and himself.

Marina's and Howard's experiences have much in common: both were threatened by men they knew who took advantage of their gendered relationships and responsibilities. Nonetheless, Howard and Marina give different accounts of their agency, drawing on normative scripts of gender:

> I was saying yes to carry drugs but think we must also think about why because most people are not interested in why [...] I don't [see] myself as a criminal 'cause somehow I didn't get to choose when I wanted to see her alive. (Marina)
>
> I take responsibility because I said yes. No matter what. I said yes. No matter how you were threatened or how you were cajoled, you said yes, so therefore it's yours. It's on your back. It's on you. (Howard)

Their differing interpretations (and subject positions) arguably reflect the different contexts in which they gave their accounts (see Chapter 3). Marina's reflects the institutional context of prison, and her need to maintain a 'non-criminal' sense of self to remain respectably female. Whilst Howard describes himself as an agent who is 'responsible', he still makes clear that his actions nonetheless took place in the context of threats.

Unknowing mules: 'set ups'

Two women described being 'set up'. Both came to Ecuador under unremarkable pretences. Sara came to help an old family friend organise papers for immigration to Europe (he was in transit in Latin America). Tisha came to Ecuador with her boyfriend for a romantic reconciliation. Both were arrested with drugs concealed in suitcases. The 'traffickers' in their accounts only became so after they were arrested. Tisha explained, 'I feel like I was...*raped* of my right to say, "Are out of your *damn mind*? What the hell is wrong with you?! You know, what kind of person are you?!"'

The metaphor of rape is extreme, but it conveys the sense of powerlessness and gendered victimisation that underpins Tisha's experience. It was precisely these gendered relationships characterised by trust that enabled both men to deceive them. Although Tisha and Sara had known the people who set them up for many years, legal investigations following their arrests revealed that Tisha's boyfriend and

Sara's friend had been living under pseudonyms and had lied about their pasts (and even their nationalities). Both gave a detailed explanation about how the drugs had come into their possession (exchange of suitcases, false names, warning signs that they had ignored, and so on); however, they were not positioned to understand why they were set up.

The recruiter's perspective on set ups and coercion

Claims of being 'set up' are often met with suspicion. It is virtually impossible to prove, in a legal sense (Kalunta-Crumpton 1998: 327; Fortson 2012: 2–29). Recruiters were able to help explain this phenomenon. I interviewed five people (four men and one woman) who recruited mules, or sent drugs by mule as an organiser/investor. They thought that the incentives offered attracted an ample quantity of willing workers. None had sent drugs with an unknowing mule, but most had heard of others who had done so. Ryan knew of someone who had successfully sent a friend's sister with a package of t-shirts impregnated with cocaine. The unwitting mule never knew that she was carrying cocaine. From a trafficker's perspective, there are some advantages. Costs can be significantly reduced. Some also argued that it would be 'safer' for the mule, as they were less likely to be nervous and more likely to pass security. It also reduces the chance of mules absconding with drugs. However, some also thought it was a gamble since drugs could be lost or damaged. Although the risk of losing the drugs might be high, the risk of arrest is extremely low.

It is notable that Tisha and Sara were set up by someone they knew. Although it is impossible to fully understand what happened, after discussion with traffickers, I would tentatively suggest that there are differences between a professional 'set up' and the experiences described above (and possibly Paula's experience, described in the previous chapter). Tisha and Sara noted that the person who set them up acted randomly and irrationally when they were in Ecuador. It is possible that the person who set them up was not an organiser/investor, but someone who was under coercion or pressure to pay debts. Instead of working as a mule themselves, they sought out someone they knew or simply planted the drugs on someone else.

Coercing mules appears counterintuitive, fuelling widespread scepticism.[8] Experienced mules stressed the importance of being calm and relaxed and looking like any other traveller – something a mule under threat or coercion is unlikely to be able to do. Intriguingly, no professional traffickers or recruiters admitted to coercing people into acting as a mule. Bobby (a Colombian who sent drugs internationally by mule) was extremely sceptical:

> Believe me, no one travels under obligation. Nobody. Nobody! This thing that people travel under obligations is a tale. No one is going to kill the father or brother of someone because they didn't want to travel. If I go and kill your brother, then you might speak to the police and... No one wants problems. Everyone wants to *distance* themselves from problems.

Yet, learning about 'set ups' perhaps throws some light on Howard and Marina's experiences of coercion. In both cases, threats came from people who were drug users and had violent, unstable tendencies. It is possible that both Marina's ex-boyfriend and Howard's friend were asked to work as a mule to pay back drug debts (this happened to Graham and is described below). Aware of the risk, they found someone else to carry the drugs for them and chose someone they knew and exploited existing (power) relations (in Marina's case) and knowledge (in Howard's case) to gain compliance. Indeed, coercion was probably a last resort, noting that Howard's contact tried to persuade him to work several times before he threatened him into working.

My aim here is not to offer a fulsome explanation about 'set ups' or coercion, but rather to demonstrate that the accounts above are plausible. This aspect of mule-work is not well researched, and the above shows that interviewing professionals adds important context to mules' accounts. It is impossible to say how common it is. I did not purposefully seek out respondents who had been coerced; nonetheless, they may have sought me out as a listener (see Chapter 3). Furthermore, to counterpoint the experiences of the willing and knowing mules, it is necessary to acknowledge that a minority are involved against their will or knowledge. Most respondents were not set up. The rest of the chapter examines mules' connections to drug trafficking.

Are people targeted for mule-work?

It is often thought that traffickers target women to exploit their poverty and naivety (Dorado 2005; Sudbury 2005b; Jeavans 2005). This was not borne out in this research. Age, being well travelled, having a passport, speaking a foreign language, and being socially connected were much more significant.

The mule's perspective

Some women were told that customs or the police would not pay any attention to them because of their gender. However, it was not being female alone that was important, but the intersection of nationality, age, skin colour, ethnicity/nationality, and experience of travelling: 'They said I was eighteen, I had an innocent face, I knew the procedure [at immigration], that I was [North American].' (Caroline)

As a young North American exchange student, Caroline would appear no different than the many thousands who travel to Ecuador every year. She had made several journeys between Ecuador and home and would have several stamps in her passport as evidence that this was a routine journey.

Indeed, some mules were approached precisely because they did not fit the stereotype of a mule as a poor person from the developing world. For example, many mules were employed, or came from countries that participated in the visa waiver scheme. Frank was in his fifties when he got involved in trafficking. His contact knew his was 'skint',[9] but Frank also explained that he had useful skills, including speaking Spanish. Like Frank, few thought they had been targeted due to some vulnerability (even those who were coerced), and most thought their contact had approached them for some specific quality that made them a 'good mule'. Howard thought that he was targeted because of his age, and being an experienced traveller (like Caroline):

> To them I was Mr. Ideal. Why was I Mr. Ideal? Because at this point, I'm in the third age of my life, I'm semi-sophisticated, and I can walk around with enough stamps in my passport to say, This guy travels all the time, not only to Ecuador, but to every other country in Latin America. Nobody questions me when I get to the border.

Frank and Howard were both in their fifties and were not the only older mules in prison. Jensen (an experienced mule also in his fifties) knew of several others who worked as a mule to supplement their government pension. He thought customs were less likely to suspect a pensioner.[10] Although historically women *were* perhaps less likely to be suspected, this is no longer the case. Zaitch contends that there was an important shift after 1991: 'Increasing global drug enforcement efforts pushed cocaine exporters to use less vulnerable couriers, more men, younger or older people, better off individuals with steady jobs, frequent flyers and more Colombians living abroad' (2002: 146). Respondents seemed to reflect these changes – many were older men from the global north, others were young 'backpacker' types (for example Caroline, but also Paula) and many were employed. This seems to indicate that traffickers tried to recruit mules who they thought would successfully be able to undertake the job, rather than someone they thought would be easily manipulated or 'groomed' into working as a mule.

The mule-recruiter's perspective

Recruiters looked for a number of qualities in a mule, including those they hoped would increase the likelihood of a mule passing customs. Ryan looked for people who were 'more normal than normal': people who could fit in at the airport and were unlikely to draw the attention of airport security. They had to look 'presentable', which excluded people with serious drug habits. Ryan also thought heroin users were unreliable and 'not worth the hassle'. Ryan also liked to recruit young, European 'backpacker types', and he concealed cocaine in sports equipment. Some recruiters mentioned that recruiting older people (like Frank, Howard, and Jensen) was ideal as they were the least likely to be suspected.

Some recruiters had also carried drugs across borders before, and they spoke about the importance of performing a credible role. Stefan wore a suit and carried a briefcase. Sometimes he would pay a woman to travel with him to play the part of a secretary. This is similar to 'contextual assimilation' tactics employed by drug dealers, which involves performing non-deviant roles that may also be gendered (Jacobs and Miller 1998; Fleetwood 2014). Similarly, Miller found that male street robbers involved women in supporting roles to successfully accomplish street robberies (1998). In other words, recruiters looked for people they thought would be best positioned to assimilate with other passengers.

Donna looked for someone with street smarts who was likely to be able to hold their own when going through customs:

> Most of the people that I sent are people that have been to jail before; they've already dealt with drugs before, so it wasn't people...I would never take someone that's innocent and that's quiet. I would never do that. I would always know people that knew what they were doing. If they got caught, they got caught.

Donna mainly recruited people that she knew of, but who did not know her well. As a drug dealer, she was part of a large network of loose contacts that she exploited. Donna didn't mind recruiting women but did not deal with friends since she would feel 'guilty' if they were caught. None mentioned that they would look specifically for a woman to do the job. This is perhaps not surprising, given that the majority of drug mules are men. Although gender was part of the picture, age, experience and nationality were equally if not more important. Indeed, recruiters said they would tend to avoid recruiting women since they were more likely to 'snitch', especially if they had children.[11] Ryan explained:

> Often men at upper levels say they don't want women involved. It's a sort of base instinct: you don't want to see women get arrested, you try not use women who've got kids. Women seem to think about the risk more, it tends to put them off. For example, for the women I've tried to get to work as a mule. Italians see it as more macho; for women it's not such an ego thing. They've got more to lose. They're more conscious of the consequences. Maternal instincts: they've got children.

Nonetheless, when I pushed him on the issue, he could think of many women that he knew who were involved in drug business. Rather than as mules, he often involved women in 'backstage' roles, such as managing and minding finances:

> 'How did they get into it?' I encouraged them, usually! Friends, getting them into business... Drivers, warehouse folk, it's the more trusting side [of business]. I suppose you tend to trust women friends more than male business associates. Men are more likely to sell it [drugs] on 'cause they're business associates. Also, women didn't have the contacts, so I specifically picked someone [who didn't have the contacts to sell on] or dispose of it [cocaine]. It's a bit harder with money. Anyone can spend [money], and frequently did.

Social connections were also important to avoid recruiting undercover police. They also ensured trust and acted as form of insurance against the mule absconding with the drugs (which had happened to Ryan):

> I look for someone that needs cash. Someone you trust, you know, responsible. I would actively go out 'n look for a mule among people I know. Usually once you find one, their friends see and put themselves forward. Ideally, I'd look for someone you can trust or frighten into not stealing [the drugs]... or at least have some control over them, maybe know their family. (Ryan)

Donna once tracked down a mule who had gone missing after returning with the drugs. Although investors thought she was trying to steal the drugs, it turned out that the mule thought she had been followed from the airport and so was lying low. Donna was able to find her relatively easily since she knew a bit about her background, friends, and family (and picked up a 'finder's fee' in the process). This echoes prior claims that social networks form a useful basis for trust (Adler 1993; Ianni and Reus-Ianni 1972; Dorn et al. 2005; Matrix Knowledge Group 2007). However, a fine balance had to be struck: recruiters looked for someone they could track down if necessary, but at the same time not someone who could identify them too easily. Some recruited through a specialised mule-recruiter, like Donna; however, even she sometimes recruited through a third person, suggesting mules may be recruited through chains of people. Although Donna would meet the mule, they would only know her by a false name. In sum then, it was clear that recruiters did seek out particular kinds of people for mules; however, there was little evidence to suggest that traffickers sought to recruit women, much less women who were vulnerable. Rather than gender, recruiters looked for a number of other qualities, including nationality.

Social connections and the drug trade

So far this chapter has demonstrated that it was not simply the case that traffickers sought out mules. The next section demonstrates that the connections between mules and drug trafficking 'contacts' tended to be incidental rather than instrumental. As such, most mules (male and female) were not coerced. Most came across an opportunity whilst a small number actively sought it out. Webs of social connections varied from close, romantic social ties to an apparent cold call from a stranger. These relationships were of course gendered; however, the influence of gender was not straightforwardly connected to victimisation. These social relationships also shaped respondents' interpretations of working as a mule, transforming it from risky to a realistic opportunity.

Romantic partners

Many women were connected to the drug trade through romantic partnerships, for example through husbands and boyfriends who were traffickers, or whose friends were involved in trafficking. In some cases, this set up subtle obligations. Marta's boyfriend, Gee, was the head of a drug trafficking organisation that sent mules all over South America.

Following the death of her father, Marta started smoking crack cocaine regularly and hung around 'the ghetto'. She was arrested for robbing a house and was imprisoned and deported with her daughter, who was under five years old. She met Gee on the flight 'home' to Africa (where she was born but had not lived since she was a child):

> He's like, 'Where are you gonna go?' I just broke into tears, girl. I got 20 bucks in my pocket, I've got all my clothes and my daughter's clothes [...] and I ain't got nowhere to go. I ain't got no phone numbers. I got nothing. He's like, 'Well, come hang out with me.' I'm like, whoa...I mean you don't do that kind of stuff in [this country]. I'm like, OK, what other opportunity do I have?

Marta and her daughter stayed with Gee, and they became involved. After they had been together for awhile, he proposed that she make a trip as a mule. The original plan was to work for him as a mule (but in the end she worked for his friend). This was presented to her as an opportunity. Her boyfriend may not have intended her to feel obliged, but she certainly did:

> In a way, I owed these people. They took me into their home, and they were feeding me and my daughter. One way or the other, I made my own decision, it was my own choice, put it that way. But in the way he looked at me and said, can you do this? I couldn't say no either.
>
> JF: t's like a subtle form of persuasion. [...]
>
> M: Yeah, but more than that, 'cause they treated me nicely and my daughter, too. I couldn't sit there and wait for someone else to collect the cash. I was always independent in relationships. I was always the one with the money, so I felt kind of helpless and....What's the word...(long pause).
>
> JF: Frustrated?
>
> M: Oh, very, I was very frustrated.
>
> JF: So, what did having the money mean to you?
>
> M: [pauses to think] Control and independence.

On the one hand, Marta spoke about obligations and lack of control over her life. At the same time, she also saw trafficking as a credible opportunity: 'I'd seen the deals go through in Brazil. I believed it.'

Rather than seeing working as a mule as dangerous and risky, Marta saw it as not especially difficult:

> I had to go bra shopping, and I bought 2 cream bras – it had to be cream – and, um, one was one size bigger, which was the outside one, and they put it in the cups and sew it up, and then you just put it on, and it fits around your breasts, you understand, you just look a lot bigger. And I thought, well, *that sounds pretty fucking easy*, you know.

Furthermore, Marta interpreted the way her partner helped organise the trip as a reflection of their relationship: 'He said to me, "You're not going to carry it in your stomach: it's very dangerous." So, I'm thinking OK, this guy really cares.'

Manuela was in her late 30s when she became involved. Manuela was also asked to work as a mule by her boyfriend (the contacts were her boyfriend's friends):

> He promised that we would get married and have a future together, but he said that we needed money. I was working as a prostitute, and he started to get really mad about it. He started to treat me like shit, screaming at me and cheating on me.

He suggested that she work as a mule instead. After Manuela agreed, he treated her well, and she felt like they were in love and starting a new future together. It is very difficult to tell whether or not this manipulation was planned before they became involved; however, the balance of power likely lay with her partner. Manuela is learning disabled and was placed in social care as a child. Without drawing overly simplistic conclusions, it is important to note that having a stable life situation and being taken care of were particularly meaningful for Manuela; during the interview she talked about how she considered herself to be getting too old to be a prostitute and worried about the future. Thus, her involvement was not only due to pressures from her boyfriend, but also the draw of domestic security. In sum then, for Marta and Manuela, relationships with their boyfriend/contact were also frequently bound up with a positive wish for love and security, as well as obligation.

It is possible that Manuela (and even Marta) were 'groomed' from the start. It is possible that their 'boyfriends' were merely traffickers who sought to gain their confidence through emotional manipulation as Dorado would claim (2005). Nonetheless, a trafficker such as Bobby thought that seemed unlikely:

> These things don't happen because trafficking is a business. Firstly you have find a girlfriend, then you make her fall in love with you, then convince her to carry a suitcase... no... It's much simpler to pay some guy $2,000 to carry a kilo, knowing that I would be making about $20,000, and if he wanted more, I would pay him more!

It seems more likely that drug trafficking connections simply coexisted with romantic relationships. This was the case for most women who became involved through their boyfriend's or husband's friends (including Caroline, Bonny, and Anika and Angela). For example, Caroline was a North American exchange student who attended a high school in Ecuador for a year. While she was in Ecuador, she met her boyfriend. She was hanging out with him and his friends in an Internet café that was an established landmark in the touristic neighbourhood, La Mariscal. Caroline's boyfriend's friends were talking about trafficking cocaine and asked if she wanted to get involved. She said yes. Although her boyfriend was present, he actively discouraged her. So although she knew her contacts through her boyfriend, he played no role in recruiting her and in fact tried to persuade her to back out several times.

In sum then, women tended to be connected to drug trafficking through men in extended social circles and milieu associated with the men in their lives. This is not surprising, given that the international drug trade is male dominated (Adler 1993). No men became involved in trafficking through female partners. For example, Paul (an independent trafficker) married a Colombian woman; however, it was not her suggestion, or her connections that created the opportunity. Their relationship (and visits to her family) created an opportunity to be exploited, rather than the source of gendered obligations as it was for some female respondents. Thus, these kinds of connections were undoubtedly gendered, but relationships were not, per se, exploitative.

Through successful mules

Three women became involved through successful female mules. Catalina became involved through her friend. When I asked her how she became involved, she promptly replied 'I fell in love', but this is only part of the picture. She met her boyfriend (and became involved in trafficking) through her friend, Diana, who invited her on a trip to Europe (paid for by Diana's boyfriend):

> It was really fun, but Diana thought something strange [was going on]. The guys had a normal house, like not luxury, but they had

> everything. In the evenings we were going out, having fun, you know, but how the hell do they have the money? There's nobody working, but they have the good clothes, expensive perfume, etc. I was like, I don't know! I didn't care, I was young – I was 23, it's not my business. When it was Christmas, he asked if I wanted to go shopping to celebrate. He gave me $400 in my hand, so we went shopping!
>
> Three months later they sent us tickets to travel [to see them]. Diana didn't have the courage to tell me, but she knew. They asked her how's her family, economically, and if she wants extra money, she can make a good amount. She asked, 'What do I have to do?' At first she was scared, thinking it had to be prostitution. The guys said 'Do you want to travel?' Said he'd get her a visa, passport, everything she needed. In the end, they told her what's going on, and she accepted, then she came and explained to me. She said she'd get $6–7000 and for the country I'm coming from [Eastern Europe], the salary is like $150 a month so imagine! For $5000 you can buy a house. I mean a very good house. So, she travelled first, and she succeeded. She went to [EU country] for one month. She wanted to stay! She went everywhere. Part of the expenses you receive are to travel like a tourist: she got clothes, camera, everything. She called and said she's having a really good time, seeing all the sights and everything. Of course it's exciting – it's really hard to leave my country. Some people are selling their home, people are risking their lives, crossing the river and forests, so for her, imagine! Travelling and coming back with good money in her pocket. When she came back she said that it was great, really fun. So when my boyfriend asked if I wanted to do it, I said yes.

For Catalina, the opportunity to work as a mule was embedded in several social relationships – not only her trafficker boyfriend, but also her friend who worked successfully as a mule. Catalina saw it as a lucky opportunity:

> The first to travel was my friend. When I see her walk through the door, I see she's happy, she has money, she can buy a house for her sister. I think wow, its cool. I didn't see the danger in there.

Amanda became involved through a friend who had worked successfully as a mule. Like Catalina, she sought out the opportunity after seeing someone else return successfully:

> [Judy] was a friend of the family for years. She was my sister's best friend. They would go out dancing together...her daughter used to go to my kids' school, so I used to meet up with her for our kids to play together, and I'm the type of person, if I know you, from like years ago, I'll still go see you...I'll go visit you, have a cup of coffee, and um, I didn't see no harm in it. I knew her father sold drugs though, so I'd always stay in the house minimum an hour 'n leave, and um, since I was into *that* at that time, we would steal her father's stash and just, get high.
>
> She was like, 'I'm going to Ecuador.' I was like, 'What're you talking about?' She was like, 'Yeah, they're gonna pay me $9000.' I was like 'What?! Are you nuts?' She went through with it 'n I saw her months later. I think 2 months later I would say, and...she got away with it.

Later, when Amanda was in debt, she sought out the opportunity to do the same (see Chapter 5). Amanda's connection to the trade were unremarkable – paying old friends a visit was a normal part of her social life, but they also connected her to opportunities to traffic as her friend's boyfriend was able to connect her to someone who could employ her as a mule. These findings echo Zaitch, who concludes that 'strong identification with surrounding successful couriers' reduced mules' conception of risk (2002: 149). Furthermore, seeing other *women* as successful mules had a role in making mule-work seem a viable avenue for (illegal) money earning. Both Tanya (below) and Amanda had been involved in illegal forms of money making (benefit fraud, cheque fraud, and drug dealing) and as such, they may simply have been attuned to take note of new ways of making money. As Dorado notes, these kinds of connections suggested more agential routes into trafficking than has previously been suggested (2005).

Street-level drug market

For three women, the street-level drug market offered connections to the international drug trade. Sharon (early 30s, white African) was a regular crack cocaine user. Her dealer offered to connect her to people who could employ her as a mule. Sharon was not indebted to her dealer, and no obligations were attached to the offer. Although recruiters tended to avoid employing people with drug habits (see above), this was a viable route into trafficking, if not an especially common one. Some women were dealers before they were mules. Tanya (a European woman in her 20s) met a successful mule through dealing ecstasy and other 'dance drugs' (in her words) in clubs and sought out the opportunity for herself. Donna (from North America) dealt cocaine as part of her active social life in the Latin community. She recruited mules through these connections for a fellow cocaine dealer and long time friend (who was also her ex-boyfriend). When she could not find someone to work as a mule, she decided to do the job herself. This was common – several male traffickers had also done the same thing. This route into trafficking was also reported by some male mules, including Graham. He became involved through a school friend who he had also sold drugs with. So, even connections through the street level drug trade could also be based on shared history and friendships.

'Cold call'

Only two respondents were recruited through people not already part of their social circle. Frank was in his fifties when he was offered mule-work by an acquaintance. He was unemployed at the time and relying on social benefits. He met someone in his local pub:

> We used to go to restaurants, bars 'n so on, then he said 'Do you want to earn a few bucks?' 'Yeah, why not.' [It was a] free holiday, and because I spoke Spanish, he latched onto me. He knew I was skint.

After Frank's arrest, his contact was able to disappear, free of the kinds of social ties that conventionally connected mules. The offer was presented to him as an opportunity, in many ways resembling a conventional offer of informal work. There was little obligation provided by either the social relationship or the conditions in which the offer was made. Similarly, Nan was approached by a customer when she was working in a bar. She was in her mid-twenties at the time, living in a large city in Southeast Asia:

> In my country, I was with my boyfriend, and when he went home, I was broke, no money, so I worked in a bar. I met an African guy, and he asked me if I wanted to work. I asked, What work? He said, Do this, do this...it was drug traffic.

Nan had worked for her boyfriend before, travelling with mules and watching them in case anything happened. I prompted Nan about if she had met this man before since her boyfriend was also African. Nan was sure she had never met him, but said, 'I lived with Africans before. I know what they do.' It is impossible to know if this was a cold call, or if this man had heard about Nan. Nevertheless, from Nan's perspective, the offer came from a relative stranger and so had no obligation attached.

Risk and opportunity

The socially situated nature of drug trafficking connections played an important role in how women interpreted the possibility of becoming a mule. Rather than seeing traffickers as dangerous individuals, and mule-work as exploitative and risky, meeting successful mules or traffickers did much to transform this into an opportunity rather than a risk. These subjective interpretations are extremely important, given that trafficking is a hidden activity, and it is impossible to account for risk in any objective way. Although law enforcement agencies continually emphasise the likelihood of mules being arrested, conversely almost all professional traffickers, mule watchers, recruiters, and contacts in this research were convinced that very few mules were caught (despite being in prison). Nonetheless, the simple fact that sending drugs by mule continues in spite of increasing arrests worldwide suggests this method of transportation remains successful and profitable. It is impossible to estimate the odds of a mule getting caught. Mules had to make their assessment on the basis of considerably less information, and so drew on existing webs of meaning connected to the social relationships, which formed the basis of their involvement.

It was also the case that recruiters could be quite skilled at presenting themselves as experts in the business who were in control and could assure safe passage. Contacts commonly offered a variety of reassurances such as: the police were paid off; no one ever got caught; they knew of a safe route; the drugs are packed in a way that cannot be detected; they would pay for a lawyer to ensure they were released, or they offered a cover story that would enable the mule to claim they did not know what they were carrying. Whilst these claims seem implausible, it is impossible to know if the police were ever really paid off, or if there really are routes that are safer than others. Meeting successful mules would certainly give credence to such claims. Nonetheless, the fact that I was interviewing arrested mules suggests that these may have been half-truths, at best. At worst, respondents may have been set up as decoys to divert customs officers (who had been tipped off by the organisers) to allow another mule with considerably more drugs through undetected.

One afternoon I was sitting in the patio of the men's prison talking to Ryan about recruiting mules. He reckoned he had sent at least ten (he assured me that none had ever been arrested). At my request, he explained how he would outline the deal to a potential mule. Several kilos of cocaine would be chemically camouflaged as part of some sporting equipment. He explained that it did not look or smell like cocaine; you could cut it, melt it, put it in water and it would maintain its integrity. Ryan was careful to emphasise that this was not an amateur job; white powder was not going to start spilling out of rickety suitcases.

Next, he explained that he would always give the mule a cover story in case of arrest. In one such cover story, the mule would claim to be carrying the sports equipment (in which the drugs were concealed) home for someone else they had met travelling as a favour. He could even set up an e-mail address to show that the mule had corresponded with this person. This was a plausible cover story. Ecuador is an international tourist centre and home to the Galapagos Islands, with a variety of sports available: mountaineering, water sports, kayaking, cycling, and many more. A large number of tourists pass through Ecuador each year; it was typical to see surfboards, diving or climbing gear, and mountain bikes on flights to/from Quito. Many tourists are young backpackers, and there is a lively backpacking scene that would make this kind of interaction common. Furthermore, he explained to me convincingly (in spite of my knowledge to the contrary) that if the mule *was* caught, their case would be watertight in a court of law. Since they could 'prove' that they had no idea that they were carrying drugs (due to the highly effective chemical camouflage) and could legitimately claim that they were carrying it home on behalf of someone they had met backpacking (and would be able to produce their e-mail address and correspondence as proof) the court could not hold the mule legally responsible and would have to let them go.

In part, Ryan was so convincing because of the way he portrayed himself: as professional, friendly, and concerned for the mule. He also explained that whenever it was possible, he would meet the mule to hand over the drugs. As much as this had an important function of making sure that nothing went wrong (i.e., drugs being stolen by either party), he said that he would also

> make the mule feel comfortable, send them on a holiday, let them think you're taking care of them [...] That's how come I could recruit people. I can persuade them in person, I know the ins and outs. I can make it sound extremely good. [But] obviously there's more risk than I can make out.

His account successfully played up the ease and professionalism of the project. However, he also admitted that his job involved minimising apparent risks.

Interestingly, some mules were given detailed information, which did turn out to be accurate (see Marta, above). Nonetheless, mules rarely had the cultural capital to be able to understand the implications of such details (regarding likelihood of getting caught, and sentencing should they be arrested) (Fleetwood 2011). For example, kilo amounts were often meaningless when they could not judge what a reasonable (or unreasonable) quantity would be:

> Yeah, I know it's a lot [5 kilos]. I didn't think about it though, you know. I just wanted to do it fast, get the money, and just forget about everything, you understand. (Anika)

Mules were typically provided with a variety of partial truths about the work they would undertake. Some mules believed they were travelling to one country, and then were sent to another (sometimes another continent) at the last moment. Mules arrested with heroin were almost always under the impression that they were carrying cocaine. Many simply knew it was dangerous and had no interest in finding out *how* dangerous. This was especially the case for those recruited through someone they did not have any trust in.

Conclusion

This chapter explored women's connections to the international drug trade, or in narrative terms, who the 'traffickers' were in their accounts. Rather than the 'Mr. Big' that features in policy and political discourses about traffickers, women's narratives revealed a heterogeneous array of 'contacts', including friends, boyfriends, and their friends, fellow drug dealers, fellow drinkers, and customers. Prior sociological research on trafficking has revealed that most men become involved in trafficking through personal connections (Decker and Chapman 2008: 96; Ianni 1974), and in this respect, women are no different. It was notable that most contacts in women's (and men's) accounts were male, but this is hardly surprising given that the drug trade, like crime in general, is male dominated. Some women were connected to the international drug trade in similar ways to men, such as through friendship networks, or drug trade connections (Matrix Knowledge Group 2007; Caulkins et al. 2009). One respondent, Donna, was arrested as a mule but had also recruited others, blurring neat distinctions between 'traffickers' and 'mules'. Nonetheless, women's connections to the trade were also distinct. Several women were connected through romantic partners (or indirectly through partners' friends). These social connections played a fundamental role in shaping how women encountered and interpreted the possibility of becoming a mule. Rather than risk and danger of exploitation, many saw an opportunity. This was especially the case where respondents became involved through successfully mules. Understanding the nature of women's trafficking connections is central to understanding how their involvement in trafficking could be a reasonable, and even agential action (albeit in limited circumstances).

Overall, the kinds of connections that facilitated women's involvement in trafficking tended to be incidental, rather than instrumental. While it has been argued that women may become involved in drug traffic due to 'grooming' (Dorado 2005), traffickers and recruiters privileged other qualities (nationality, having a passport, being well travelled) over gender. Indeed, men preferred not to work with women, lending credence to theories of homo-social reproduction in crime networks (Steffensmeier 1983; Mullins and Wright 2003). In spite of this, men also reported employing women to undertake a variety of other roles (working as accountants, recruiting and minding mules). Although researchers have encountered women who have become involved through exploitative and abusive relationships (Sudbury 2002, 2005b), it was far more common for women here to report subtle forms of obligation. A minority of respondents were coerced or threatened into carrying drugs, but this was the exception rather than the rule. Coercion (and set ups) appeared to be opportunistic rather than routine. Gender power was significant, but coercion did not occur *solely* in the context of gendered inequalities, and not all relationships were exploitative. Rather than gendered inequality and exploitation, interviews with recruiters showed that knowing who the mules were was more important than the mules being desperate, indebted, or poor. In this way, mules' connections had much in common with connections between traffickers: social networks were a basis for trust (Adler 1993; Decker and Chapman 2008: 96; Zaitch 2002). However, these connections were not mutual: recruiters like to know about mules but concealed information about themselves.

Whilst drug war discourses conceive of traffickers as foreign 'others', respondents knew traffickers as participants in local social circles, first and foremost. According to Hobbs,

> Networks are the media through which individuals and groups move between the local and the global, but this does not indicate the kind of structural determinism suggested by many writers on organised crime. Networks here refer to metaphors for relationality. (1998: 419)

These networks of relationality were transnational. Interestingly, it was not the case that shared ethnicity/nationality formed the basis for trust, as in prior research (i.e., Colombian immigrants in the Netherlands (Bovenkerk et al. 2003; Zaitch 2002) or Jamaican mules in London (Ruggiero and South 1995; Dorn et al. 2005). The picture here is quite different: most contacts were of a *different* national and ethnic background than mules. Most contacts were Latin-Americans or Africans living in Europe, North America or Southeast Asia; most mules were North Americans living in North America, Europeans living in Europe, and so on. Rarely mules were Europeans or North Americans visiting or living in South America. It is possible that mules may have been specifically chosen because they were *distantly* connected to national groups of migrants. There is good reason to recruit mules from distantly known people, especially because of the risk of arrest. Furthermore, it is worth reiterating that mules were rarely 'groomed', so it seems likely that these kinds of national connections were, for many respondents, simply a fact of everyday life and relationships, albeit ones that take place in the context of globalisation (Ray 2007; Castles and Miller 2009). Although drug trafficking has been constructed as an 'alien invasion' (see Chapter 1), the picture here is one of criss-crossing, international flows of people. Given that my knowledge of contacts is filtered through respondents' interpretations, it is difficult to conclusively say much about the role of ethnicity and nationality in trafficking networks, so a degree of 'ethnic skepticism' is necessary here (Murji 2007).

At the end of this chapter, a complex picture is emerging: one in which the majority of women mules are neither 'volunteers' nor exploited victims in any straightforward way. This picture becomes further complicated in the next chapters, which examine mules' motives, and what mules did when they trafficked drugs or tried to back out.

5
For Money and Love: Women's Narratives about Becoming Mules

Amanda was ten months from the end of a four-year sentence when I interviewed her about the circumstances that led to her involvement in the international cocaine trade. She was in her late twenties, Latina (but grew up in North America), and was living in one of the newest pavilions of El Inca. This was our third interview. We had agreed to talk about the trafficking part of her story, and she began by reading me a short passage written in her journal:

> I was with my children's father since the age of 13 [...] and had my son at 15, my twins at 19, and my other son at 23. [...] So [he] was the first man in my life. He took my virginity, and I have my kids from him. I guess I could say I watch 'Little House on the Prairie' too much, cause I'm like, you know, I didn't marry him, but he took my virginity, so that calls for me to stay with him no matter what. Even though he put me through hell. I would work; I would do so many things and on top of that, hustle the system to get extra money.

Throughout the interview, her narrative described other aspects of her life, including school, family, and her relationship with her boyfriend. I have quoted at length to give readers a feel of the complexity of her narrative:

> I was working in the city, and uh...I wasn't really doing too good 'cause I was like *stressed* out. Taking my kids to school in the morning, I wouldn't be able to...I don't know. I had to take them to school, I had to take my son to day care, I had to get to work, sometimes the trains wouldn't be running regularly 'n I'd be late (laugh), it was a disaster for me. I'd get there late sometimes, you know, I was a

> temp, but I was a very respectable one, you know, I had good credentials with the company, so they just admired what I did for them. So everything was OK until the towers, the twin towers fell down.
>
> To cut a long story short, I lost my job after [my country hit an economic crisis]... Well, practically a lot of people did. The economy was terrible. It was like red light all over [the city]. [...] I already told you I was like an alcoholic basically, you know. I started going out into the world, into the bars 'n stuff like that 'n talking to people, 'n I started beginning to know about the type of person [my husband] was 'n everything, so I decided to leave him [He had been violent towards her, and she discovered he was unfaithful]. I decided to leave him, 'n I went to my mum's house 'n left my apartment that I had suffered to get by going through a shelter with my three kids (because I didn't have the last one yet).
>
> I left that apartment to give it to [my husband], to give him time to leave. I stayed in this little room with my mom and my four kids. Four months later, he called 'n [told me] he's leaving. I go back to my apartment and find nothing there. He took my furniture. He took my sofas, my bedroom set, a TV in my son's room. So I called him 'n cursed him out... [Later] I get this letter that I have to go to court. Apparently I owe $4000 in rent for the 4 months I haven't been there... The light bill was $1000, a little over, and the gas, you know. So I'm like I have four kids to take care of, what am I gonna do? You know.
>
> So, after I had that hearing with the judge, and the judge said I have a week to come up with the money, and I'm like, with all my bills in front of me on the kitchen table. I can't eat, I can't sleep; I started to smoke cigarettes. My kids are sleeping. I walk two blocks over to her house 'n just knock on [Judy's] door. I go upstairs and her boyfriend was in her bed, she was there. 'I wanna do it.' They're like, 'Are you sure?' 'Yes, I'm sure.' [...] In a week's time, I had my passport, I had a thousand dollars, 'n I had directions of what to do when I get to Ecuador.

Quoting Amanda at length shows the meanings are embedded and suspended in her narrative (Reissman 1993). Her account was not chronological, and I steered her back to talking about trafficking several times. This 'difficulty' in giving her account reflects taboos about talking about trafficking in prison, as well as the fact that Amanda is struggling to give me a 'true' account that reflects the events, feelings, and relationships that were important to her at that time. Alongside her narrative of a respectable hard working mother is another about the stress and exhaustion of temporary work, commuting, single-motherhood, reliance on an under-resourced welfare state, and cycling between her mother's house, the women's shelter, and a place of her own. She hints that her response to the stress was to go out to bars and try drugs, including cocaine. These experiences and feelings were harder to articulate. In a later interview, she explained:

> I told you about [my husband], right? And about how [he] drove me crazy? I told you about me 'n my rent, my kids 'n everything like that. I don't know. I guess I was thinking selfishly [...] I don't know, thinking very selfishly. You know it hurts me when I think about that... I wasn't thinking... just thinking to get away from everything. [...] But it's like, I wasn't only a mother to my kids. I was a mother to [my husband]. I was a mother to my mother; I was a mother to... I was just tired. I was too tired

Amanda's involvement cannot be adequately described as the result of either compulsion or choice: it clearly reflects elements of both. It is certainly the case that her choices were objectively and materially constrained in ways that were gendered and raced. As a temp, her employment was precarious, and the first to go in times of economic crisis. Furthermore, since her name was on the rental documents; the magistrate judged her to be responsible for debts incurred. As a single parent, she was financially and materially responsible for her children. Certainly her experiences fit well with the concept of the 'feminisation of poverty' (Dorado 2005; del Olmo 1986; 1990); nonetheless, the meanings of poverty are locally specific and shape both the background and forefronts of crime (Miller 2002). Amanda's job loss was a crisis but she also gives a sense of many years of grinding poverty and insecurity in temporary employment and reliance on meagre benefits, leaving her with little to fall back on.

Her narrative also shows that her involvement in trafficking was also led by her sense of self as the basis for evaluating her options and priorities. Throughout, Amanda emphasises *who* she was/is, more than what she had done. She describes herself as a respectable, hard working, loving woman: emphasising her traditional values regarding relationships and her hard work against all odds (including unreliable public transport and her unfaithful boyfriend). Her self is connected to significant others in her life (children, boyfriend, parents, employers). She also told me that her mother's rent was overdue, and she was worried that they would all be evicted. If she didn't do something, 'everybody would be in the doghouse'. She draws on discourses of poverty (which were common in El Inca), to explain her offending by emphasising her lack of choice. In these respects, her narrative is a common one, albeit drawing on her unique biography and circumstances.

The centrality of Amanda's *selves* in her narrative indicate the importance of her sense of self as protagonist in shaping how she interprets her circumstances, the actions she should take and the future selves she wishes to be. In other words, drawing on her narrative identity as mother ordered the events as they unfolded and shaped priorities, and possible outcomes. Amanda describes herself as a woman who placed (and continues to place) her children and motherhood as central to her sense of self. As a Latina, she learned to cook, clean, and care for the men in her life from an early age and was now the matriarchal head of the family. These experiences and contexts are an important part of her habitus, which shapes *how* she evaluates, reflects, prioritises, and acts. These form the basis of her 'practical reflexivity' (Bohman 1997; McNay 2004). Her identity is not solely about her as an *individual* but is also about her relationships to others: 'We would *all* be in the doghouse.' In other words, her evaluations of social action are based on an identity that is fundamentally relational (Eakin 1999; Gilligan 1982; Somers 1994).

Nonetheless, she also has ambivalent feelings about that identity and responsibility, so involvement in trafficking also offered her the possibility of escape and respite, if only for a short time. She defined these desires as 'selfish' and said it 'hurts... to think about that'. Thus, Amanda's narrative about becoming a mule reflects contradictory feelings and identities. It is underpinned by a sense of fatalism: she could simply see no alternative. As McNay puts it so memorably, 'individuals act in certain ways because it would violate their sense of being to do otherwise' (1999: 318).

Introduction

This chapter approaches women's motives for involvement in trafficking as narrative evaluations in response to material circumstances and possibilities. In other words, this chapter draws on the claim made by Presser that individuals act on the basis of the self as an imagined protagonist in an evolving story (2008, 2009). This is described in more detail at the end of Chapter 2. To recap, narratives are subjective evaluations and interpretations of circumstances and events (Holstein and Gubrium 2000). These subjective accounts occupy the intersection between structure (possibilities are materially and discursively limited) and agency (individual interpretations and appropriations of culturally available discourses) (Presser 2009: 179; Sandberg 2010: 455). In other words, 'narrative criminologists should understand self-narratives dialectically – as agency conditioned by context – and as attempts at coherence that draw on a wide variety of cultural narratives and discourses.' (Presser and Sandberg, forthcoming).

Prior research into the relationship between self-narratives and offending has tended to focus on men, describing how offending behaviour enables men to enact particular kinds of narrative identities, for example as hero (Presser 2008, 2012). Tricky questions about how, or whether, women fulfil gendered identities through crime remain (Miller 2002). Arguably, women's discursive 'work' is especially interesting, given that women's offending is more heavily stigmatised (Lloyd 1995). Women's motives clustered around money, romantic love, and to a lesser extent, excitement. Each of these narrative themes will be discussed in turn.

Women's narratives about money

Given the significance of poverty in prior research and in El Inca (see Chapter 3), it is not surprising that most mules described themselves as motivated by money (as Amanda does above). Rather than absolute poverty, individual narratives reflected local economic circumstances, as well as women's interpretations according to local expectations about the role of women (as well as respondents' age, family circumstances, ethnicity, and nation). They reflected relative deprivation, refracted through narratively constructed selves (Holstein and Gubrium 2000).

Nan came from East Asia. Like many young women of her generation, she moved to the city in search of work and sent money home to her family. She was working in a bar when a man offered to pay her to carry cocaine from Brazil to Southeast Asia (plans were later changed, and she travelled to Ecuador). The offer of mule-work came at the same time that she learned that her grandmother (who had raised her) was sick. Nan planned to traffic to pay for her treatment. Other mules have claiming to have been motivated by hospital bills for family members (Sudbury 2005b; Green 1998). It is possible that Nan's narrative is more strategic than truthful. Nonetheless, it does reflect her national background, which does not have the kinds of government welfare that are taken for granted in the global Northwest.[1]

Although paying for the operation for her grandmother was an important motive, it was not the only one. Nan explained that the amount she would have been paid would have allowed her to return to the village to live with her family. She said she had 'grown tired' of life in the city. While living away from her family, she smoked amphetamines and had a devastating relationship with a man who left her broke, taking the money he had promised to pay her for minding mules (she did not speak to mules, but watched over them from a distance). Most painfully, she described how he pushed her towards having an abortion, which she still felt very emotional about. When she accepted the offer of mule-work, she was working long hours in a bar to make ends meet with few opportunities to change her situation. Nan's narrative expressed a strong sense of longing to be home in her family's village, and sadness that she did not see her grandmother one last time before she died. She had also wanted to 'do right' to make up for the years that she had been away from her family. For Nan, working as a mule represented an opportunity to gain the economic capital to return home, provide for her family, and embrace a positive identity as good daughter. So, rather than the continuation of a pre-existing narrative identity (as in Amanda's case as 'struggling mother'), the opportunity to traffic represented the opportunity to enact a new, 'good' identity, according to locally significant ideals about what good daughters ought to do.

Tanya lived in Western Europe and was also in her late twenties. She was educated and had been employed (but was unemployed when she became involved in trafficking). Like Nan, her narrative incorporates 'failing' to fulfil her gendered role and represents involvement in trafficking as a route towards new opportunities, fulfilling gendered responsibilities and sense of self. Tanya's drug career began by selling in a club, which she described as a busy, but fun time. Tanya loved music and dancing (she danced whenever possible in prison and choreographed a dance group). The birth of her baby radically changed her life:

> I didn't like how it changed. Like, before I was always in the street, only going to my house just to sleep. [...] I never used drugs before my child, but I was always around people, never on my own. Every four hours, I had to give her food; I was changed totally, and I don't like this. I will not get a child again for sure. It's too much changing for my life.

Tanya put her baby in her mother's care. She explains:

> I didn't traffic when I had my child, only after [...] On one side I wanted to be with her, on the other side I saw it's not good...but

> everybody was hoping about it, that I could make a choice to say it's not good for my child to be like this, I have to do something, and she cannot live with me. I could not find the way out alone out of this drug world. [It was] not because I was a drug trafficker, but because I was a drug user. It was better for my daughter. I cannot give her things that my mother can give her.

Tanya planned to use the money she would make working as a mule to support her mother and daughter financially, which would have enabled her to enact another kind of identity: the decent working mother (Tanya planned to make several trips). This was an extension of an existing way of life and conception of self and a way to enact a positive mothering identity.

She became involved through a successful mule she met when she was dealing drugs in clubs, but she did not work as a mule until after she gave her child to her mother years later. Only then did taking the opportunity to traffic hold this particular set of meanings. In contrast to Amanda and Nan, Tanya was not facing a financial crisis or urgent need for money, but saw trafficking as a way of providing for her family in the long term.

The theme of meeting the material demands of parenthood was very common in mule's narratives. The term 'provisioning' is useful here. Adam Smith used 'provisioning' to refer to 'the creation and distribution of the necessaries and conveniences of life' (Ferber and Nelson 1993). This term has been adopted by feminist economists Ferber and Nelson, for whom it describes 'having the basic goods and services consistent with a society's social norms' (Strober 2003: 148, see also Davies 2003). Successful 'provisioning' was deeply intertwined with Tanya's assumed identity as mother; however, the exact meanings differed, reflecting local, culturally embedded expectations as well as an individual's particular circumstances.

Anika lived in Western Europe (like Tanya) and was in her early thirties and married with a daughter when she became involved through her husband's friends. Her narrative centres on providing adequate housing for her family in accordance with local norms:

> I wanted to move, you know, I needed money, and I was thinking of taking an opportunity just once to make some money. Just once. I wanted to because I never did it before [...] I wanted to make [it] for another house. I just wanted to move so that she [daughter] could have her own room.

Marta was in her early twenties when she and her daughter were deported to Africa after she was arrested for robbery. She was white, described her family as financially very well off, and had previously been employed in a job she enjoyed. After she was deported, she found it very hard to get work. Providing for her daughter was also important in her account:

> JF: So, what did having the money mean to you?
>
> M: [pauses to think] Control and independence. Being able to say... like I would go to the shops with my daughter, and she'd see something she liked. One day she saw a comforter – one with moons and stars which she always liked, and it was [expensive]. I didn't have the money. I couldn't say 'at the end of the month we can get it, or in a few days', so I ignored it, just said 'come on, let's go'. The next time she told my friend about it when we passed by the shop, and he said that he'd buy it for her. And I felt like, Oh my God, where's my life got to? I felt like a worthless mother, actually. I felt like I couldn't provide for her.
>
> JF: It's expensive being a mother, eh?
>
> M: Being a mother costs money, and it really hurts when you can't give them what they want. Before, in a way, yeah, I could buy her toys, not everything but like when I would get paid I'd buy her some clothes or whatever, and she always had what she needed. [Not being able to do that], I kind of felt helpless, insecure. Everything in one.

Marta's account speaks of motherhood as a multiple identity in which provisioning plays an important role in her self-esteem. Although she wanted to be able to provide for her daughter materially, she wanted to be able to do so on her own terms, which she describes as having independence and control. As a single parent, the sole responsibility fell on her, and she felt a strong sense of disappointment at not being able to fulfil this role. In the previous chapter, Marta described how she was deported after being arrested for robbery and moved in with a man she met on the flight home. The incident with the comforter was perhaps more strongly felt since she and her daughter were not living in their own apartment at the time and were facing an uncertain future:

> [My boyfriend said] go do this trip for me. And I'm thinking great. I don't have to ask Mum for money anymore. I can buy myself a little nightclub, 'cause we had plans to buy a nightclub, and a car, and I could rent an apartment, or take an apartment on a loan.

For Marta, trafficking was a way to regain her lost sense of self as an independent woman in control of her life and as provider for her child. Rather than reflecting long-term poverty and lack of opportunity, it reflects her newfound status as an immigrant living under precarious circumstances. Like Tanya, she had come across the opportunity to work as a mule before; however, under those circumstances, it was simply not meaningful:

> When I was [home], smoking, this one guy, he was a dealer of mine, because from [home to next island] it's about 20 minutes, it's not far and [island] is where all the drugs are. It's all the crack cocaine...Jamaica and Holland is where it comes from, right. And [he] was like, do a trip for me, and I was like, 'You're fucking crazy, man! The day I do trafficking is the day I go with 20 kilos because I'm not so stupid to do it!' You know. It was always a joke, it was never something I wanted to do, and then it just popped up...It popped up ridiculously.

Angela was also African, but as a black woman her narrative differs greatly from Marta's (who is white African and grew up abroad). Angela was in her mid-thirties when she became involved in trafficking through a friend of her husband's who she knew from church. Her narrative centred on providing for her children, specifically to be able to give them opportunities which were previously unavailable:

> For me, I'm not educated, so like my dream was always that my children must be better than me, but I think I made a big mistake. But for me the most [important] thing was my children because I've got four babies. The first trip I got good money, I bought me a plot, and I was thinking this is good 'cause like the money you make in 2 weeks, two months, you make in 10 years. [...] It's a lot of money [...] it's a lot of money for a black woman, for a domestic worker to have that money.

Her narrative draws on discourses connected to local and historical changes. When she speaks to me, she draws on these narratives to describe herself as an *African* woman, for someone who is not. In particular, she emphasises ownership of land and education – possibilities unavailable to her historically, and which were therefore particularly meaningful in terms of having a stake in a rapidly changing country. Working as a mule enabled Angela to fulfil her hopes (for a time). Her first trip enabled her to buy a plot of land and send her children to a good school (which she described as a 'white school'). Angela's motives for continuing traffic are complex:

> I didn't go to school much, so like, so like the aeroplanes and the countries, it was like something exciting, something good because you could take like first class in the aeroplane, and stay in good hotels, so it was like something good. It makes me feel good about myself.

In the same way that working as a mule gave her the capital to engage in material forms of entitlement, Angela also talks about the experience of working as a mule as one of recognition. Rather than being an invisible domestic worker, she travelled first class and stayed in good hotels. These are less easy for Angela to voice; she described herself as 'greedy' when I asked why she continued to traffic. Whereas her motives of providing for her children fit with culturally dominant narratives about appropriate womanhood, she feels uneasy about wanting things for herself (bearing in mind that the cultural narratives she grew up with offered her little entitlement, either as a black person, or a woman).

Finally, not all narratives about money forefronted women's domestic responsibilities, or drew on 'mothering' identities. Sharon accepted an offer of mule-work to have 'more money to smoke [crack]' and to 'treat' her daughter, in this order of priority. Sharon was in her early thirties, was white, and lived in Africa. At the time, she was recently divorced, and her brother had been killed in the preceding year. She supported her mother and daughter through her legal job but relied on a variety of strategies to support her drug habit:

> [It's] funny because some drug addicts you see, they'll steal to get money to smoke [crack], they turn to prostitution to smoke and stuff like that, but not me, never. I never stole one penny from anybody to support my habit. No, with me, it was just like that: if I didn't have money, I just didn't smoke, y'know. But selling things for smoking, now that I've done a lot... [prompt] I once went to this pawnshop and pawned my TV, my microwave, and everything just to support my habit. It was bad, but steal from anybody? Never. I just don't have the heart for it. I just don't have the heart for it.

Sharon emphasised that she did 'not have the heart' to do other types of crime, explicitly rejecting discourses of 'pathology and powerlessness' about women's drug use, that offer only passive subject positions

(Anderson 2005; Maher 1997). Instead she constructs a more active narrative, morally justifying her choice as less harmful and non-violent: she is a good-hearted woman. Having money to smoke would have meant a respite from the month-to-month work of providing for her family and supporting her habit. By describing herself in this way, she suggests that her involvement was the continuation of her existing sense of self: as someone who smoked crack as long as it was convenient to do so. Thus, engaging in trafficking was a way to continue using drugs, whilst keeping her drug use marginal to her sense of self. For Sharon, as long as drug use and trafficking were hidden, they required only minimal incorporation into her self-narrative.

Constructing 'mule-work'

Respondents' narratives constructed mule-work as a particular type of crime that was preferable to other types of crime. A minority of women were involved in acquisitive offending before they got involved in trafficking: prostitution, selling drugs, and fraud were all cited. Manuela wanted to get out of prostitution, and working as a mule would have enabled her to do so. Similarly, Marta described mule-work as more 'respectable':

> The only person that knew [I was going to work as a mule] was Emma. [...] She was 19 and was working as a prostitute. [...] I met her one day when she was picking up her cheque. She said, 'Why don't you think about it?' She said, 'Come and sit at the bar and see how it goes.' So, OK, I went, I hung out. I couldn't do it. There's no way I can fucking do it! So from there... I had to do trafficking. [...] It was hard, and it still is, to get work. I've worked once in my life in an office – I couldn't do it! [My profession] didn't really exist [in this country] and what there was, was a big drop in salary. It doesn't boost your ego now, does it? I felt like, how have you fucked your life up?

Marta describes prostitution as very far from her sense of 'self'.[2] Her boyfriend was a trafficker, and knowing him may have had a role in shaping how she felt about working as a mule. This may also have been the case for those mules who became involved after seeing friends work as mules.

The majority of mules had no history of involvement in offending, and in fact many were employed. Working as a mule pays relatively highly for a short period of work for which no specialist skills are required. Unlike other forms of work or criminal engagement (robbery, or even drug dealing), it is possible to do it only once (as many planned to). Since trafficking happens 'elsewhere', most respondents hoped to do it under the guise of a work trip. It is this particular feature that made it radically different (and in the eyes of some respondents more attractive) from other criminal or legal income generating strategies. Like Sharon (above), they hoped to avoid having to incorporate it into their self-narratives in the long term. Understanding this is crucial to understanding the apparent paradox in getting involved in crime as a way to enact identities as mothers. So, the proceeds of trafficking were a way to do motherhood, but only under the condition that trafficking played little role in their sense of self. Only very rarely (for example in Tanya's case) did women see trafficking as a long-term activity to be incorporated in self-identity.

What do women talk about when they talk about money?

The large financial rewards of working as a mule supposedly make it difficult for poor women (and men) to resist (Heaven 1996; Dorn et al. 1992). In fact, mules' pay varies considerably. Green reported that mules were paid between £300 and £1,000 (1998: 86) to carry cocaine into the UK;[3] Zaitch found that 'the broad range of backgrounds and motivations of *mulas* is further evidenced in their payment, which can fluctuate, according also to the amount transported, between $1,500 and $10,000' (2002: 145). Caulkins et al. report that mules were, on average, paid £10,778 (based on data from six respondents carrying approximately two kilos into the UK (2009: 73)). The least well-paid respondent in this research received $6,000 to cross the Ecuador-Colombia border with around a kilo of cocaine in his stomach (he was Ecuadorian). The best paid were offered $15–20,000 to carry two kilos to North America and Western Europe (where they lived). This is a greater payment than previously reported and probably reflects respondents' nationalities. It was also the case that those who expected the largest payments were men (although generalisation is difficult with such a small sample). Research on mules arrested in California found that gender was not statistically significant in terms of mules' pay (Bjerk and Mason 2011). It was unheard of for mules to dictate or negotiate their wage, even those who were professional or experienced (more in Chapter 8).

Most mules expected to be paid between $6,000–9,000; the majority were from North America and Europe. The value of this sum varied across continents and economies: although it could buy a house in some countries, in others it was about enough to redecorate a flat. Some expected payment in cocaine (in full or in part). Marta expected to receive just $500 and half a kilo of cocaine to sell. This would have been worth around

$7,500 wholesale, or if they had cut it and sold it in smaller quantities (as they planned to) they could have made around $12–15,000 (prices based on UNODC 2005: 183). Most of those who were coerced did not get paid (see Marina's account), nor did some willing participants (see Paula's account).[4]

Nonetheless, in most cases, the amount offered was not so large as to be 'irresistible', nor did all respondents become involved due to financial crisis or grinding poverty. Furthermore, the geographical diversity of respondents in this research demands a critical perspective on 'poverty'. Previous research that focussed on mules from a particular country, such as Nigeria (Green 1991), Jamaica (Sudbury 2005b) or Colombia (Dorado 2005) enables a geo-political level of analysis. Here, using a narrative approach centres women's subjective experiences of being in economic need, or wishing to fulfil economic goals relative to their neighbours.

For respondents in situations of sustained poverty, mule-work offered a route to material gain where legal opportunities were blocked or very limited. For Nan, working in a bar enabled her to get by, but offered little hope of being able to change her circumstances in the long term. This echoes Merton's theory of strain (1938, 1968): when legitimate routes to material gain/status are blocked (usually by poverty of education, structural subordination) individuals take illegitimate routes. Having said that, 'strain' theory remains problematic in relation to female offenders (Broidy and Agnew 1997). Furthermore, if there is evidence of 'strain' here, it was oriented toward local norms, rather than the riches of the global North (cf. Young 2003).

Women's narratives about money were about a relative sense of poverty (Townsend 1979; Young 1999). They were commonly about desiring to 'provision' for children, parents, and sometimes partners, and fulfil their gendered selves (as mothers, daughters and girlfriends). The exact meaning of this varied 'consistent with a society's social norms' (Strober 2003: 148). Provisioning is underpinned by the idea of providing for the whole social unit (usually the family) counter to rational choice theories premised on an individual actor (Ferber and Nelson 1993). Whilst explanations based on 'the feminisation of poverty' implicitly refer to the experience of those in the developing world, 'provisioning' can better take into account the diversity of women involved in trafficking as mules worldwide. Furthermore, 'provisioning' highlights a broader range of activities beyond survival, such as enabling children to attend a good school. It also usefully captures the fact that, for many respondents (especially those from the global Northwest) provisioning was tied to norms about consumer culture (Power 2009). Additionally, narrative connects with their subjective interpretations of poverty and the moment at which simply getting by 'crystallised' into discontent (Baumeister in Paternoster and Bushway 2009). In some cases, trafficking offered the possibility of returning to an original self, or achieving a desired self (Paternoster and Bushway 2009). For example, Nan wanted to be return home as the 'good' granddaughter who could look after her family. Often these moments were connected to major changes in offenders' lives, such as being deported, having a child, or the death of a family member. Nonetheless, some narratives reflected a long running self-narrative of motherhood, which women were heavily invested in upholding. These narrative identities were so central to their sense of self that failing to maintain them was unimaginable (McNay 2004). Women were in a sense 'driven' by these identities, yet they were also engaged in creative constructions of them.

Women were responsible for children in a very real sense. Yet, it was also the case that women understood their role drawing on cultural discourses which held women responsible (rather than the children's fathers or the state) (Somers 1994). At the same time, women's financial position was precarious, and their options to provision were very limited (especially in nations without a welfare state). It is not surprising that women also held ambivalent feelings about motherhood (as in Amanda's account at the start of this chapter), although they were difficult to voice. Further, Sharon did not feel compelled by her self-identity as a mother and did not see herself as 'failing' (although others might have). It was notable that women rarely spoke of wanting to have more money for themselves, despite the global influence of discourses about women as empowered consumers (Power 2009).

Women's narratives about romantic love

Romantic love was an important theme in women's individual narratives, much like in El Inca. While public narratives about love tended to mainly offer passive subject positions (such as being 'led astray'), respondents' personal narratives made space for agential subject positions. Manuela was in her early thirties when she became involved in trafficking through her boyfriend. She is white, from mainland Europe, and draws on western ideologies about love in her account:

> He promised that we would get married and have a future together, but he said that we needed money. Then he changed his attitude. I

> was working as a prostitute and he started to get really mad about it. He started to treat me like shit, screaming at me and cheating on me, but I was so in love that I forgave it all. [...] One day he presented some friends, and I met with them and my boyfriend, and they said they wanted to send me to Brazil.
>
> Marina:[5] Why did you go to the meeting?
>
> Manuela: Because I wanted to keep my boyfriend. I wanted to keep him by my side, not for him to leave. I'm the kind of person who doesn't like to lose someone from my life. He was also telling me that he thought I wanted to leave him, and he said he didn't want that. After the meeting, he also threatened me with the police if I tried to leave him. Then after that he was always by me, we were sleeping together again, and I was thinking that everything was good.

One reading of Manuela's experience would emphasise manipulation and exploitation, rendering Manuela's involvement passive. Yet, Manuela tells us her boyfriend was someone she loved and valued. In this respect, she draws on mainstream romance narratives that emphasise coupledom in the fulfilment of the self and as a route to happiness (Fraser 2003; S. Jackson 1993; Weatherall 2002). At the same time, cultural discourses about romance also incorporate control, possessiveness, and jealousy (Fraser 2003: 15), making it easy for her to interpret his controlling behaviour as 'romantic'. In addition to being caught up in the first throes of romance, Manuela also gives a reasoned account of the value that this relationship meant to her:

> I was getting older. I wanted a man and to get married and have a good family. To have a real job and a family. [...] I was happy. Thinking that I'd found the right man, and I was believing in him.

Being married and having a 'normal' domestic arrangement were symbolically meaningful and materially significant: 'Many [single women] fear – quite rightly – that they will slide into poverty and/or endure social stigma.' (Fraser 2005: 16) In contrast to the material realities of poverty and stigma that she had already experienced in prostitution, attaining a normal family and upholding the normal tenets of femininity were a way to improve her social status and long term prospects (Richie 1996: 135). Her desire for this status was informed by her current lack of it: 'to not be respectable is to have little social value or legitimacy. [...] Respectability embodies moral authority: those who are respectable have it, those who are not, do not.' (Skeggs 1997: 3) Being in love and in particular being 'settled' are tied up with capitalist consumerist markers of social 'success', in particular getting married and buying a house together (Fraser 2003: 278; Illouz 1997). Seeing herself as a loving girlfriend was the basis for acting as one by working as a drug mule. Yet, Manuela is not merely a passive participant in her 'love story', but plays an active role in constituting it, albeit in circumstances that are materially and discursively constrained.

Paula also got into trafficking through her boyfriend (see the start of Chapter 3). She is white, middle class, and European. Her narrative is shaped by her sense of self as his girlfriend:

> It was too dangerous for me, but it was the only possible solution to take my boyfriend at that time out of the danger because they had him; they were threatening his life; there was no way he could do it, because they didn't trust him to let him do it, he might run away or something, so I felt like there is no way I could get that much money. He owed a lot of money.
>
> So... I was just like, 'What's more important? I'm just going to do it.' Kind of like a lesser evil. It wasn't like I pondered it for a couple of days and decided what I should do. No, I just... It was an impulse, but it wasn't forced on me. It wasn't like I was just manipulated... Well, in a sense, yeah, but... I still knew that eventually I was the one saying I'm gonna do it, you know.

Paula's narrative draws on dominant western cultural narratives of love, in shaping her priorities. When she says: 'What's more important?' she implies that nothing is more important than his life/love. Before this, they had been together for two years, and had discussed getting married. In some respects, Paula's narrative of 'doing it for love' is similar to Manuela's; however, she adopts an active subject position, describing herself not only as obligated but also as heroic: rather than being 'saved', she would do the saving (Weatherall 2002). She also draws on very traditional ideas of love and sacrifice, prioritising others before oneself (S. Jackson 1998; M. Jackson 2002; Somers 1994).

Narratives about love were frequently also about building a future with others. Marta described wanting to provide for her daughter (earlier in this chapter), but she also hoped to start a small (legitimate) business with her boyfriend so that he could move away from crime, and they could plan a life together:

> I said, 'Alright, after this you're gonna stop [trafficking]. But you can also change your life.' It was a way to change my life, and I thought I had someone who loved me.
>
> JF: So, the money represented a way to change your life, but also his, too?
>
> M: Yeah. It was stupid, but yeah.

Like Manuela, she hoped for a future together, with all the markings of financial success: having a house and a man. She also wanted a business to enable her to work and pay for things herself. In this regard, her narrative is both traditional – in that it centres on her role as the carer and nurturer of others – and also distinctively modern and western in its emphasis on independence and financial success (Power 2009).

What do women talk about when they talk about love?

> Our subjectivities are…shaped by the social and cultural milieu we inhabit, through processes which involve our active engagement with sets of meanings available in our culture. We create for ourselves a sense of what our emotions are, or what 'being in love' is through learning scripts, positioning ourselves within discourses, constructing narratives of self. (S. Jackson 1993: 44)

Paula's willingness to work as mule to save her boyfriend, Marta's hopes for building a life together, and Manuela's excitement about settling down with her partner all show how their subjectivities as 'women in love' made their entry into drug trafficking meaningful. Love was a uniquely female motivation, reflecting the cultural dominance of 'narratives of the heart' in the global North (where respondents had grown up), and their significance in contemporary social life (Fraser 2003; Jamieson 1998). Love is not solely personal and sentimental, but also a 'social construction which was its own logic and rationality' (Torres 2008; Hochschild 1979).

Respondents drew on these cultural narratives to make sense of events as they occurred, and to think about and guide possibilities for action (S. Jackson 1998; McNay 1999). In particular, identities offered guidance about 'about how a woman "should" be, think and act' (Fraser 2005: 14).

Cultural narratives about romance situate love as central to happiness and self- realisation (Illouz 1997). Nonetheless, women were not cultural dupes, but actively located themselves within these discourses, appropriating them selectively (Brunt in S. Jackson 1993: 44; McNay 1999). Whilst typical discourses of love tend to offer women passive subject positions (S. Jackson 1993), respondents did not solely see themselves in these terms. For example, Paula situates herself as the 'rescuer', rather than the 'rescued', but at the same time, her discourse is traditionally 'other-oriented' (S. Jackson 1993; Somers 1994). Similarly, Marta's motive incorporates relationships with her daughter and boyfriend, as well as her personal desires for independence and control over her life.

Love relationships are a context in which power relations play out (Connell 1987; Fraser 2005). Although 'romance seems to erase power in its image of mutuality' (S. Jackson 1993: 132), discourses of romance have been widely noted as problematic for women in that they justify oppression and make women vulnerable (Firestone 1972; S. Jackson 1993, 1998, Fraser 2003). Julia Oparah (née Sudbury) concludes that 'women's relationship with male traffickers is one of exploitation, not partnership' (2005b: 175). In contrast, Torres describes respondents as agents of their decisions (2008). This research seems to show that both are possible. As with narratives about poverty, adopting a narrative perspective draws attention to women's active role in constructing narratives about their involvement. Yet, within love discourses, Paula could not imagine *not* acting to save her boyfriend, as doing so would interrupt her sense of self. So her actions were in a sense 'driven' by cultural discourses about how women in love should behave.

'True' love?

It is impossible to know if these women were cynically manipulated by their boyfriends. In retrospect, Manuela thought that was probably so, but Paula and Marta did not. Nonetheless, in hindsight, respondents were critical about how 'true' their partner's love was. At the end of the interview, Manuela described her feelings after she was arrested:

> I was crying. Then I was hoping that somehow, it all comes good. I was really confused.
>
> JF: How did you feel about your boyfriend?
>
> M: I was calling him a bastard, but then when I called him later, I was still loving him. I was still believing that he will help somehow, and then he changed his [phone] number. Three months after I got arrested, I called him and he said he would send money to get me out [escape], but he never did. [...] I want never to see him. I want nothing to do with drugs. I want to kill him (indicates stabbing him)!

When she said she wanted to 'kill him', she indicated stabbing him with hands shaking from rage. This dissolved into an embarrassed smile, apologetic for her violent sentiments toward someone she had loved. She still felt embarrassed about trusting him and believing that things would work out, even after she was arrested. Her boyfriend stopped calling, as did Marta and Paula's boyfriends. Indeed, the vast majority of women were abandoned by their partners after they were sentenced. As such 'doing it for love' was sometimes understood as a form of deception, re-interpreting their love as mistaken, and not true love. And so, although publicly women preferred to emphasise their victimisation, in private, remembering falling in love and subsequently losing it was difficult and poignant. Catalina was involved for several years, working in partnership with her boyfriend:

> [I was] with this guy for so many years, as lovers, living together, promises, being engaged, then I end up in prison, and it's like nothing ever happened. [...] I felt I'd been used, not been loved. I thought that he loved me, but then I found out that he used me, you understand how I felt? [...] We'd been together for so many years – suffering together, laughing together, going through everything together. In the beginning [after arrest] he was keeping contact, sending money, asking about the lawyers, and then he disappeared just like that [clicks fingers].

I return to Catalina's narrative at the end of this chapter.

Travel and excitement

Many respondents had never been overseas before or expected to ever afford to. Their narratives constructed travelling as excitement and in some cases, as escape. International travel and global mobility are intertwined with new kinds of inequalities of mobility (Bauman 1998). Drug mules do not neatly fit either of Bauman's typologies: they are neither hypermobile elite 'tourists' who are a part of the capitalist system, nor 'vagabonds', who are immobile, extraneous to global capitalism (1998). Yet, their motives reflect a world where travel is a marker of economic success and participation in social life on a global scale. At the same time, their motives also reflect circumstances in which travel was otherwise unattainable, and lives that seemed mundane in comparison:

> I'm thinking great! A way to *get out*, you know. I'd just come out of prison, you know. [Marta had also been forcibly deported from her

> home country to the one she was born in]. I'm thinking it's gonna be excellent. I can go on a vacation, it was supposed to be for one week, everyone's gonna pay for it, and I can do whatever I want. I mean, how fucking sweet is that? (Marta)
>
> It was a spur of the moment decision and along with it came excitement because I was going to do something really daring. (Sharon)
>
> I had butterflies in my stomach. At first I enjoyed it. I had cheeky clothes. It was the first time when I felt like a proper tourist, like I'd seen on the TV. Like before I was thinking, how can I? I don't have money, and in my country it's really hard to leave. Before, I thought only business people [could travel]; I never thought about young people travelling. I felt cool: dressing like a tourist, visiting different countries, speaking different languages. (Catalina)

Travel is not inherently exciting – it can be terrifying, upsetting, and tiresome or boring. Being a 'proper tourist', only for a while, was a 'seduction', especially for Catalina and Annie, who had travelled many times as mules (Katz 1988).

For some, travelling was an escape and respite from extremely stressful lives marked by economic hardship, crisis, responsibility, and instability:

> I wanted to go and never come back, like when the plane took off in [home], I was like, bye. Good byeeee! You know, like, I'm *leaving*! Like I was disappearing, like something from The Twilight Zone. (Amanda)

Staying in the international drug trade: Catalina's narrative

Catalina was involved in trafficking as a mule for many years. She made multiple trafficking trips, and gives an insight into the role of narratives in maintaining her involvement in the international drug trade. She became involved through her friend (described in Chapter 4). Here she talks about her involvement drawing upon discourses of romance and financial success. She also describes herself as someone who is respected, by her family, boyfriend, and also by people that she meets while trafficking. Her narrative reads like one of falling in love for the first time. It tells of self-discovery, growing up and adventure:

> I liked that guy so much. I started to love him. I…how can I say…if I was travelling, everyone was…the person I had contact with, they had respect, they were treating me really fine…and…I don't know. I started to enjoy…It was just me and him in the house at the start. He was the person who took me out from the country I could never leave. Having money, I could keep my family. Friends from home, they saw me in expensive clothes, changing the family home with expensive things in the house. They start to see me differently. It's like, how they say, money is everything.
>
> It's not that he taught me directly but…We talked a lot. I learned from his attitude. I thought that trafficking has no character or status; that traffickers would be just bullshit, only knowing about trafficking, but that's not true. At home, if that guy walked down the street, everyone will say hello. He gets respect. […] With him, I learned to be stronger, to face life differently. My husband was the one who taught me to drive, to use the computer, to speak English…So many things. We were teaching each other the way to dress up. When we were going out, we were not going to just any place; we were always selecting a good place carefully.

Just as she describes herself as falling in love and into trafficking, she describes her eventual disaffection with it in similar terms:

> I never felt like a business partner…Sometimes when he paid me, I would feel smug, but then [after] we have some time together in a relationship, I asked: 'Are you going to do something for our lives?' But it never happened. Was it just business together? No. Sometimes I even asked him if there is any trip to do [as a mule], but he never pushed me to travel. He organised everything, but sometimes he asked me for advice, too.
>
> My life was starting to be empty. I understood, for him, I wasn't the half he needs. For me, it wasn't love between us, just business talk. He was always out; we didn't have a good relationship. We didn't even have sex, just a good morning and a kiss goodnight. Imagine! Engaged but not having sex! […] It's funny because I was so in love with him, but then I don't understand why… There was no relation. Apart from bringing him money, there was no relation. I started to be so tired, Jennifer. Not physically tired but psychologically tired. Travelling for the money, enjoying things, different countries, but I didn't have what I wanted: my own peace. [I started to miss] my

> family. My mother was begging me to come home. I just started to feel tired. Then, I started to think, what am I travelling for? I had a good job before, I knew people, I always had cash in my pockets, I finished university. I was like, why do I have to sacrifice my life for all this shit?

Catalina's story ended with fights, and eventually her partner withheld her passport from her. It was a false document, and she could not replace it. Since she had travelled into the country on a false passport, she was not free to leave. In the end, she decided to make one last trip to make the money to be able to leave her boyfriend and the drug trade and go home. The final trip was to Ecuador where she was arrested for the first time. For Catalina, this arrest was a betrayal by her boyfriend: he had always ensured that she had well concealed drugs. In this instance she was arrested with a small quantity of poorly packed drugs. Shortly after she was arrested, he stopped answering her calls and fell out of contact.

Male mules' narratives

Briefly looking at men's narratives helps reveal the ways in which women's narratives were gendered. Men's narratives were constructed differently, drawing on discourses of autonomy and entrepreneurship as well as hegemonic masculinity (Connell 1987, 2002; Messerschmidt 1993, 1997, 2005).

Michael was a student in his early twenties when he was arrested leaving Ecuador with two kilos of cocaine in his suitcase. He was white and middle class. This was his first trip as a drug mule to Latin America, but he had previously been involved in overland cross-border drug trafficking in Europe. He first got involved to 'maintain his style of life' through people he met partying while at university. Michael grew up in an Eastern European country emerging from communism. His style was influenced partly by the influx of young tourists, bringing western culture and ideals with them. He had hair down to his shoulders, smoked marijuana, dressed like an American skateboarder, and finished his sentences with 'man'. He simply saw his involvement in drugs as a way to pay for that while maintaining his independence from his parents.

Graham was just twenty when he was arrested. He grew up in North America, was white and described his background as working class. He was offered work as a mule to pay back a drug dealing debt that was largely his brother's fault. His narrative combines entrepreneurial discourses as well as family responsibility:

> I wasn't forced to do it, but my conscience forced me. It was either me or my brother would come down [to Ecuador], and I knew he could get killed. I made the choice that I had the better chance of returning. It was either that or seeing my nephew grow up without his father and his wife without him. I had less to risk.
>
> JF: Did you have any other options to pay the debt?
>
> G: Yeah, money, but there was no cash. I was working, but I'd just paid off my debts, so the cash was already spent. I would have had to wait for the next pay cheque and sell something from my house. I was not the kind of person who buys stuff thinking I'm gonna sell it. Once I buy something, that's it. It's mine till it's broken, then I'll throw it out! It wasn't an option.

Graham's solution to their problem (which he viewed as a collective one) was based on his sense of self as entrepreneur, brother, and uncle. He describes himself as a self-made man (paying off his debts and buying things for his apartment) and in later conversations he told me he would also have made a small amount of cash that he planned to invest in setting up a nightclub. He also speaks of responsibility to his family. The trip as a mule was not only solving the immediate problem of how to pay back his brother's debts, but it also meant that he could fulfil his (gendered) responsibilities and desires for the future: his account is underpinned by a gendered 'duty' that is relational, much like many women mules.

Lastly, Frank was sick long term and unable to work. He was white and from a working class background. Before he became a mule, he was nearing retirement age and was living meagrely on a government welfare program. Working as a mule would allow him to materially improve his living conditions:

> The usual reasons, short of cash, ill health, things that I needed to redecorate my council flat etc., etc...and somebody said 'Do you want to do this? We'll pay you [$10,000] a kilo' 'Yeah. Why not? Nothing to lose.'

Frank's circumstances sound much like those described in previous research: 'relative poverty, a sense of desperation and opportunity to rise above the grinding misery of economic hardship in the developing world all contribute to a rational explanation of the phenomenon' (Green 1998: 18). Rather than having something to gain, Frank saw nothing to lose. His account was the shortest, and was barely a narrative at all. He was very reluctant to do an interview, and quickly steered it away from why he got involved towards what it was like to be a mule. Rather than a tale of woe, his was a rueful, farcical account of working with a bunch of incompetent idiots. What made his narrative so hard to tell was that he was very ill and, at the time of the interview, the future looked bleak.

These men's narratives are gendered in that they did not deal with stigma connected to offending (as women did) and were able to rely on discourses that closely link masculinity and crime (Messerschmidt 1993). Michael's narrative normalises his involvement in trafficking as simply something he does so he can party. Graham's narrative draws on culturally dominant narratives about financial success. Yet there are also similarities; men's narratives sometimes centred on relational identities, as Graham's did. Like women, men's narratives also reflected local norms about standards of living that reflect global capitalism and consumer culture.

Conclusion

Respondents' narratives reflect a heterogeneous array of national, ethnic, and social backgrounds, ages, and experiences, making it hard to draw straightforward conclusions. The last two chapters have explored whether women participate in mule-work willingly, or are compelled by circumstances or traffickers. Women's narratives show that their involvement could rarely be attributed to either choice or compulsion. Instead, they give a sense of the on-going process of making meanings, making selves, and making lives.

Undergirded by the concept of 'practical reflexivity' (Bohman 1997), this chapter demonstrates that women's involvement in trafficking was the outcome of a narrative evaluation of emergent circumstances and opportunities that was itself structured by respondents' habitus. Here, gender was a lived relation, structuring women's material opportunities, as well as ways of thinking about them (McNay 2004). Setting aside those who were involved through coercion and threat, most women reflected, evaluated and took action towards future goals (Emirbayer and Mische 1998). As such, women acted with a degree of agency. Nonetheless, as Bohman explains: 'We are not [solely] trapped by the structuring effects of the habitus into which we are socialized, but by processes of cultural and political exclusion from interpretive processes over which we do not have sufficient control or input.' (1997: 184) In other words, gender played out in women's economic disadvantage *as well as* through cultural notions about women's role and responsibilities.

Women mostly explained their involvement in trafficking through discourses about poverty and economic circumstances, echoing previous research (Green 1991, 1998; del Olmo 1986; Huling 1995, 1996; Dorado 2005; Bailey 2013). Adopting a narrative perspective centres subjective interpretations of poverty, and the moment when discontent becomes 'crystallised' (Baumeister in Paternoster and Bushway 2009). Doing so helps to explain why not all poor women with opportunities to become involved in trafficking do so. Women's narratives were often about the financial difficulties of making a life as mothers/daughters, often as head of household and in precarious or underemployment. Thus, women's involvement was a response to gendered poverty, mediated by gendered identity. Women's narratives were also the product of particular cultural and historical circumstances (S. Jackson 1993, 1998). Remember, for example, Angela's narrative was connected to contemporary political and cultural changes. The influence of global capitalism and consumer culture could also be heard.

Whilst individuals creatively adapted discourses about gender, they tended to narrate themselves as 'other-oriented' (S. Jackson 1993). Rather than being compelled by others, women described doing 'whatever it took' to ensure that their loved ones were safe and taken care of (although the exact meaning of this varied). Doing so was extremely difficult for some respondents, especially in countries where the welfare state had been rolled back (Sudbury 2005b), or where there was no welfare state at all. Unsurprisingly, women's narratives often contained ambivalences about financial and caring responsibilities.

It was notable that women's narratives centred on remarkably western, traditional forms of femininity. With few exceptions, respondents were strongly invested in relational identities, primarily as mothers, daughters, and romantic partners. This may simply reflect the material reality of women's lives, since they are arguably characterised by relationships with others (Gilligan 1982; Broidy and Agnew 1997; Steffensmeier and Allen 1996). However, this would tend towards gender essentialism, which does not sit well with interactionist perspectives that underpin this research (West and Zimmerman 1987). Somers offers a second interpretation: cultural scripts about womanhood rarely offer women subject positions as autonomous agents (1994). For example, it was very difficult for women to say, *as women* 'I wanted to make some money', or 'I wanted to travel'. In fact, they did so rarely, but usually buttressed these statements with normative ones. Women nonetheless did describe excitement at the prospect of international travel.

While most women framed their experience primarily through their sense of a female identity, this was not universally the case. Yet, it highlights the difficulty in voicing narratives that do not 'do' female gender. Although gendered discourses were not necessarily determining, it was difficult to have a sense of self that is *not* gendered (M. Jackson 2002; Butler 1990). As in El Inca, it was difficult for women to narrate themselves without 'doing' gender: 'For a narrative to be meaningful and to acquire some degree of social authority, it must draw, to some extent, on culturally dominant discourses of truth telling.' (McNay 1999: 327) As Stuart Hall puts it, 'some stories have a much longer structuration, a *longe durée*, almost a historical inertia. Some stories are just bigger than others.' (cited in McNay 1999)

Given that respondents came from all corners of the globe, the similarity in the kinds of gender respondents drew on is surprising. There are two possible explanations. One is gender is a social structure with global reach and scale. Some aspects of gender are globally continuous: women undertake the majority of unpaid work, receive less pay, and do the majority of caring work (Connell 2002). This is not to say that gender arrangements are the same the world over, but rather that similarities and linkages do exist (ibid). This can be seen in the case of neoliberal globalisation, which has, on the whole, worsened women's material wealth, although not in an equal or uniform way (Walby 2009). On the other hand, this similarity may be accounted for by cultural imperialism (Mac an Ghaill and Haywood 2007). For Haywood and Mac and Ghaill (2003), globalisation not only reshapes economic relations, but also has an impact upon the constitution of subjectivity, identity, and desire. This is not to displace the significance of the material, however (Mac an Ghaill and Haywood 2007).

Contradictions and ambivalences were also incorporated. McNay notes that even as individual practices of gender have changed, traditional ideals about gender persist (2004). Amanda wanted to provide for her children, but also wanted to escape her responsibilities. Women's sense of self is not unitary or fixed, so some women had multiple narratives about their involvement. These did not always fit together neatly and involved a degree of contradiction. The greatest contradiction was trying to 'do' gender through their narrative, given that involvement in the drug business is socially deviant and seemingly incompatible with female gender (see, for example, Harper et al. 2000; Steffensmeier and Allan 1996; Messerschmidt 1993). However, as Elizabeth Wurtzel neatly sums up: 'to be a do-right woman [...] sometimes you've got to do wrong' (1998: 2).

A common criticism of narrative approaches is that they are superficial, constructed after the fact, and are of limited value in explaining 'real' life. This kind of criticism assumes that reality and representation are separable; however, a constitutive view sees reality as *narratively constituted*, offering plots, themes, and categories for making sense of flows of emergent events (Bruner 1991; Somers 1994; Presser 2009). Therefore, there can be no experience that is prior to narrative (Scott 1992).

A more precise criticism is that mules' narratives were constructions oriented towards the going concerns of prison, and as such are more like justifications than motives (as described in Chapter 3). Nonetheless, narrative ethnography enables a more careful interpretation of women's narratives, taking into account these going concerns and discourses in practice (Gubrium and Holstein 2008), as well as methodological interventions to open up space for ways to say things differently and to talk about taboo subjects. Doing so has helped make space for the contradictions and multiplicity in women's narratives. Understanding the complexities of the processes involved in constructing a narrative is methodological work, but reading respondents' accounts as mere record would disregard their agency as storytellers (McNay 2000). Ignoring this complexity would also risk misinterpreting what women mean when they talk about poverty, love, or victimisation. Furthermore, the division between motive and justification may not be so distinct. As Presser says, 'people talk themselves into engaging in some behaviour even as they also talk after doing it.' (Presser 2012: 9). The fact that women's narratives centred on selves, to which they held deep emotional attachment, adds weight to Presser's statement. Finally, connecting interpretations to habitus through practical reflexivity anchors them in social structural factors, since the habitus is durable and portable (Bourdieu 1990; Erel 2010). Since the habitus makes available particular discourses, narratives are not easily rewritten.

6
Beginning Mule-work

After respondents agreed to work as a mule, a chain of events was set in motion. Contacts spoke to traffickers; organisers bought aeroplane tickets and communicated with a second set of contacts in Ecuador who would ensure that drugs (usually cocaine, but sometimes heroin) would be packed and ready for the mule. Donna's first trip as a mule was organised by a close friend. She had worked with him recruiting mules. She wanted to postpone the trip, but could not:

> The first time that I did it, I was scared. I had to leave on my birthday. I said to the guy I was working for, I go, 'Let's wait a week, I don't wanna go now... I wanna have my birthday party here with all of you not... [but he said] 'Donna, I need it now, I need the money now. We need it now.'

In Bourdieuian terms, Donna had abundant social and cultural capitals (1986), including 'street capital' (Sandberg and Pederson 2009). Yet, despite having a friendship with her contact and being able to draw on experience working in the drugs business, the objective circumstances of the drug trade left no room for negotiation. Since someone had agreed to work as a mule, and then backed out at the last minute, processes had already been set in motion, so Donna could not choose when she left. In contrast, Amanda, a first-time mule who knew nothing about trafficking and did not know her contact well, was able to negotiate when to leave. This seems counterintuitive since greater capitals would normally widen opportunities. Nonetheless, since Amanda volunteered herself, her contact would have organised around Amanda's preferences (at least regarding when she would travel).

Amanda and Donna's experiences show that mules were sometimes able to negotiate some aspects of their labour. Nevertheless, the capacity to have control was not solely the result of having capabilities for action or resources to draw upon, but was objectively limited by drug trafficking processes. Thus, in order to understand gender and agency, it is necessary to contextualise women's experiences in the processes involved in drug trafficking.

Introduction

The next three chapters examine gender in drug trafficking by looking at the processes and interactions that facilitate international transportation of cocaine and heroin by mule (or mule-work for brevity's sake). There is an almost complete lack of research examining how mule-work is organised, and that which does exist does not examine questions of gender or exploitation in any depth (Caulkins et al. 2009; Fleetwood 2011). In part, this is due to assumptions that women's involvement in trafficking is passive, combined with notions of traffickers as exploitative (see Chapter 2). These chapters therefore fill a gap in knowledge by examining what drug mules do and how mule-work is organised. In particular, the following chapters consider how much control mules had over their labour, and in what ways gender was significant. Understanding how mule-work is organised opens up new questions about the relationship between gender and agency in drug trafficking. Contextualising women's involvement within mule-work more generally helps disentangle *gendered* forms of exploitation from exploitation of mules more generally. Although this chapter focuses on mules (and women in particular), interviews with recruiters and organisers are used to compare women's experiences with male mules', and understand the processes surrounding mules that place objective limits on action.

The following chapters show that the relationship between gender and agency was far from straightforward, and in general, gender was less significant than might have been anticipated. Overall, the position of the mule offers few opportunities for them to have much, if any, control over their labour. This was largely systemic (due to the processes surrounding mule-work), but was nonetheless 'done' through social interactions.

The role of the contact in Ecuador was key, and so this chapter explores mules' interactions with them. Contacts undertook specific tasks relating to the mule (such as looking after them, fitting them with drugs, or persuading them to travel to the airport). They were the only 'traffickers' that many mules ever met. In order to make sense of emergent events and circumstances, mules drew upon discursive categories. Drawing on the social interactionist tenet – that people act on the basis of the meanings that things have for them, and that these meanings are negotiated through social interactions (Blumer 1969) – this chapter explores how mules interpreted their role, and their relationships with their contact in Ecuador. Respondents' reflections drew on narratively constituted categories from prior experience, and so this process can be thought of as another kind of 'practical reflexivity' (Bohman 1997). Mules drew on habitual, stable categories of the self, as well as roles such as worker, tourist, or girlfriend. The role of 'mule' was established through interactions with contacts. As 'mules', few respondents expected to have any control over their tasks. Many drew on discourses about work to normalise traffickers' instructions and control. However, some women also drew on their sense of self as friends or girlfriends, rather than mere mules, to negotiate freedom from traffickers' control, at least during the first part of their journey whilst 'holidaying' in Ecuador.

Leaving home

Most mules reported that travel arrangements were organised quickly, leaving them little chance to reconsider. At this stage, mules collaborated with their original contacts who were trusted boyfriends, or friends of friends. As described in Chapter 4, these relationships were often characterised by trust. All mules travelled to the airport of their own accord, even Marina (who agreed to trafficking following threats of violence). In general, respondents described themselves as willing volunteers at this stage of the process. Most were excited about travelling and having a holiday. Sharon is typical:

> They didn't give me only the feeling of excitement; it like gave me this feeling of being in charge of something. I'm doing it, y'know, I'm actually going to do something dangerous! My God, the first day I got on the plane I was so excited. Woo! I'm telling you. Mixed emotions, you know, because it was my first, so it didn't know how it was going to be like, but I did it anyway.

Marta's contact (her boyfriend's friend) took her shopping, checked her into a hotel, gave her spending money, and made sure she felt comfortable and relaxed. She had expected it would be like a 'cool free holiday' and her expectations were met:

> He picked me up, bought new clothes, shoes, everything. He left me in the hotel and gave me cash and said 'here go to the airport and off you go.' So I thought it was pretty good.

Amanda was hesitant about leaving and remembers her goodbyes poignantly:

> I left the money with my Mum 'n I brought $200 [...] and um, I told my mother, you know, 'I'm going on vacation' (half laughing) and she's like 'what are you talking about, 'you're going on vacation?!" I'm like 'yeah' and she's like "Mandy, what are you up to?" 'N I'm like, "Don't worry about it Mom, just pray that if I come back all our problems'll be solved." 'N my sister and her husband, they didn't like the idea. My brother started crying cause I took them all one by one to reassure them to take care of my kids.

Amanda's contact paid her $3,000 in advance, enabling her to pay off the most pressing debts. In spite of the sadness of leaving the family and fear (of aeroplanes and getting caught), Amanda was also looking forward to having a holiday and also remembers feeling excited:

> I was like...happy, I felt like I was a person that travels; I was alone; I didn't have no responsibilities, something I always wanted to feel I guess. I was thinking selfish at the time. [...] Just, you know...I'm getting on a plane! I'm leaving and I'm gonna go to Ecuador! And I'm gonna go to Ecuador: live it to the fullest.

Most women told their families they were on a short work trip, or were going to visit friends. Few told anyone they were flying to South America for fear of arousing suspicion. Those who had children left them in the care of the extended family. All expected to return soon: most trips were planned to last between five days and two weeks, probably so that mules would blend in with business travellers or tourists.

Guests, tourists, mules, and traffickers

For most mules, leaving home was a step into the unknown, but nonetheless, respondents had expectations about what they would do in Ecuador, where they had to stay for a week or so. Respondents drew upon discursively constructed categories to make sense of this new situation, and events as they unfolded (Sacks in Holstein and Gubrium 2000).

Some women expected to be met as guests; others expected to be tourists (like Amanda, above). Most adopted the role of mule as soon as they left home. Only one respondent described herself as a trafficker. These roles were negotiated, confirmed, and denied through interactions with contacts. This session also describes what mules did while they were in Ecuador to give some background to the chapters that follow.

Few mules had any knowledge about Ecuador or how everything would be organised. They were not usually told who or when they would be met by contacts in Ecuador, and they were never given specific details such as names or addresses. Typically they were given only very basic instructions about which hotel to check into, or a number to call once they arrived. Manuela's experience was typical:

> I heard from my boyfriend that I must call him to know what to do [once I arrived]. I was staying in Quito for a few days, then I was sent to Guayaquil.[1] I was told which hotel to go to. They were telling me all this by telephone. Every time I went anywhere I had to call. That's how I got the number for the contacts to call in Ecuador.

Although Manuela was a first-time mule, her experiences were similar to Catalina, an experienced mule. Catalina describes how she communicated with contacts at home and in Ecuador:

> First you call them [contacts in Ecuador] by phone. Before you leave, they [contacts at home] give you a number. You have to hide it or memorise it. When you arrive you call, or sometimes when you arrive you call back [home].

Guests

On Donna's first trip as a mule, she was met at the airport by her contact, who was a friend of her friend. She describes him as a good host who treated her like a mutual friend:

> The next day was my birthday, he brought me a bottle of champagne and another friend of his and I didn't have to feel alone. 'Cause my friend told him, 'Please take care of her. It's her birthday and she's *really pissed off* with me right now.' (laughs) He goes, 'Please take care of her. Please make sure she has fun and then put the drugs on her, whatever, but make her have a nice week of vacation.' And I had a good time. I travelled a lot. He made me travel. I ate well, I slept well.

Marta became involved in trafficking through her boyfriend's friends and anticipated that she would be treated as such. She had also been promised a holiday as part of the deal. When her contact treated her as a mere mule, she resisted, drawing on her drug trade connections and background:

> I came in to Ecuador [...] in the evening. I went straight to my hotel. I was told not to come out. Uh! No fucking way! I'm in a different country. I love travelling. With [my work] I've always travelled. I love travelling. So I'm like no, fuck this, I'm gonna go 'n find something to eat. I don't eat plain food and I wanna go get a bottle, you know...I mean, shit I can't smoke anything, I don't know where to get weed, so I'm gonna get something to drink, chill out in my room. What are you gonna do? Sit sober in your fucking room watching TV? How boring! You know.
>
> So, I'm like alright, I walk down the road. On my way up, this guy calls me and he's like calling me in English. I'm like, 'My God you speak English?' And he's like, 'Yeah, I'm [contact name].' I'm like, 'OK...oh! You're [contact]!' He's like, 'Yeah. Go back to your room I'm coming up.' This was the guy; he had to meet me in the hotel. He's like, 'Why did you come out of the hotel?' I'm like 'because I was fucking hungry, dude, what do you think I'm gonna sit 'n wait for you all day 'n starve?' Fuck that shit. So I went back to the hotel. He said to me, 'You know, you shouldn't be coming out,' 'n I'm like, 'Well, I'm not going to sit in this hotel all day. I'm here on vacation 'n I'm gonna fucking enjoy it'! So he's like 'OK.'

While some mules drew on discourses about traffickers as menacing and violent to make sense of interactions with their new 'contact', Marta's partner was a trafficker, so she didn't give credence to her contacts unreasonable requests. Since Marta knew her initial contact well, and had a history of international travel, she had no reservations about doing what she chose in what she saw as her own time (rather than working as a mule). After that, her contact did not ask her to stay in the hotel again and treated her in a friendlier manner:

> So I went walking around during the day 'n everything. He came to visit me on the Friday. I was here two days, OK, and he says to me that he's going to the coast, or I don't know where, but he's going away for the weekend to go get the drugs, do I want anything. So I'm like 'Yeah, I want some marijuana,' so he bought me some marijuana, he bought me some wrappers [rolling papers] and...that was it.

When it came to packing and preparing to leave with the drugs, Marta felt quite differently about taking orders:

> JF: How did it feel being told what to do?
>
> M: Umm...normal, actually. Just like normal work. I looked at it as a job, he told me what to do 'n I did it. I really trusted them. I really did. I think that was my problem.

Marta made an analogy with her previous job and explained that when she started a new job, she simply took orders from others. Only later on, when she knew what she was doing could she query these orders. When it came to mule-work, she would not have known what was right or wrong: 'You listen to what they say 'n you just do it. Just like any other job, girl!'

Tourists

Like Marta, many mules were told they would have a 'holiday'. Most stayed in Quito's tourist area called 'La Mariscal'. It has a large concentration of hotels, restaurants, tourist markets, museums, clubs, tour agencies, bars, and cafes. Spanish is spoken everywhere, and English is a close second (followed by German and French). The majority of foreigners visiting Quito are tourists of all ages, including backpackers, gap year volunteers, and college students attending university.[2] It was a bustling centre during the day, and at night the streets were filled with tourists, rich Quiteños, salsa music, and street traders of licit and illicit goods, as well as police with large dogs at every corner. At the weekends, traffic jams at midnight were common. It was carnivalesque, hectic, and offered no shortage of opportunities for tourism and excitement.

Some mules did not meet contacts until the very end of their trip, leaving them plenty of time for a holiday first. Amanda met her contacts the day before she left. Before that, she holidayed in Quito and even made a short trip to the Galapagos Islands. She understood Spanish and quickly found people to hang out with:

> I went to the spot [bar] (laughs), I went to exercise room...I went to Galapagos and I drank wine, I looked at the view, you know, I tried to block out of my mind that I was there to commit a crime.

Frank met his contact in his hotel on the day he arrived. They met every other day until he left. Frank was aware that he was being controlled, but he also described this time as a holiday:

> The contact wanted to see my passport to confirm who I was, etc. I gave him a copy [of my passport]. I had a copy in my pocket then went to [money transfer service] 'n got the money. A few days later, the contact comes again and asks me to go out for a meal. At the hotel, they had two-for-one cocktails during happy hour, but they extended it for me. I was putting this on the hotel bill 'n was running out of money almost. I was paying every other day because they only gave me money in small amounts. I met the contact, asked for money; I said I needed at least *x* to pay for the rest of the stay. I would go out at about six or seven a.m. and walk about, then I'd come back for breakfast [...] I got friendly with the security guard 'n we'd go out drinking together and to a few clubs, etc. I didn't leave; I just got to know the town well.
>
> JF: How much did you feel that you were in control of what you were doing rather than being controlled?
>
> Frank: I was being controlled. Mainly through the money situation. This fellow would run up, and I'd go 'n see him and get enough to last a couple of days. I was controlled money-wise.

Although Frank collaborated with his contact (and enjoyed his holiday at the same time), his reliance on his contact for money meant he had little option but to stay in town. Control was also explicit: Frank had to hand over a copy of his passport. Most mules left home with only a small amount of cash and were reliant on their contacts to pay for hotel bills, food, and so on. Frank was indifferent about being minded: after all he had plenty of things to do, and enjoyed taking advantage of happy hour and exploring the city. Like Frank, most respondents collaborated with their contacts: they had everything to gain by staying where they were told and checking in with their contacts regularly as expected. Frank was subject to comparably little control compared to other mules.

Mules

In most cases, respondent accepted being minded by their contacts as part of their new role as 'mule', which started as soon as they left home. Most collaborated with their contacts in adopting this role and submitting to the expectations placed upon them. Nan rarely left the hotel without supervision. She had little money and spoke no Spanish and only a little English at the time:

> [The contact] would come and take me to go and eat. Then I rested. Then in the evening, he would come and get me again. He was always

> with me because the hotel was locked up at night; you cannot go out. They didn't want me to know anyone here.

Nan had minded mules before (following them in case they tried to abscond), which she said was easy and like a free holiday. She thought that staying in all the time was boring but complied partly because she did not see resistance as meaningful or useful. Since she had minded mules before, she understood that this was at least partly to stop her speaking to anyone about what she was doing in Ecuador. As a young woman from East Asia, her presence as a tourist may have been more likely to be questioned (unlike white mules from Europe – like Frank – who would have blended in with other tourists). Her experience as a mule-watcher may also have shaped her expectations of her role. Nan did not want to anger her contact: she assumed that if he was in drug trafficking, he might also be violent. Her ex-boyfriend had been a trafficker, so she was also drawing on her knowledge of him, and other traffickers she had met as well as dominant discourses about traffickers.

Interestingly, the degree to which mules were supervised had little relationship with their experience. Angela had made several trips as a mule, yet she was also subject to high levels of control while in Ecuador. She did not mind being asked what to do since her contacts asked her 'in a nice way'. Angela reflected on how her experiences varied in different countries:

> Imagine you go to a black country, and only you [are] white, and you do get scared, so it's a little bit danger for you, so you don't go out. Like in Brazil, I don't understand what they saying because they're speaking another language so what'm I going to do outside? [...] In Australia was nice because they speak English; in Pakistan they speak mostly half, half-English, but they speak Punjabi – but I understand because I had a Punjabi friend for years, and I was wearing their clothes, so they respect me.

Also, as seen in the last chapter, Angela enjoyed travelling, and here she took advantage of room service:

> Like if you stay in a hotel, you stay. Only if they come to fetch you, then you can go out. Like for me, I was respecting their rules. The room service people, they talk to them, they know exactly what to bring you
>
> JF: How did you feel to be told what to do by a man?

> A: You [are] told in a nice way, so you don't feel uncomfortable, you know, 'cause it's like a nice way.

Contacts made various requests of mules, mainly about keeping in touch and staying at the hotel. Some mules were asked to move to another hotel, which they found worrying:

> I did feel that I pretty much had everything in control until I got here. When I got here... the first day I felt I had it under control, the second day – when they came to pick me up to tell me to change hotel cause the one I was in was 'too expensive' – that's when I felt, alright, I'm starting to lose control. (Graham)

Moving to different hotels had no apparent rationale. Graham recalled that one hotel seemed to be much like the next; nonetheless, it served to reinforce the hierarchical relationship between contact and mule. Graham was well versed in how the drug trade works. He found this kind of arbitrary control disconcerting and was uncomfortable losing control, but saw little choice other than to do as he was asked.

Traffickers

Catalina (an experienced mule who had travelled widely) was given 'training' about how to pass as a tourist when she was travelling as a mule. She was clear that this was an important part of her role. As a professional trafficker, she had no contact in Ecuador who minded her. Catalina organised most aspects of the trip herself, but reflected on and performed her role as a tourist to fulfil her role as a professional trafficker:

> They're training you. Like... how to react if the police are around you, or if you're tired, don't go to expensive hotels, to go to touristic [sic] places and not just for shopping. As a tourist, you have to do tourist things, but not just for shopping. Well, shopping yeah, but with your own money, and not to spend the whole day in the hotel – go out and visit places.

Catalina travelled to many countries as a mule, but this was her first-time in Ecuador. Being foreign was a key resource for passing as a tourist in this milieu. Although some mules were encouraged to take a holiday and enjoy themselves, few were given the kind of instructions and 'training' described by Catalina. For her, the 'holiday' part of the job was not only a performance. She loved to travel, especially experiencing new cultures, and she loved going shopping. While she was working away from home, she travelled autonomously. Nonetheless, maintaining the performance could be isolating:

> It's very lonely. You have to be on your wits, if you like meet tourists; they ask where you're from. I was travelling on a false passport, so you must be careful about what you're saying, etc.

Even for professionals like Catalina (and Angela), travelling was sometimes exciting and pleasurable, but could also be nerve-wracking and lonely. Indeed, most mules remembered being in Ecuador waiting to travel as characterised by moments of insecurity and worries.

Gendered interactions

Interactions with contacts in Ecuador were inevitably gendered (West and Zimmerman 1987). The drug trade is male-dominated (Adler 1993; Zaitch 2002), and so most contacts were men. Some mules established fairly mutual relationships with their contacts, seeing them as friends, but many drew on popular discourses about traffickers. As seen in Chapter 2, the role of trafficker has been constituted in dominant discourse as masculine and violent. Sharon describes the role of gender in her relationships with her contacts:

> I think in a way men, especially those guys that are contacts, in a way they start to control your life like 'We're in charge. You're just a mule, so you do what we say.' But in the end, it all comes down to 'It's a man'. The woman will start looking up to that man because he is controlling everything; he is the one supplying the money.

Although Sharon thought that traffickers could be commanding because of their gender, men could also find their 'contacts' vaguely threatening:

> JF: What was it like dealing with your contacts?
>
> Graham: It was... I didn't like it at all, to tell you the truth. Only one of them seemed genuine. The other one was shady as fuck. I met the old guy in the lobby. He was watching HBO in English – the only English I heard the whole time I was here. The guy spoke broken English. We had some beer, smoked some cigarettes. [...] So, the guy

> in the lobby, he sat next to me for like four hours. We just chatted. He played it cool, laid back. He was actually testing *me* out. To see if I would talk or anything like that [...] Then the other guy told me he was actually the other contact I was dealing with. After that I was like, alright...now I can really talk. I felt cool. I felt like he wasn't going to fuck me over. But the young guy, he was always nervous, jumpy. He was the one always telling me, 'You have to wait here', 'do this', 'do that', 'don't worry', it...That's when I thought that shit was starting to get shady.

Graham and his contacts watched TV, drank beer, smoked cigarettes, and chatted. Despite being from different cultures and having little in common (including language) this form of 'manly' interaction put Graham at ease. Similarly, Caroline's interactions with her contact took the format of stereotypically female interactions. Instead of hanging out in a public place, they spent time in her contact's home:

> The woman talked to me more than anyone else; [it was] just her and her husband. She was educated, well-dressed, she spoke English, she gave me money, bought me clothes, brought me to her house. She made me feel comfortable, and the fact that she was a woman, I felt very comfortable with her.

The kind of femininity they shared was also co-constituted by class. Caroline emphasises that her contact was (like her) educated and well-dressed: both indicators of middle class, loosely conceived. Nonetheless, although their interaction was shaped by gender, it was also shaped by the need for secrecy: training and discussion about trafficking inevitably take place in private. Giving Caroline money and buying her clothes was also a subtle way to indebt her. Nonetheless, having a female contact was rare. Three female mules reported that their male contacts tried to have sex with them. One respondent thought it was romantic; two others rejected the offer outright.

Traffickers on managing mules

Interviews with people who recruited and managed mules helps contextualise respondents' experiences within typical practices and processes surrounding mule-work. At this early stage, traffickers were concerned that mules would change their minds about being a mule and back out.[3] This sometimes did happen, according to Ryan (who recruited and managed mules). Bobby recruited and sent mules as part of his role in a small Latin American 'cartel'.[4] He explained that because mules sometimes changed their minds, they gave the mule as little information as possible:

> We only told them what we had to, up to a point, you know? Every day, things move forward a bit more. [...]The thing is that we were not the typical Colombian organisation that...There it's like...if you promised to travel, too bad: you travel, because we already bought named tickets, and everything is in your name. No, not us. We didn't go around armed, we didn't go around killing anyone, not anything like that...So, if you do not want to travel, OK, don't travel. Because equally, they don't know anything, so it will not have consequences for us. Problems, yes, but that's another thing.

Ryan organised mules in a similar way, giving them as little information as possible, to limit problems that could happen if the mule got frightened and tried to back out. He was also worried that they might talk to police: 'I see mules as the weak factor in it all. If they get caught, they're going to talk. As far as I'm aware, none of ours have talked. And mules are expensive.'

This was borne out in mules' experiences. They usually knew nothing about their contacts in Ecuador, having nothing more than a phone number to call, or the name of the hotel they should check into. Mules did not typically receive the drugs until the day before they would travel, at the earliest. Even if mules had wanted to back out and go to the police, they would not have had any concrete evidence to back up their claims (see Chapter 8).

Traffickers described mules as a valuable resource to be carefully managed. Sending a mule involved a significant investment of resources (money, effort, and time) by those involved (see also Zaitch 2002: 156). It involved an upfront investment of at least $10,000 (much more for mules travelling from Africa or Asia).[5] Popular accounts of mules in the printed media and in films have described mules sent in groups (Carvel 1990; Marston 2005) as dispensable, 'kamikaze couriers' (Green 1998: 103). However, losing a mule (should they go missing or back out) could represent a significant loss; hence, the kinds of control that were evident to mules (making sure they had only small amounts of money, asking them to stay in the hotel etc.). Traffickers were cognisant that it was advantageous to make mules feel comfortable, but this was secondary to making sure mules could not abscond, and in particular that they could not go to the police.

Despite the fact that drug trafficking is a global enterprise, there was remarkable similarity in the way that mules were managed (see also Caulkins et al. 2009). This may be because they were all managed in Ecuador (and possibly even by the same minders and contacts). Interestingly, although relationships were gendered, men and women described being controlled in similar ways. Gender seems to be less significant than respondents' role as mule. Interactions with minders made clear that respondents were implicated in a hierarchical relationship in which the mule was expected to submit to the contact's requests. Nevertheless, collaboration and co-operation were typical.

Conclusion

Leaving home was a step into the unknown for mules. Some respondents enjoyed the 'holiday' they had been promised, but for most, the time spent in Ecuador was an anti-climax. After the initial excitement, they found themselves without much spare cash, language, or any idea of what to do. This period was ambiguous: a few respondents did enjoy a holiday, but most found themselves under various forms of supervision, from someone popping by every couple of days to give them spending money, to being unable to leave the hotel. Given the ambiguity of the situation, mules relied on interactions with contacts to understand their role. Since most were first timers, they were happy to comply with their contact's requests. Most mules saw good reasons for doing so: they relied on contacts for money, and some wanted to perform the role well in the hope of doing more trips in future. Furthermore, doing what you are asked to by employers (who are paying for hotels, food, and so on) is very similar to legal work. Lastly, drawing on what they had heard about drug traffickers as dangerous, some expected being a mule to involve doing as they were told.

Mules could sometimes renegotiate their role, drawing on relationships or experience, to differentiate themselves from mere mules. In fact, those who were able to successfully adopt other roles (as 'guest' rather than mule) drew on social capital to do so. Rather than seeing themselves as workers, they saw themselves as friends of friends, or girlfriends. This was validated by contacts: Donna was treated to a birthday celebration. Marta drew on her social capital in the form of her social connections with her boyfriend (who was a trafficker) to establish herself as an equal. Unlike many mules, she did not assume that her contact was a dangerous trafficker and did not treat him as such. Interestingly, cultural capital (drug trade know-how) played a relatively minor role.

Graham had previously been involved in trafficking but nonetheless found himself in roughly the same situation as other mules who had very little knowledge or experience.

Prior research has tended to see mules' involvement in trafficking in passive terms, yet here there was a large degree of collaboration between mules and contacts. Overall, gender was less significant than might have been expected, as interactions were primarily organised according to roles: contact and mule. Rather than gender, ethnicity seemed to play a role in the degree to which mules were supervised. Whereas some mules could easily blend in with the social milieu in Quito (especially those who were North American, European, and white), women who were black African or East Asian were more likely to be asked to stay in the hotel, and were subject to a greater degree of supervision. This was possibly due to traffickers' concerns about them attracting attention.

7
Mule-work and Gender

I had the natural reaction like [the capsules are] really big, and it's in your throat, and I just kept coughing the capsules up until I got really, really tired and kind of frustrated with myself, but once I said yes, I felt like I could not back down now. [...] I was just like... 'I really *cannot* do it,' you know. And I tell this guy, and he's like, 'No, you can, and it's safe, and people do it all the time,' and I'm like *'How?'* And he's like, 'No, try again.'... and, OK... and he's telling me it was more in this time... It definitely wasn't... and he kind of opened my jaw and like really... like *pushed* it in. Basically... so that it went through this barrier. By this time I was really exhausted, and I could not feel in control because it was against my body.'

JF: How did you feel when he was putting the capsules down your throat? Did you feel like he was helping you or [that it was] somehow kind of violent?

Paula: It did feel kind of violent, you know, it's like your mind is one thing and your will... I guess... you make up your mind, and its one thing, but then still, it violates natural ways of your system... And also at some point... I really got to feel like... I have no more strength, you know. I was exhausted, and he forced it, and I was trying so hard first myself, and then eventually I couldn't force it down and just... I have no strength, and he's like, 'Get up and walk around,' and I feel like: forget it! We will wait until I have to go to the airport, because I have no strength, I feel sick, I need to rest, you don't really know what's going on.

But also... It's something – I know nothing about this, and I have to trust him. Whatever he has to do for this whole thing to get done, for my boyfriend to be safe, then... you know, I said, 'Yes, ok *I give*

> *you control over me,'* because obviously they're going to use me, and I don't know how to do it myself. (Paula, her emphasis)

Paula agreed to traffic drugs to clear her boyfriend's debt (see the start of Chapter 3 for a reminder). It is difficult to interpret Paula's narrative as either voluntary participation or coercion. She labours under intense pressure, and she describes the work of swallowing capsules as violent. Nonetheless, she also explains that it was the act of swallowing the capsules that felt violent (as violating the natural functions of her body) rather than the circumstances. She struggles to describe what happened, yet doesn't draw on discourses about either work or victimisation to do so. Her account is underpinned by a paradox: she says that she 'could not feel in control', but at the same time says that she gave her contact control over her. She describes herself as a willing participant, albeit in a process over which she has no knowledge, or control.

Introduction

This chapter examines the next stage of mule-work in which respondents prepare to traffic drugs: collecting, packing, or swallowing drugs. Examining the way which labour was organised is a way to understand the gender 'regime' and local power dynamics: 'the current labour practice gets embodied in technology designed with given social arrangements in mind, among them the sexual division of labour' (Connell 1987: 102). This chapter explores what mule-work was like, and in particular the extent to which women's involvement was active and agential, and the ways in which mules' actions were controlled by contacts. As in previous chapters, attention is paid to material and discursive resources available; in other words, this chapter asks, to what extent was active involvement imaginatively and materially possible for mules?

Mules' experiences were diverse, yet on the whole, mule-work is characterised by lack of mules' involvement in their labour. In short, the processes surrounding mule-work effectively design out their involvement. Few mules had any say in what they carried or how it was concealed, but surprisingly, those who did were women. Furthermore, women were not more exploited than their male contemporaries. In some instances, women had more influence over processes, and were better able to negotiate their conditions due to close social relationships with contacts at home (as was seen in Chapter 4). This chapter examines the three ways that drugs were packaged, looking at the process involved and mules' experiences. This

Table 1 Methods of smuggling

	Drug	Weight (kilos)	How drugs were concealed
WOMEN			
Catalina (1)	Cocaine	1–2*	Body
Manuela	Cocaine	2.5	Body
Sharon	Cocaine	2	Body
Angela (2)	Cocaine	2	Body
Donna (1)	Cocaine	2*	Body
Donna (2)	Heroin	1.5	Body
Bonny	Cocaine	6.5	Luggage
Amanda	Heroin	6	Luggage
Anika	Cocaine	5	Luggage
Catalina (2)	Cocaine	3.3	Luggage
Marina	Cocaine	2	Luggage
Tanya	Cocaine	2	Luggage
Angela (1)	Cocaine	unknown	Luggage
Caroline	Heroin	1	Swallowed
Paula	Cocaine	0.9	Swallowed
Nan	Cocaine	1.5	Swallowed
MEN			
Frank (2)	Cocaine	2.5	Body
Wilfred	Cocaine	2*	Luggage
Graham	Cocaine	2	Luggage
Frank (1)	Cocaine	1	Luggage
Michael	Cocaine	2	Luggage
Howard	Cocaine and heroin	2 and 3	Luggage
Lorenzo	Cocaine	1	Swallowed

Note: Only where mules were arrested were they able to find out what and how much they were actually carrying. Those marked with * were successful trips, so the quantity is approximate.

chapter also draws on interviews with traffickers to contextualise mules' experiences.

Methods of smuggling

Drugs were smuggled in three main ways by respondents: concealed in luggage and packages, on bodies and in clothes, and swallowed in capsules. Although mules are typically depicted swallowing cocaine in capsules (for example Marston 2005), in fact in general, cocaine is most commonly smuggled in luggage, then on the body. Swallowing is, in fact, the least common method used by both men and women carriers (Green et al. 1994; Harper et al. 2000; Caulkins et al. 2009; Unlu and Ekici 2012).[1] Harper et al. found that women were slightly more likely to carry drugs in luggage than men, and that men were slightly more likely to carry drugs by swallowing them than women (2000: 107).[2] They noted that women tend to carry larger quantities of drugs than men – this may be due to the differences in methods used, as greater quantities can be concealed in luggage than swallowed.

During fieldwork, I encountered a small number of traffickers who were arrested carrying their own drugs (rather than someone else's, as mules do). They might be thought of as 'self-employed couriers' (Caulkins at al. 2009) or 'independent traffickers' (Zaitch 2002). Overall, independent traffickers smuggled cocaine in similar ways to mules: in luggage (compressed into mechanical parts, loose in a talcum powder bottle, compressed into drilled out parts of wooden objects, particularly souvenirs), worn or strapped to the body (in the soles of shoes, or in clothes) and swallowed (although only one reported this). Overall, men and women in this research were carrying drugs concealed in similar ways, but gender influenced the way that drugs were packaged.

Luggage and packages

Around half the mules interviewed carried cocaine and heroin concealed in luggage, either in double-lined or false-bottomed suitcases or concealed in objects in their bags. Cocaine (and sometimes heroin) was concealed inside items such as cartons of wine, compressed into souvenirs, paintings, shoes, or a briefcase. Drugs were always packed and concealed before the mule received them, so mules did not do anything except wait for their contacts to bring them the package to carry. Packing drugs in luggage and packages is a relatively gender neutral method of transportation. Suitcases can be fairly gender neutral (although contents could 'gender' the suitcase), and objects such as paintings and souvenirs could be equally typical in a man's or a woman's suitcase.

Suitcases (and objects inside them) were usually made by a specialist. Stefan (an independent trafficker and organiser) explained: 'You pay what it's worth for a well made suitcase.' His supplier guaranteed that his bags could pass sniffer dogs and could even be drilled without leaking cocaine. Ryan contracted someone to process the cocaine into a form of plastic that could be made into outdoor equipment such as the ground-sheet for a tent. This made it very difficult to know how much cocaine was concealed, and in fact he routinely sent large quantities (5–6 kilos) in this way. Oscar (an independent trafficker) paid $5000 for the collaboration of his specialist (more than the wholesale value of the drugs he carried). He asked for cocaine to be packed into mechanical car parts. Since Oscar is muscular and had a shaved head, he had no difficulty passing himself off as a mechanic. Tanya received her drugs packed into a briefcase. She spotted immediately that carrying this would draw attention to herself, as she could not pass as a business person, so she packed it inside her check-in luggage in the hope that it would pass undetected.

The handover of the package was usually arranged to 'design out' opportunities for either the mule or the contact to rob the drugs. Ryan claimed he once lost $30,000 as a result of a fumbled handover: he could never work out whether the mule or his contact stole the cocaine. Following this he always spoke to both the mule and the contact on the phone while the handover took place, or he would organise to collect the drugs and give them to the mule himself. Exceptionally, Frank collected the drugs himself following his contacts' instructions; however, his initial contact kept in close contact with him:

> I got a taxi to a big church and then I picked up the drugs there; it was in two cartons of wine. Chilean. So I didn't know what or how much was inside. Then [initial contact] rang and gave me the address of where to drop off the package once I arrived.

The fact that cocaine always arrived pre-packaged meant that mules had very little information about what or how much they were carrying. Since carrying drugs in luggage required minimal involvement from the mule, those who were coerced tended to be carrying drugs concealed in this way. Marina (who was coerced) had no idea what she was carrying:

> When the guy brought me that bag in the hotel, I was looking inside the bag, and I couldn't see it because it was in [the lining]. And I'm so stupid how I was, I was thinking, Hey, they forgot it! Yah! (both laugh), so I go really cool to the airport, and then when they come to control me, and they put the knife in the bag, and this white power comes out, I said, 'Oh shit, I didn't see it.'

Although Marina was perhaps optimistic in thinking that her contacts had forgotten to pack the drugs, in fact no one could check what they were carrying because drugs were already concealed, designed to pass through customs. Howard explains:

> I didn't know what was in the bags. All I knew was 'product'.
>
> JF: Do you know how much you were carrying?

H: I had no idea. I found out later it was 5 kilos: 3 kilos of cocaine and 2 kilos of heroin.

JF: That's a lot.

H: It didn't weigh anything. 10 lbs. But I didn't know. They were bags, they were items... nothing more, nothing less.

Strapped to bodies or packed in clothes

Five respondents (four women and one man) carried drugs strapped to their bodies or hidden in clothing. The male mule had the drugs strapped to his abdomen. Women mules often carried drugs packed into underwear: usually in a bra or packed around their buttocks and hips. Marta carried around a kilo in her bra, and Manuela and Donna both carried around two kilos packed around their hips and buttocks. This reflected the heterosexual male 'gaze' which designates those supposedly most natural aspects of the female body – curves of breasts and hips – as the normal object of men's view. Interestingly, Schemenauer found that US customs officials viewed women through a sexualised gaze, and exoticised Latina women, drawing on racial, colonial discourses (2012). So although traffickers may have hoped that packing drugs in women's hips and buttocks would have been able to avoid suspicion, Schemenauer's research found these parts of women's bodies to be under additional scrutiny.

Unlike packing in suitcases, this was customised for the individual's body shape. This required some specialisation, and interestingly, this role was sometimes filled by a woman:

> [The contacts] are men, the ones I met in Brazil – men, it's men, you never talk to a woman, you talk to a man. The only time you talk to a woman is when she's going to look at you to see your size to go and buy the clothes you have to wear. The men don't know the size. (Angela)

The ways that drugs were concealed on bodies reflected gender norms. For example, women carried drugs strapped to their breasts and buttocks. Miller suggests that 'gender may be used as a resource for women to accomplish participation in and avoidance of crime' (2002: 452). However, she also found that male robbers use women as accomplices in particular ways according to gendered stereotypes – for example posing as prostitutes to lure men into quiet areas where they can be robbed

(1998). In the same way that Miller's male robbers were the 'author' of female robber's gender performances, investors chose the method of concealment and mules were not the 'authors' of their gendered performances.

In most cases, mules had no input into where the drugs were packed on their bodies, but Donna was a rare exception. She was good friends with her initial contact (Nino), had recruited mules for him before, and spoke Spanish fluently. She had an unusual amount of cultural capital and was able to take advantage of a rare opportunity. Donna described her contact, Perla, in Ecuador:

> Perla told me that she was very poor. She told me how much she was getting paid for this. I was getting three times more than she was, and the most dangerous is to carry the drugs from Colombia to here [Ecuador].
>
> JF: So she was working like a mule.
>
> Donna: She was like me, she was like a kind of a *mula* [mule] herself, and she told me, she said if she didn't do this job, she was gonna get killed. It showed that she was poor. She was well-dressed 'n all, but still.

Recognising that Perla was a mule rather than an organiser, Donna changed where the drugs were concealed. Rather than seeing herself as a mule who should merely do as she was told, Donna acted less like a mule and more like an organiser. Donna told Perla that Nino had decided that she should carry the drugs on her body, instead of in her luggage:

> I was supposed to have drugs in my suitcase, and at the last minute I changed the place of my drugs. They gave me a jacket with the drugs [instead]. But I didn't tell nobody; I didn't even call Nino to let them know I didn't have the drugs in the suitcase anymore, I have it somewhere else.
>
> JF: How come you made that decision?
>
> Donna: Just to see what would happen, I guess. I said to the person who was going to bring me the drugs to come 'n get my suitcase to put everything in, but then I said, 'Can you put it somewhere else?' She asked, 'Does Nino know?' 'Yeah, yeah, he's the one that told me to ask you.' Bullshit. And Nino changed his phone number, and he told me to give Perla his phone number and I didn't.
>
> JF: So you had control of what was going on?
>
> Donna: Mm hmm

It was pure chance that Nino changed his number, but Donna seized the opportunity. Having worked as a mule before, she decided to carry the drugs on her body (as she had done on her successful trip). Nonetheless, despite having a high degree of control, Donna was arrested with heroin, not cocaine as she had agreed.

Swallowing capsules

Some mules carry drugs inside their bodies. 'Body-packing' refers to the practice of smuggling drugs in the body in the carrier's vagina, rectum, or stomach (Gregory and Tierney 2002; Stewart et al. 1990; Traub et al. 2003). The only method of internal concealment used here was swallowing capsules of cocaine compressed into capsules inside latex (fingers of gloves or condoms). The 'swallower' in press reports is overwhelmingly female, but in fact most are men. Data on mules arrested at London's Heathrow Airport showed that three quarters of 'swallowers' were men, and that a greater portion of men than women had swallowed capsules (Harper et al. 2000: 107). Similar data collected in Schiphol Airport in the Netherlands found that 77.3 per cent of 'body packers' were male (Dorn et al. 2008). The majority of 'body packers' requiring medical attention are male (Heinemann et al. 1998), but the demographic may be changing to include pregnant women, teenagers, and children (Traub et al. 2003: 2519; Vale and Kennedy 2004; Sturcke 2007). Four respondents swallowed capsules of drugs. Caroline, Paula, and Nan were all first-time mules. Lorenzo swallowed capsules on his first trip as a mule, and later as an independent trafficker.

Respondents usually knew from the start that the job involved swallowing capsules of cocaine.[3] Nan's contact explained that the chances of arrest were high, and 'hiding' the cocaine inside her body was 'safer'. The punishment for trafficking drugs into her home country included life imprisonment and the death penalty.[4] She was most worried about being arrested and trusted her contact's expertise.

Caroline spent a week with her contacts while they trained her to swallow the capsules. She was living in Ecuador at the time:

> They gave me food and medicine, vitamins, said I needed to be healthy, I needed to be strong, I need to eat three times a day. They taught me how to swallow [prompt]. They taught me how to open my throat, first by swallowing grapes, then with cocktail sausages, then sausages with the plastic on them and plus I was stretching my stomach by eating a lot of food and being healthy. So the last day, I

> only ate chicken broth, and that was to like clean out my stomach. They gave me vitamins B12 complex, they gave me vitamins to clean my liver, and then that night I swallowed [the capsules].

Zaitch's description is very similar:

> Two weeks before they are due to leave, the training starts. They are trained by swallowing grapes, carrots, or banana pieces and they follow a diet to regularise their digestive cycle. The last two days, they eat very light meals: vegetables, fruits, and no fat. The painful loading process takes, in some cases, a few hours, walks and massages helping to accommodate the balls, and some yogurt, olive oil or Vaseline to swallow them. (2002)

I also interviewed Guillermo, a young Ecuadorian man who travelled to Colombia to begin his training as a mule. He was given extensive instructions about the process of swallowing drugs:

> They told us that we should not ingest anything at all, nothing solid. If it was liquid, it had to be water only, pure, because if you, let's imagine, drank Coca Cola or some other drink with bubbles...they would burst. Your body's evolution would not take it...This would burst and you would die. Even if one capsule burst, you would die. They said that we should not ingest any food in the plane, and in order not to cause suspicions, you had to eat the food and chew it awhile, so they would see you, and you would have a bag hidden, and you had to spit the food in there because if you would eat it, it [the capsule] could burst.

Although it is widely considered potentially fatal to eat while carrying capsules of cocaine in one's stomach,[5] I have not been able to find evidence to confirm or deny this. Lorenzo claimed that he would eat to avoid appearing suspicious and had never experienced any problems with his capsules.

Conversely, Paula and Nan were given no training or advice about swallowing capsules. Swallowing capsules was a long, uncomfortable process. Respondents described them as about the size of their thumb. Capsules are typically about 2 cm in diameter by 6cm length (Dorado 2005: 320). Dorado describes the process of ingesting capsules:

> The process of ingesting can last all night. [...] They can ingest more than 100 units with a total weight of around 900 grams. [...] The

> process of swallowing is slow: after a certain period of time they have to swallow 5 or 6 units, helping them down with water, oil or silicon jelly. (2005: 320).

Prior research has stated that those mules who swallow capsules are subject to greater exploitation and threats: 'these particular couriers are often even more ill informed than conventional unskilled *mulas* [mules]. [...] In some cases *boleros* [swallowers] report to have suffered some sort of pressure from the *cargadores* [loaders]: psychological blackmail or explicit threats' (Zaitch 2002: 150). Similarly Dorado and Huling report that mules were physically threatened and intimidated to swallow capsules (Dorado 2005; Huling 1995, 1996). This was not borne out in this research. Nor was it the case that 'swallowers' were the least educated and most vulnerable (cf. Zaitch 2002: 150). In fact, Paula made clear that she was under no financial pressure and could have said no.

As in other methods of concealment, capsules arrived pre-made. Nan and Paula were arrested with cocaine; however, Caroline discovered that she had swallowed heroin (she thought she was swallowing cocaine). Had she been arrested arriving at her destination country (rather than in Ecuador) she would have received a much higher sentence for heroin than cocaine.

There are numerous documented incidents of capsules of cocaine (or heroin) bursting and quickly causing death in medical journals and forensic scholarship (Deitel and Syed 1973; Heinemann et al. 1998; Kelly et al. 2007; Stewart et al. 1990; Traub et al. 2003) and in the press (Bosely and Radford 1992; Morris 2007; Stuart 2003). Between the mid 1990s and 2000, one to three mules were found to be dead on arrival at Schiphol airport in Amsterdam each year (Zaitch 2002: 149). Nonetheless, it is impossible to estimate accurately what the chances are of capsules bursting. Some forensic researchers have claimed that increased mechanisation of capsules has improved quality and safety (Traub et al. 2003; Veyrie et al. 2008); however these studies were conducted in Western Europe and cannot be considered representative of global trends. Furthermore, not all capsules are equal. Carlos (a Colombian broker of cocaine) showed me a capsule of cocaine that had just arrived into the men's prison (presumably smuggled in by a visitor). He unwrapped it and counted out seven layers, including multiple layers of latex, one of carbon paper and a final layer of candle wax, which he claimed stomach acid could not dissolve. This represented considerable hours of work (given that a mule can swallow about 100 capsules). Forensic scientists have developed a typology of 'capsules' (Kelly et al. 2007), ranging from type I: loosely packed, covered by just 2 layers of latex; to type IV: tightly packed cocaine wrapped in tough latex and finally covered by a hard shell of fibreglass or paraffin. Whilst these are the most likely to pass through without bursting, they are the most easily detected by x-ray.

Lorenzo made and swallowed his own capsules. When I asked him about the risk of the capsules breaking, he described how once he had driven a truck over one to see what would happen: the capsule was a bit bent out of shape but survived intact. He claimed that he had swallowed capsules many times without problems. Lorenzo was rare in admitting to working with capsules; other professional traffickers, including investors, said that they would never use capsules and considered them to be simply not worth the risk of someone dying.

Experienced mules

Whilst first-time mules knew very little about trafficking, it might be expected that more experienced mules would have more control over their work. However, as my research shows, that was not necessarily the case:

> JF: Did you say, 'I want to wear it. I want to put it in my bag?'
>
> Angela: No, you don't say nothing, they just bring. They don't tell you how they gonna make it, how they gonna give it, they just... last minute somebody just say you have to go, then the stuff is ready, so you don't know.

Angela worked in different places each time (so met different contacts on each trip). She did not have a clear idea of what was going to happen, but simply accepted this as part of her work. Catalina, an experienced mule, worked with her boyfriend, but had limited control over her labour:

> JF: What about how it's packed? You get to decide that?
>
> C: No, but if I'm not sure about the packing, I just call back [boyfriend] and we pack it again. [...] My boyfriend was taking advice from me. He knows my strong character, and he asks me if it's ok like this, or if I have another idea. He would tell me what I was supposed to be picking up, and if I arrive and it's not what we talked about at home, then I call him. He thought it was better that I should feel in control while I'm there, like I'm his eyes in his place. He respects this because

> I'm gonna put myself in the shit, so it's better like this, so that I'm in control.

Although cultural capital was an important resource for gaining control over her work, arguably her relationship with her boyfriend played the most significant part in enabling her to take an active role in her labour.

Drug quantities

When respondents first agreed to traffic cocaine as a mule, the way that drugs would be concealed was agreed. Mules were often told the quantity of drug they would carry at the same time. There was little scope for discussion or negotiation. Sharon explained: 'You get told what to do; you either accept it or not. It had already been discussed by contacts.'

Investors decided what and how much the mule would carry and how it would be transported. Ryan described himself as the employer and the mule as an employee. He recruited mules directly: 'It's like a wage to do a job and that's it. There's no negotiation. We say, "Here's the option to do a trip, take it or not. You'll get paid x amount."' Ryan uses the vocabulary of the market, describing the task of carrying drugs as a 'job' and the payment as a 'wage'. He also makes it clear that this 'job' involves a hierarchical relationship in which he maintains control throughout. The only decision made by the mule is either to 'take it or not'.

In order to make a profit, investors had to send a critical quantity (see also Fleetwood 2011). Paul (an independent trafficker) started by carrying a relatively small amount (about 40g) in a talc bottle. Although this was (in his own judgement) neither a particularly sophisticated method nor a particularly large amount, it covered the expenses of his holiday. In contrast, if a small collaboration of people sent a mule, several people have to be paid and a profit made.

Ryan was part of a medium-sized smuggling enterprise. In order to make a profit, they needed to send each mule with at least 2.5 kilos of cocaine on a regular basis. The quantity that mules carried was the result of several factors, including the availability of drugs, available capital, and technological expertise. For example, Ryan employed scientists who could chemically camouflage cocaine (Krebs et al. 2000); however, this could be costly, which also had an impact on the minimum quantity needed to make a profit.

The minimum quantity smuggled by mules in this research was around a kilo, and the maximum was 6, which probably indicates a variety of sizes of trafficking collaborations, and the professionalism of those involved as well as the kinds of technologies that were available. For example, only small quantities could be carried using capsules (Zaitch reports 400g – 1 kilo (2002: 149)). Those carrying drugs on the body carried 1–3 kilos, whilst the largest amounts were carried in suitcases (5–6 kilos).

Conclusion

This chapter fills in an important gap in knowledge about the work undertaken by mules. It shows that the vast majority of mules had almost no control over their labour since the way that mule-work is organised effectively designs out the possibility of their involvement. Mules were subject to the control and choices of investors, managers, and minders throughout the process – from travelling, as in the last chapter, to collecting and ingesting drugs, in this chapter. They were unequivocally labouring under the control of others, regardless of whether they became involved through coercion or choice in the first place. This is also the first research to examine the role of gender in the work done by mules. Surprisingly, men and women were equally subject to control and exploitation as mules: gender was much less significant than might have been assumed.

Zaitch reported that 'cocaine was carefully weighed and packaged in front of them [mules] to avoid misunderstandings, others claimed to know just the weight carried and the very basic instructions.' (2002: 147) No such transparency was reported by respondents in this research. Mules were given only basic details about where they were going, and investors acknowledged that misleading mules about the quantity or drug they were carrying was not that unusual (see Chapter 4).

Examining the way that mule-work is organised reveals that no mules could know what they were carrying, and in a significant portion of cases, they found they were carrying vastly larger quantities, or a different drug, than previously agreed. This was especially the case for those mules carrying drugs concealed in luggage. Those mules who were coerced also tended to be carrying drugs packed in luggage. This runs contrary to previous research that has seen 'swallowers' as the most vulnerable.

Few mules took much interest in what they were carrying. In fact, none considered the possibility that they might be carrying a different drug, or a larger quantity than they had agreed to, until they were arrested. Nonetheless, quantities and categories of drugs have important consequences in sentencing. For example, in the US, 3 kilos of cocaine would result in a minimum sentence of five years, but the same quantity of heroin would result in a minimum sentence of ten years (United States Drug Enforcement Agency 2013). In England and Wales (until February 2012) and the US, carrying more than 5 kilos of cocaine will receive a much longer sentence (Fleetwood 2011). At the time of writing, drug quantities play a primary role in determining sentences for drug importation offences in England and Wales (Sentencing Council 2012). Few mules were aware of this, although professional traffickers were (Matrix Knowledge Group 2007; Fleetwood 2011). Those mules who were carrying heroin when they thought they were carrying cocaine tended to be destined for countries where the sentences for carrying heroin are higher, suggesting that mules were intentionally misled by their contacts.

Only in very rare circumstances could mules have influence over aspects of their labour. Those who were (rarely) able to control aspects of their work were able to do so by dint of circumstance, or by drawing on their social capital where contacts were well known, for example as boyfriends, or friends of boyfriends. Men were less likely to be involved through someone they had a close relationship with, and therefore rarely had this kind of social capital to draw on. Although neither male nor female mules had much control over their labour, gender was important; the 'styles' in which drugs were concealed reflected gender norms, but these gender performances were 'done' by organisers rather than by mules.

8
Backing Out

> That night, I was dreaming about police everywhere, and I didn't want to go. They said, 'No, you have to go, you can pass the x-ray.' I didn't want to go but they took me in a taxi to the airport
>
> JF: What happened when you tried to back out?
>
> N: He said, 'You have to go. You can't do thinking now!' They're pushing me out of the country! They said I have to go because they already sent you, spent money on you for the ticket for nothing... all this. [He said the ticket cost $3000] I just do what I'm told. I don't want to be here anymore. I took the choice to be here already, and that's what I have to do. It's lots of money for the ticket: if I go back without the drugs, I think they're gonna kill me.
>
> JF: Did they ever say that to you?
>
> N: No, they don't say, but I knew from my country: African people [her contact was African] are working with the police and the mafia. If you make them spend money for nothing, they're gonna put you in trouble.

Nan's experience of trying to back out was fairly typical. Up until this point, she collaborated with her contact, obeying his requests that she not leave the hotel without him and undertaking the difficult task of swallowing a very large quantity of capsules. Until now, Nan's participation could be described as more or less voluntary, but mechanisms of control only became visible when she tried to back out. At first, her contact tried to assuage her fears by reassuring her it was safe to travel and that she would successfully pass the x-ray. Then he explained that they had spent money on her ticket, which she would owe them if she returned without the drugs. Although their persuasion may have become more desperate ('they're pushing me out of the country!'), no direct threats were made. Instead, Nan drew on racial stereotypes about her contacts and drug trafficker myths about the violence that would ensue. At this point, it became clear that she could not choose *not* to continue. Nan's narrative is therefore one of resignation: having agreed to traffic, she saw little option but to carry on. This final chapter examines what happened when mules attempted to back out. Doing so brings into focus the blurry boundary between mules' collaboration and contacts' control.

Of the fourteen mules I interviewed (who were not coerced into trafficking), half did not consider or try to back out.[1] Most simply caught a taxi to the airport and had no further communication with their contact, although they were possibly accompanied by a watcher/minder on the flight. Others were accompanied to the airport by their contacts; for example, Howard's friend (who had coerced him), stayed to watch him check in and pass customs to ensure that Howard did not try to inform the border agents, or try to dump the drugs at the airport.

No men who were mules thought about backing out. This is an interesting gender split, but it is impossible to know if this reflects wider trends. Paul (who recruited mules) thought that women were more likely to reconsider:

> Women wimp out more than men. Women think more, speak more, communicate more. They think about the odds more, see things that men might not see, and perhaps they're not happy with the risk.

Paul's explanation clearly draws on cultural scripts about men being tough and apt for criminal work in a way that women are not (Messerschmidt 1993; Mullins and Wright 2003; Mullins 2006; Steffensmeier 1983). These same cultural scripts may inform men's understanding of their role. Men who were mules could not explain why they didn't think about backing out: most simply did not see it as either possible or desirable.

Thinking about backing out

Caroline thought about backing out but decided to do it anyway. She was living in Ecuador at the time, so unlike other mules, she was in her usual social milieu, arming her with resources to change her mind and back out of the trip:

> Before I was going to swallow, I said, 'I don't want to do it.' I was afraid and [my boyfriend] says if I don't want to do it, don't do it.

> And I said, No, I've gone too far. And it's kind of like this thing when I start something, I finish it. I want to prove that I can do whatever I want to do.

Caroline was not obligated to travel by her boyfriend, nor were her options constrained by debts, financial crisis, or poverty. Since she had not yet travelled, she did not owe her contacts anything. She spoke Spanish fluently, and, unusually, her boyfriend was with her and offered to help her negotiate backing out with her contacts (who were also his friends). Caroline was able to imagine successfully backing out and also had access to the kinds of social, cultural, and economic capitals that could have enabled her to successfully do so. Yet, she decided to traffic anyway. She explains that she was driven by her self-conceptualisation as someone who 'finishes what they start'. Caroline's involvement in the drug trade was the most agential in that she could have chosen otherwise, even after she had agreed to traffic and had undergone training to swallow the capsules of drugs. Nonetheless, her experience was very rare.

Half of the mules interviewed thought about backing out (Anika, Caroline, and Donna) or attempted to back out (Amanda, Marta, Nan, and Manuela) but in fact none were able to, either due to lack of opportunity, assumptions of violent reprisals, or actual threats of violence. Anika thought about leaving without the drugs. She was supervised by contacts who had her passport. She could not see any way to leave the country without taking the drugs with her:

> When I was in the hotel the last night before I was supposed to travel...I was just looking at the things [the drugs]; they were packed already in my luggage. I was just thinking, should I do it? Should I not do it? I was a little bit scared, but I was thinking, Where [can] I put the drugs now? I already have them, I am inside the hotel, they have my passport, where can I put five kilos? So I was thinking, Just once, and nothing's going to happen to me.

Marina also wanted to back out. She was involved due to coercion and threats from her ex-partner. She could not imaging taking the risk of not seeing her daughter again:

> I was thinking, really, I will leave that bag here, and I will go without drugs back; then I was thinking, I can't do it, because when I do it, I will not see her [daughter] again. So I was really confused.

Unlike Anika, Marina was not heavily supervised, and could have left her suitcase at the hotel, or dumped it at the airport. However, Marina was convinced that her violent ex-partner would not let her see her daughter again if she returned without the drugs. He had previously been violent towards her, and she was extremely anxious about his threats of reprisals against her or her daughter.

Trying to back out

Marta had to change her flight twice because of delays in the drugs arriving. She became increasingly anxious and called her contact at home, threatening to return home without the drugs:

> I said that if the drugs didn't come by the next ticket I had booked, I'm going. He said I couldn't do that. I said, 'Yes, I can.' I had a bit of control but not that much ... but if you look at it, we don't have much control. Not really.

Unlike Anika, Marta still had her passport and a valid ticket and arguably could have caught her flight home. Despite knowing her contact well, she was also aware that her control over the situation was limited by her role as a mule. She did not have the authority to legitimately make the decision to leave. Although she drew on her identity as a friend (and fellow trafficker's girlfriend), her actions were also an enactment of her subject position as mule, which she sees as powerless: 'we don't have much control. Not really.'

Amanda spent most of her time in Ecuador unsupervised. After several phone calls home to her friend Jane (whose boyfriend was her initial 'contact'), her contacts in Ecuador came to collect her:

> It was this man and this woman; they were like drunks, you know. I was like, 'So pathetic, oh my God, they're supposed to be professional people?' (laughs) I was like, 'What did I get myself into?' But there was no way of turning back, you know? So, um ... I was like, fuck it; I have to go with it. I have to go through with it.

Her contacts arrived, took her out, paid her hotel bill, and left a suitcase packed with drugs. They took her old suitcase away with them. When her contacts left, Pablo (a minder) stayed with her to watch her. She initially pleaded with him, but then called Jane:

> [I was] with that Colombian guy [Pablo]. I was arguing with [him] 'cause he wanted to sleep in the bed with me, and I wanted him to sleep in the sofa bed. So, [anyway] he was like, 'Don't worry about it. You're gonna get away with it – you're not the first one, and you're not the last one,' he told me.
>
> But I had this gut feeling that I wasn't going to go through with it, plus when [Jane] called, and I told her, you know, I can't do it. Well, she was like, 'Well, you can't back off now because if you don't do it, you're going to owe us $4000.' So that's why I didn't back down. Because I was already in debt; $3000 for my rent, $1000 for my light, $600 for the gas, my mother was in debt by $4000 in her rent, and that's what I wanted it for.

Amanda received an advance payment of $3,000 (as seen in Chapter 6), which her mother had used to pay off the most urgent debts. Although Amanda was not threatened, her debt effectively bound her to the task of carrying drugs.

After reassurances and discussions, contacts got more desperate: hurried persuasions were replaced by violent threats. Manuela's contact came to check that she was wearing the package just before she left for the airport:

> It was really heavy: two and a half kilos. It was really uncomfortable. [Indicates where it was: all round her posterior and lower abdomen]. I felt like a lemon being squeezed! It was *pressing* on me! And then I changed my mind and I told him, 'I don't want to do it.' So we had a discussion. He told me that if I don't want to wear the drugs…he threatened me. Said he would kill my family. He said it was not good to come here and then not take the drugs. Then I was really scared. I didn't know what to do, so I was wearing the slip [which contained the cocaine]. […] I had no control over what I was doing. I was totally nervous; I was thinking a lot about what I was doing. [prompt] I was asking him [contact] if he can see it in the clothes. And he said no. [He said], 'It's too late to change.' I was thinking that he was scared, also.

It is impossible to know if Manuela's contact did in fact know anything about Manuela's family, but she believed that he did. Her initial contacts knew her boyfriend well, and her boyfriend had met her family. Conversely, Manuela knew nothing about her contact and was not able to give any information about him to police. Manuela saw little option other than to go to the airport and try to go home.

Bonny was threatened with violence against her family, and her child in particular. Bonny (a single mother) left her child with a good friend and his family (including her contact). She did this willingly and did not think twice about trusting a friend with her child while she was out of the country for a few days. When Bonny called her contact and said that she wanted to return without the drugs, her contact replied, 'Remember I have your daughter. You come back with the drugs and everything will be OK.'

It is difficult to say if this strategy was planned by her contact, or whether he acted opportunistically. Interestingly, this seems to echo other practices in the international drug trade. Stefan (a professional trafficker who had recruited mules) told me that traffickers sometimes left family as a guarantee in return for receiving large consignments of drugs in place of cash:

> In big deals, it's ugly, but... If you are coming to Colombia to do a deal, you have to bring a family member with you, and they stay in Colombia 'til the deal's done. If you steal or fuck up, then they'll kill your friend/family member. That's the Colombian way. It's ugly, but there's so many traitors, that's how it has to be. It's a form of kidnapping, but that's the way it goes. Your friend or whoever gets looked after. If you get arrested, get a lawyer to send a report or copy of documents to confirm, and they'll go free. They might even send you [person in jail] money.

In short, people could be employed as a deposit or insurance. Stefan explained that his friend had once volunteered to act as his guarantee so that Stefan could get drugs on credit, smuggle them, sell them, and then pay for the drugs trafficked. Although he emphasised that in this case, his friend had volunteered to do this for him out of his own free will, this practice is underpinned by violence. Violence is typically seen as an intrinsic and inevitable feature of dealing and trafficking markets (Dorn et al. 2005; cf. Zaitch 2005) necessary to highly structured, hierarchical organisations to enforce a rule of law where no legitimate enforcement exists. However, Pearson and Hobbs contend that violence is 'bad for business' as it draws the attention of the police, and therefore should be understood as a sign that things are going wrong (2001). Respondents' experiences suggest that although threats of violence were occasionally used to coerce mules *into* traffic, they were more commonly employed when women tried to back out, and even then only as a last resort after persuasion had failed.

Since no male mules in this research tried to back out, it is difficult to know whether men may have experienced threats of violence against their families, if they tried to back out. The experience of having one's family threatened may be peculiar to women, as they were more likely to have children (the male mules in this research did not have children). Nonetheless, as seen above, Howard's partner received threatening phone calls, and he felt compelled to traffic to protect her.

Using threats and intimidation seems counterintuitive, since a scared mule would seem more likely to be obviously nervous or scared while passing through security and boarding the plane. Mules raised legitimate concerns about suitcases that smelled strongly (or badly), or about poorly packaged drugs, but minders seemed uninterested in delivering the mule to the airport calm and mentally prepared. Manuela noted that her contact seemed scared. It is plausible that 'minders' were employed solely to mind mules and ensure that mules travelled to the airport.[2] Having done their job, they were less interested in the success or failure of mules trying to pass customs.

Experienced mules

Since respondents were recruited in prison, it is difficult to know if any mules ever successfully backed out. Interviews with investors, recruiters, and minders suggest that mules did rarely back out at the early stages, before they left home, but almost never once mules had started travelling. Nonetheless, Catalina (an experienced mule) did manage to delay and back out of working as a mule, on separate occasions. Her experience sheds light on what most women lacked to enable them to do so, too. Unlike first time mules, Catalina had considerable capitals at hand: her relationship with her partner/contact was important as a source of legitimacy (and social capital), as was her experience as a mule, providing her with cultural capital. On one occasion, she had a nightmare the night before leaving:

> I woke up at two am. I say, 'I'm sorry. I can't leave at seven am.' They asked why not. So I said, 'I can't travel. Can we change the day?' They said, 'OK, it's better, so no one will be in danger.' They gave me a day or two. There was no bad reaction from them. No forcing. It was just OK (shrugs shoulders). [...] When I told him I can't travel, I thought they're gonna... I was scared for a few minutes how to say... I thought they were gonna slap me. [Then I was thinking that] their reaction is business; I have to take that. But no! They said 'OK, another day.' So I waited two days, then I travelled.

Although she could not back out completely, she delayed the trip until she felt ready to leave and passed border security successfully. She anticipated some form of violent retaliation, but in fact this was not the case, possibly because of her close relationship with her boyfriend.

Later in her career, Catalina refused to pick up the drugs. She was in charge of meeting her contacts to collect the packages of cocaine. Her boyfriend was many thousands of miles away:

> I refused to pick up the drugs that trip. I think that was the first time when I wanted to change my life. I didn't want to [do it]. I lied to my husband: 'I called the people; they don't answer.' He says, 'Are you sure?' I don't know what happened; my husband was not stupid but... He said, 'If you say like this, I will take it [believe it].'

Unlike other mules, Catalina was in charge of liaising with her contacts, and she normally organised the collection of drugs herself. As an experienced mule, she had gained a lot of knowledge about her labour (cultural capital); however, arguably social capital was more powerful. Catalina was sure her boyfriend knew that she was lying: they had been together (romantically and as business partners) for some time. She thought he decided just to let her do what she wanted this time since she had already done many successful trips.

Threat: nationality, intimidation, masculinities, and 'the mafia'

Several mules cited their contacts' nationality when they described being threatened, or referred to organised crime groups, especially 'mafias' (meaning any organised crime group rather than Italian or Italian-American mafias specifically). Mules' initial contacts were often known through social connections (see Chapter 4) but contacts in Ecuador were a mystery. Respondents drew on stereotypes of drug traffickers as ruthless, scary, and violent. This was especially true where contacts were 'Colombians'. Amanda remembers:

> I felt pressured. [prompt] Especially after seeing the Colombians, you know, *reunidos* [together], together like... There was the woman: the woman was like 'Oh yeah. She'll do what she has to do.' [threatening tone of voice] It was just like something out of that mafia movie with Al Pacino, you know, 'Scarface' or whatever they call it. They were all meeting there, and they were talking over the suitcase like... Before

> anything went down, I couldn't feel like I was doing this; it was like in a fantasyland. Reality hit me exactly at the moment when I saw them that night, together, with the suitcase on my bed, on the hotel bed. I didn't speak Spanish too good at that time, especially when the Colombians talk really fast. So when I was watching that, it was like I wasn't there. Like I was watching; I put myself like I was watching from the outside, and I wasn't in with them, but I was actually in *with* them. [...] I was their puppet. I felt like I was a puppet with strings and they were controlling. Yeah, I wouldn't move, wouldn't speak, you know, 'cause I would only speak when I was spoken to. I asked one question, and he was like, 'Don't worry about it.' I felt like, uff... I'm not even gonna mess with them, 'cause they'll probably just kill me and take the suitcase and...

Paula had been visiting Ecuador to learn Spanish. Quito is home to many Colombian migrants who are employed in various industries. However, Paula interpreted her contacts' nationality as a source of threat: 'He was... I didn't understand him well... he was a scary person... in himself... He was a Colombian, and they kidnap people.'

Similarly, at the start of this chapter, Nan (from Southeast Asia) read her contact's African ethnicity as evidence that he was part of a violent group: 'African people are working with the police and the mafia. If you make them spend money for nothing, they're gonna put you in trouble.' She drew on popular stereotypes, as well as personal experience, since her ex-boyfriend was an African involved in trafficking. Howard's response was similar: 'We weighed the idea of going to the police, but to me, the immediate image I got was cocaine cowboys.[3] And gunfire.'

In Chapter 4, Howard recalled visiting 'cartel headquarters' (p. 73) while he was working in the music industry in the 1980s. Donna (who had dealt drugs and was a Latina) similarly remembered a man she knew of who had been subject to retaliation, even after completing a prison sentence:

> I knew a guy once that came back from [her family's historical home], a guy that I used to know as a kid with my mum and her husband. He was disappeared. He had just come out of jail. He was starting back again: he'd started to sing, he made CDs 'n everything. He started clean, [but] he was still in this shit. And he disappeared for two months. After two months, they found his body without a head and missing a hand.

Empirical research on Colombians in Europe sheds some light on the role of national reputation in trafficking. Bovenkerk et al. contend that ethnicity is fluid and performative (2003). Trafficking organisations and individuals managed their 'ethnic reputation': 'playing with reputations that already exist, either by obscuring ethnic ascription or exaggerating stereotyped images' (2003: 28). They describe one Colombian who traded on the reputation that his surname, Escobar, gave him. To those who knew little about Colombia this was used to considerable effect; however, other Colombians would have been aware that his was actually a relatively common surname, and that he was probably not related to the infamous Pablo Escobar.

It is not clear from mules' accounts whether contacts actively manipulated their nationality as a means of control; mules nonetheless interpreted their behaviour in this way. Reuter contends that 'the mafia may be a paper tiger, rationally reaping the returns from its reputation while no longer maintaining the forces that generated the reputation' (1983: xi).

It is impossible to know whether or not contacts were in fact violent, organised criminals. There is a strong possibility that they were (at least in some instances) people contracted solely to mind mules with little further knowledge or control over business. Ironically, contacts could rely on discourses about traffickers perpetuated by government, law enforcement, and popular media to facilitate managing mules. In fact, those women who did not treat them as if they were 'traffickers' (but rather as friends, or boyfriends), were able to successfully negotiate aspects of their role, including backing out.

At the level of interaction between mules and contacts, threat and violent potential were attributed to contacts on the basis of (presumed) criminal connections, but also relied on the immediate presence of masculine 'bodily capital' (Hobbs et al. 2002). Sometimes this potential for violence was explicit, but more commonly, no explicit performance was necessary: mules drew their own conclusions. Interestingly, female contacts worked in jobs that did not require them to be threatening, such as specialisations associated with more pastoral roles, including recruiting mules, training them to swallow capsules, or organising where to pack the drugs on their bodies. Men seemed to fulfil roles that involved threat, such as accompanying mules to the airport and ensuring that they travelled with the drugs.

International drug trafficking, like the street level drug trade, takes place within existing structural relations. Organisers in the international drug trade arguably took advantage of gender relations to establish authority, power, and control (similarly, see Maher 1997: 203). In general, women were more likely to report being threatened; however, they also more commonly described trying to back out. In fact, no male mules in this research attempted to back out. Although threats took place in the context of gendered relations, it is important to keep in mind that women were threatened as *mules*. It was not the case that women were subject to violence and threat solely because of their gender; men were also subject to coercion.

Conclusion

This is the first research to look at what happened when mules tried to back out. Many mules' participation could have been described as willing and collaborative until this point, but when they tried to back out, they found that mechanisms of control bound them tightly to their prior agreement to carry drugs. In many cases, contacts tried to persuade mules by reassuring them that they would successfully pass customs. Another common practice was to tell mules that they owed their contacts the cost of the flight and 'holiday', which usually ran into several thousand dollars. Sometimes mules were paid part of their fee in advance, adding to this debt, and since many mules were motivated by poverty or financial crises, repaying this debt was simply not possible.

Persuasion was sometimes accompanied by violent threats, but this was not always necessary. Many mules simply assumed that backing out would result in violent reprisals, drawing on dominant discourses about traffickers. Gender was inevitably important, and threats were gendered (in that they were bound up with masculinity); however, women were not more likely to be threatened because of their gender. Threats were often made against family members. Since no male mules in this research tried to back out, or had children, it is hard to know whether threats were used against women in a different way than men. Nonetheless, overall it was the case that all mules were managed in such a way as to make it virtually impossible to back out.

Understanding how mule-work is organised contextualises women's apparent victimisation. Closely examining what mules do (and not just their motivations) allows a clearer understanding of agency by taking into account time and change (McNay 2000). By this I mean that following mules through the journey (from their narratives about becoming involved, travelling, and doing the job) shows that victimisation and agency are not static qualities of a person, but are enacted through social interaction. Possibilities for action were limited by the objective circumstances of mule-work, which was designed to keep mules tightly controlled, especially once they had the drugs. Possibilities for having influence or control over their labour were limited by women's access to capitals, including cultural capital, as drug trade know how about what was possible and social capital. In this way, victimisation and agency were not absolute, but rather, echoing previous chapters, it was possible to find examples of mules successfully negotiating control over their work, including being able to back out (albeit rarely). This was only the case for those with sufficient social and cultural capital. Nonetheless, it was also the case that, having agreed to carry drugs, most mules had virtually no choice but to do so. Looking at backing out reveals that even apparently 'willing' mules were in fact labouring within extremely constrained circumstances. When they arrived at the airport, many saw themselves as willing participants, but arguably they could not have done otherwise. In this sense, women's and men's participation was remarkably similar.

Conclusion: Women's Offending in Global Context

The study of globalisation and crime now forms a major subfield in criminology (Aas 2007, 2013; Findlay 1999; Hardie-Bick et al. 2005). One strand of such research explores how globalisation is reshaping crime, in particular the emergence of transnational forms of crime (Aas 2013; Findlay 1999); 'as social life is lived transnationally, so too is crime manifest transnationally' (Hardie-Bick et al. 2005).

Sociologists have noted that women are often missing from academic discourses about globalisation (Chow 2003) but change is afoot (Eschle 2010). Arguably, a similar critique applies to criminological study of globalisation. Approaches to global forms of crime tend to focus on the 'big scales' of globalisation, obscuring the significance of social structures, including gender. This is certainly the case with much research on drug trafficking. In contrast, this book offers a view from the fringes of drug trafficking, especially from women and mules. Whether trafficking is imagined as a hierarchical pyramid, or a loose network, those at the bottom or peripheries will comprise a significant majority. I hope this book demonstrates that they have much to add to contemporary understanding of the international drug trade, and by extension, women's role in global crime more generally.

This book offers a critical account of women in the international cocaine trade, which explores questions of gender, structure, and agency. In order to do this, I showed that dominant discourses about drug trafficking set up gender binaries that are antithetical to understanding gender, structure, and agency. I have proposed that instead, questions of structure/agency and women's offending must be approached from the smallest scale, that of human interaction (S. Jackson 2001; McNay 1999, 2004). By exploring questions of subjectivity, interpretation, and action, drawing on narrative theory, women's participation can be more clearly understood.

Rather than approach women's accounts of trafficking in a straightforward way as records of events and experiences, they have been approached here as narratives (Presser 2009; Sandberg 2010; Presser and Sandberg, forthcoming). Doing so draws attention to the social role that trafficking stories played in prison and the complexities involved in giving an account of involvement in drug trafficking, especially around claiming victimhood and agency. Some kinds of accounts, and speakers, were supported in El Inca, while others were silenced. Overall, subject positions of victimhood received greater support, both from prison staff and women themselves. Collectively, women represented themselves as drug mules to negotiate gendered stigma and to enable them to challenge various forms of 'misrecognition' (Fraser 1995). Nonetheless, talking about trafficking remained taboo (Torres 2008). As such, fieldwork entailed reflexivity about my role as a co-constructor of stories, and in particular, the role I could play in making space for alternative, conflicting, and contradictory kinds of narratives.

The question of how and why women become involved in drug trafficking was fundamental to this project. Rather than the kinds of violent traffickers that feature in political and popular discourses, mules described traffickers as friends, boyfriends, husbands, and customers who were also successful mules or recruiters. These relationships played an important role in shaping the way that respondents interpreted the possibility of working as a drug mule. Rather than danger and risk, many respondents saw opportunity. In some cases, women said they felt obligated due to these relationships. Whilst this is significant, it is nonetheless very different to the kinds of strong coercion that dominate media discourse, and some academic research about women's recruitment into drug trafficking as mules.

Whilst it has been commonly thought that traffickers recruit women due to their vulnerability, this was not the case here. Unlike prior research, I contextualised mules' experiences of trafficking processes by drawing on interviews with recruiters, minders and investors. Interestingly, gender was not the most significant factor for recruiters. Traffickers sought out people they thought would seem unremarkable to police, border agents and customs, Reflecting this fact, many mules in this research were well travelled, and some were pensioners, perhaps evidencing a trend in recruiting diverse people for mule-work (Zaitch 2002). These factors were more important than gender alone. Furthermore, recruiters sought people that they knew *about* to be mules as insurance against mules running away or backing out. Although the recruiters and traffickers said that they would not be interested in coercing someone into working as a mule, it was nonetheless the case that a handful of respondents credibly recounted being coerced or threatened into trafficking. A small number of respondents also described carrying drugs that had been put in their luggage without their knowledge. Whilst these kinds of claims are frequently met with frank disbelief (see Chapter 1), traffickers were able to explain why such claims could be plausible, even if they were not typical. This is the first research to explore coercion in depth. Drawing on interviews with traffickers was particularly useful, given that drug mules were often misled or lied to by their collaborators.

Mules in this research came from all over the world, including the global North (Western Europe and North America) and the global South (Latin America, Asia and Africa). They came from diverse ethnic and class backgrounds and had a wide range of age and experiences. Most were first-timers, but some had made several trips previously or had been involved in other roles. Their narratives about how and why they became involved in international drug trafficking reflected this diversity.

Narrative analysis was used to explore women's narratives as subjective interpretations of material circumstances, structured by the habitus (McNay 2004). Despite geographical and national distinctions, respondents' narratives drew on a surprisingly narrow range of discourses. Overall, women' narratives tended to be 'other-oriented' (S. Jackson 1993), whether they were about romantic relationships or 'provisioning' for partners, children and parents (Ferber and Nelson 1993). In this way, narratives were often about maintaining or attaining gender roles, which were oriented towards local contexts. Women's narratives were often about the financial difficulties of making a life as mothers, daughters, girlfriends, and wives. Thus, their involvement in trafficking could be understood as a response to gendered poverty, mediated through gendered selves that guided their actions. Rather than being compelled by others, women often felt compelled by their responsibilities and roles. Given that women were often in precarious or low-paying jobs, their narratives unsurprisingly contained ambivalences about these obligations.

Women rarely offered narratives based on desires for themselves as men did, for example, through discourses about entrepreneurship. This may reflect the difficulties that women encountered incorporating crime into their self-stories since crime is generally stigmatised for female offenders (Lloyd 1995). Furthermore, discourses about womanhood tend to emphasise relationships with others, rather than autonomous subject positions (Somers 1994). Nonetheless, women did speak about being excited about travelling and temporarily escaping their responsibilities. Thus, women's narratives about becoming mules are understood here as creative engagements with available opportunities, interpreted through cultural discourses about what women are supposed to be like. Whilst these were iterated through local norms, the global could also be 'heard' in women's desires, through the influence of consumer capitalism, neoliberal discourses that make women responsible for the care of others, and gender norms and values (Haywood and Mac an Ghaill 2003). Globalisation was not 'out there' for respondents, but played an intimate role in shaping their emotions and desires. In sum, women's involvement in trafficking was not solely the result of the 'feminisation of poverty', as has previous been claimed, but also reflected discourses about what women 'should be' like. Subject positions such as girlfriend or mother made trafficking make sense.

The final three chapters explored the role of gender in the organisation of mule-work. Mules' relationships with their contacts were inevitably gendered, but overall, gender was much less significant than expected. In fact, the way that mule-work is organised effectively designs out the need for mules to be actively involved. In general the work of the mule is characterised by a lack of information or control and this was the case for both women and men mules who experienced mule-work in broadly similar ways. Most considered themselves to be participating voluntarily and accepted this lack of control as merely part of their role as mule. Furthermore, when they attempted to back out, it became clear that they could not do so. Contacts tried to reassure mules and persuade them to travel, sometimes with reference to debts mules had occurred during their 'holiday'. As contacts became more desperate, persuasion was followed by threats of violence (including against mules' children and partners). Exceptionally, two women were nonetheless able to negotiate aspects of their labour, including where to pack the drugs, and even when to travel. They did so by drawing on cultural and social capitals. Interestingly women were much more likely to be connected to trafficking through close relationships, and therefore were more likely to have social capital enabling them to influence their role. Whilst has often been assumed that women's role in the international cocaine trade is passive and that women are more likely to be victimised, the picture here is more complex.

Representing agency

In the course of this research I encountered few 'cocaine queens', yet women refused to understand their involvement as passive or unintentional. Recounting women offenders' agency risks rendering them 'equally' punishable (Snider 2003; Chesney-Lind 2006), and given the epic scale of women's incarceration for drugs offences worldwide, this is something that I am anxious to avoid. Interestingly, the same problem of enacting agency whilst avoiding becoming 'punishable', troubled women in El Inca.[1] To be clear, I am not arguing that all women mules are volunteers however I do aim to show that women could and did act in purposeful and intentional ways, even in constrained circumstances. This research has described different aspects of agency. As meaning-makers and storytellers in prison, women creatively interpreted their world, their place in it, and their hopes for the future. Women's participation in the international cocaine trade was often the result of reflection, evaluation, and action. As protagonists in an emerging story, their narratives were creative evaluations of current circumstances and opportunities. At the same time, their narratives were not freely chosen, but were culturally and historically specific. They were also gender specific: women had little choice but to be mothers, daughters, and girlfriends as protagonists in their narratives. Finally, in a world that drastically constrained their access to education, employment, and financial stability, participation in drug trafficking as mules simply 'made sense'.

Beyond drug mules

The sub-title of this book is 'women in the international cocaine trade', yet the focus is on women as mules, which is of course only part of the picture of women's involvement. There were several reasons for this. Firstly, most existing research is on women as mules, and findings have much to add to this body of study, especially in examining mule-work. Secondly, women as drug mules have been the focus of drug policy reform, and thirdly, women in the international cocaine trade are undoubtedly concentrated in the role of mule. This book nonetheless hints at the breadth of women's involvement in international trafficking.

A handful of respondents had worked in other roles beside mules – for example, recruiting or minding mules. Chapter 4 found that some mules had been recruited through successful mules who were women. Male traffickers also talked about women they worked with – for example, they described women minding money and drugs, or posing as a secretary to help a trafficker pass border security dressed as a businessman. Chapters 6 and 7 describe women acting as 'contacts' in Ecuador – managing mules and organising the packaging of drugs. Nonetheless, women in prison were generally unwilling to talk about trafficking, so it was difficult to identify women who may have fulfilled other roles. This was in part due to prison taboos about trafficking as well as the 'code of silence' about speaking to outsiders. Despite spending several years visiting prison, it was very difficult for me to speak to women who were not mules. Interestingly, no Ecuadorian women participated in the research, probably due to fear of retributions. Unfortunately they are most likely to have been arrested whilst undertaking tasks such as minding mules, giving them packages of drugs and so on, as contacts.

I encountered several traffickers' girlfriends during fieldwork. All were arrested with their boyfriends as they left Ecuador and in some cases, I interviewed their boyfriends, too. Nonetheless, only one was willing to be interviewed. This may have been due to loyalty to boyfriends (and perhaps fear of reprisals). Pragmatically, most girlfriends were released after trial; none were found guilty. Data from the one trafficker's girlfriend who took part was not used due to ethical and pragmatic reasons. Furthermore, there was not sufficient data to justify a separate chapter.

Finally, in the course of fieldwork, men in prison regaled me with countless anecdotes about the drug trade, and women in it. One told me about running away with a drug boss's daughter when they were just sixteen. After several days on the run, 'associates' tracked them down in the desert and returned them both to the boss, who insisted the man marry his daughter. Most men had tales about women involved at high level, as bosses' wives, and of daughters who had inherited the family business and squandered it all. These anecdotes hinted about women's presence in the upper echelons (also Adler 1993; Campbell 2009). Arguably, such data says more about men's discourses about men and gender than it does about the women themselves.

Final reflections: on theory

As I wrote up field notes, I had a strong sense of writing from outside of the empirical, political, and national territories that I had taken for granted as a student in the global Northwest. Researchers at a local university, FLACSO, offered an important focus on Ecuador as the normal case. Academics there adopted a pragmatic and eclectic approach to theory and research from the global North (Pontón 2008; Nuñez 2006a; Torres 2008). Nonetheless, since I was writing about women who were mainly *not* Ecuadorian, or even South American, I struggled to find the kind of theory that would help make sense of their involvement in drug trafficking as a form of global, transnational crime. Rather than examine the influence of globalisation upon a particular milieu (as a 'glocal' context), the key theoretical problem here was to take into account women's lives from diverse points of the globe, leading up to their involvement in trafficking. And, if possible, try to hold in view the social constructedness of gender, as well as the global variation in the situation of women.

Since returning 'north', I have tried to hold onto this sense of marginality. I have been particularly buoyed by feminist theory that encouraged me to think more deeply about the importance of being in the 'margin', as well as my own limitation in being able to truly do so (hooks 1982, 1984; Mohanty 1991, 1993). Connell's *Southern Theory* (2007) revealed the puzzling 'Northernness' of most sociological theory. I have also been influenced by the proposal of southern epistemology (de Sousa Santos 2008). I learnt that most criminological writings were conversations within a particular community (Morrison 2006), which did not include the global South. This imbalance seems especially unjust given that countries like Ecuador have been radically reshaped by crime control politics from the global North, arguably causing more harm than good (Cohen 1982; Bowling 2011). Questions about crime control and coloniality (and post-coloniality) are now squarely in the criminological mainstream (Agozino 2000, 2003; Morrison 2006; Cunneen 2011) and there also exists a transnational feminist criminology (Reynolds 2008; Sudbury 2004, 2005a). Whilst there is a burgeoning awareness of the global in feminist criminology (Cain 2000; Cain and Howe 2008; Pickering and Lambert 2004), this is the first book (to my knowledge) to explore women's participation in transnational crime. My attempt to 'do theory', comes at a particular historic juncture in criminology.

The theoretical approach adopted in this book is not obviously global or post-colonial, and arguably it is rather old fashioned. It draws on symbolic interactionism: the idea that people act on the meaning that things have for them, which are negotiated socially (Blumer 1969). Ferrell rightly notes that this process takes on a greater complexity under the influence of globalisation (2006, also Young 2007); however, symbolic interactionism offers a way to think about social action within the transnational and global 'social worlds' that comprise drug trafficking. Furthermore, narrative analysis (which draws on symbolic interactionist traditions) offers ways of understanding how individuals construct participation in international trafficking from local points, even in the context of cultural globalisation. Since narrative is the point at which structure (as available discourse) and agency (individual appropriation) meet, they offer the possibility of connecting local and global, self and society. In this way, paying close attention to women's narratives as mules offers a way to 'hear' gender and structure/agency in the context of a globalised world.

Notes

1 Introduction: Cartels and Cocaine Queens

1. At the same time First Sergeant Alberto Arean Varela, head of the anti-drug and organised crime police unit at the Guardia Civil in Ibiza, expressed doubt in relation to their claims of coercion: 'Sincerely, with my experience, I don't think these girls were forced to do this [...] Because, particularly when you go to South America, you need to pass several controls so the first thing you [would] do is go to the passport control and say "Listen, this is what is happening to me", and the police will react – so I don't think they were forced.' (quoted in Collyns 2013).
2. Similarly, see Galloway 2013; Moir 2013; Platell 2013; Riley 2013; Malone 2013.
3. Unlu and Evcin (2011), published in Turkish, summarised in Unlu and Ekici (2012).
4. This mandatory minimum was applied sporadically, with many drug mules in prison receiving sentences of eight years (and some less where they had aided police). Sentences for drug offences were under review at the time of writing (Asamblea Nacional de la República del Ecuador 2013).
5. These same figures have been published by the US Department of State (USA Department of State 2007).
6. 'La Cárcel en Ecuador: vida cotidiana, relaciones de poder y políticas públicas'.
7. I do not know how the practice of visiting foreign inmates in prisons in Ecuador began. Some inmates thought that this custom had spread from the San Pedro Prison in La Paz, Bolivia. Rusty Young, the author of 'Marching powder', reports that he read about visiting inmates in the Lonely Planet Guide book, and his own book also publicises visiting prisons as a tourist attraction (Young and McFadden 2003). These prison 'tours' continue to be touted as 'the most bizarre tourist attraction' (Baker 2009). Young reports that inmates charged visitors for the tour, which included the chance to take cocaine and/or stay overnight for 'the best party in Bolivia'; Baker reported this fee was £25 (2003). Prison visiting in Quito was never this well organised, or commercialised. I did not pay for a 'tour', nor did I go in looking for a party or an opportunity to buy or take drugs. I heard about visiting through a local organisation called the South American Explorers Club. At that time, they collected donations (clothes, toiletries, and so on) for male and female prisoners and delivered them sporadically to the prison. This was and is completely separate from the setup in Bolivia. At the time of writing, prison visits in Ecuador have all but stopped following a pardon (*indulto*) for drug mules in 2009, which resulted in most foreigners being deported (Metaal and Edwards 2009).
8. An account of the emotional aspects of fieldwork can be found elsewhere (Fleetwood 2009).

9. Drug traffickers are not necessarily dangerous, but being connected to illegal activities is risky for the researcher due to law enforcement (Polsky 1985).
10. Although some have claimed that being female makes the researcher more (Craig et al. 2000) or less (Taylor 1993) vulnerable, gender is not the only factor involved in researcher safety and may not always be the most salient (see also Sampson and Thomas 2003). Other salient identities in this fieldwork included my nationality, language, status as visitor and friend as well as researcher. There are several good discussions of gender in ethnographies of deviance and crime control (Lumsden 2009; Irwin 2006; Hoefinger 2013; Kane 1998; O'Brien 2009; Jewkes 2012).
11. One male ethnographer was punched by a guard who mistook him for a prisoner.

2 Imagining Drug Trafficking: Mafias, Markets, Mules

1. The connection between supply and demand is complex. For example, in the UK cocaine use has decreased over the last five years, as has drug purity (Mulchandani and Hand 2010). At the same time as cocaine use has decreased, the number of people using cathinones, such as mephedrone, has increased (Measham et al. 2011).
2. Inter alia Leonard 1982; Gelsthorpe 1989; Klein 1995; Joe and Chesney-Lind 1995; Chesney-Lind and Eliason 2006.
3. Hobbs reports that only the Italians viewed the phenomenon of organised crime as home-grown (1998: 408) but even that seems to be changing (Paoli 2005).
4. This was mirrored by Andy Slaughter, Labour MP for Hammersmith, in a discussion about transparency and consistency of sentencing, and in particular the annual report from the Sentencing Council: 'The council noted that drug mules are often vulnerable people and victims of exploitation and violent coercion by organised gangs. Disproportionately, they are women, poor and poorly educated, and they are minor beneficiaries of the illegal trade, if they benefit at all' (HC Deb, 2nd February 2011, Vol. 539, part 260, Col 1051).
5. Rarely, Francis et al. (2013) note the fact that the vast majority of serious and organised criminals in their research were male; however, they do not offer any analysis regarding gender.
6. Norrie criticises the rational choice perspective from the perspective of jurisprudence and criminal responsibility. He uses the terms 'practical reasoning' and 'practical rationality' (1986: 219) to reflect the social contexts in which decisions are made.
7. The feminisation of poverty thesis as it relates to women's involvement in drug trafficking is somewhat different from the thesis as it relates to women's involvement in crime generally (Carlen 1988). Whereas the feminisation of poverty thesis has traditionally focused on hierarchical divisions of gender (i.e. patriarchy), research on drug mules examines gender inequalities on a global scale.
8. The category did not exclusively relate to drug importation but included other offences relating to producing and selling drugs.
9. Adler claimed that 'as the position of women approximates the position of men, so does the frequency and type of their criminal activity' (1976: 251). Furthermore, she thought that as women became emancipated like men, they would seek the same kinds of security and status: 'criminal as well as civil, through established male hierarchical channels' (1976: 11).

10. This research refers to Europe and North America.
11. The further two tenets are 'that the meaning of such things is derived from, or arises out of the social interaction that one has with one's fellows' and thirdly, 'these meanings are handled in, and modified through an interpretative process used by the person in dealing with the things he encounters.' (Blumer 1969: 2). This observation takes on a novel character under globalization as it facilitates greater global movement of the meanings of crime and deviance (Ferrell 2006; J. Young 2007).
12. Furthermore, it is difficult to 'read' social structure when respondents are out of their usual social context. Social class cannot be determined from statistical analysis of respondents' neighbourhoods (as in Maher 1997; Bourdieu 1990).
13. Specifically in criminology, there have been calls to better account for women's agency and empirical research has shown that even in constrained circumstances, women can and do act with intentionality and creativity (Batchelor 2005, 2009, 2011; Denton 2001; Phoenix 2000; Maher 1997; O'Brien, forthcoming; Miller 2001).
14. Studies of media portrayals of female offenders can arguably be considered a more recent expansion of this trend (Seal 2010; O'Neill and Seal 2012; Chesney-Lind and Irwin 2008).
15. In fact both sides acknowledge that material and cultural are mutually implicated in women's oppression (S. Jackson 2001; McNay 2004).
16. Broadly, larger schemas have been referred to as discourses (after Foucault) and individual self-stories have been referred to as narratives (S. Jackson 1998; Sandberg 2010; Somers 1994). Discourse here is employed in a broad sense to incorporate both dominant, institutional discourses (for example, those about family roles) as well as countercultural, temporary, and locally situated collections of meaning. Similarly, 'Narrative criminology is situated in the classical opposition between agency (what is the teller trying to accomplish?) and structure (which narratives are available?)' (Sanderg 2010: 455).
17. Several contemporary criminologists have used Bourdieu's conceptual toolkit of habitus, capitals, and field to useful effect, and offer very useful summaries of his concepts (Sandberg and Pederson 2009; Fraser 2013b; Sandberg 2008a, 2008b; Ilan 2013).
18. McNay is one of several contemporary feminist theorists who draw on Bourdieu's theory of social practice (also Adkins 2004; Krais 2006; Lovell 2000; Moi 1991; Skegg 1997, 2004).
19. In cultural anthropology, 'below' also refers to 'grounded, embodied experience' (Fraser 2013a: 258; Kenway and Fahey 2009). I use it here in a less specific sense.

3 What Do Women Talk about When they Talk about Trafficking?

1. Steamed corn cakes similar to tamales, a typical Ecuadorian afternoon treat.
2. Paula's second account of events (five years after the first interview) was very similar to her first account (above). It is included here for interested readers:

    P: The very last day I had a Colombian guy come and there was a lot of calling between me and my boyfriend. [The contact] came over to a hostel where I was staying and my plane was supposed to leave I think at

4 and ... he came in the morning, he brought me the ... capsules ... and they were in peach cans.

JF: At what point did you find out that you were gonna swallow the capsules?

P: While talking to my boyfriend and the guy was ... You know, my Spanish wasn't all that good at all, but then they just kept on saying, you know, 'It's safe. This way no one will ever find out. You just swallow them like medicine' and all that so ... it was basically, it was already there, like what were they gonna do with it ... ? So ...

JF: So the way I imagine it is that you were talking with your boyfriend, and then this guy comes round with the capsules all in the same day ... and so, in a way it's already organised

P: Yeah, it was already organised ... He told me before, a friend of mine is gonna come round from Colombia, maybe for you to bring something home, and then, you know, within the conversation it came out that he was in danger and all that, which probably before I hadn't talked about, but you know, one thing that hasn't changed. I accepted. It was like it came more from me. What can I do? If that's the only thing I can do, I'm going to do it, you know, and he was like no, no, no ... and I'm like 'OK, let me do it!'

3. Parole was reintroduced in 2006 in Ecuador but was limited to those who had the resources to undertake the necessary paperwork and who could find a job and a place to live. Paula was sponsored by a member of an international missionary group, but not all prisoners were so fortunate.
4. Paula was not compelled to traffic as a result of poverty, nor did she have any dependents. She is very clear that it was her choice to become involved. However, she also states that everything was organised by other people and happened 'fast'; in fact the drugs arrived pre-packaged before she had agreed to carry them, so her involvement was also not the result of a rational, cost-benefit type analysis.
5. Ecuador passed a new constitution in 2008, following the election of Raffael Correa as president in 2006 and his taking office in 2007.
6. The constitutional limit was 6 months for serious offences including drugs, extortion, violent offences, and rape, 3 months for non-serious offences (Edwards 2003).
7. The sentencing process was very long. Having one's sentence executed (sentencia ejecutoriada) was the final stage in sentencing, following an initial hearing, court case, and in some instances, an appeal.
8. Fieldwork pre-dated the Bangkok Rules, which offer an expanded understanding of women's distinct needs as prisoners from the previous Minimum Rules (United Nations 2010).
9. My observations relate to the period between 2002–2007. A documentary about one of these protests was made by FLACSO, examining the circumstances and process by which 361 visitors were held hostage for 48 hours in the men's prison in Quito in 2004 (Herrera 2005). Protests have continued since, including protests at the apparent suicide of a foreign national prisoner in 2011 after her sentence was raised from four to eight years.
10. This was the first account of being a drug mule that Amanda shared with me. Over subsequent interviews, we discussed what led her to that work and

multiple conflicting narratives emerged. This should be considered a public statement of self, as much as an explanation for her offending.

11. According to a survey of the women's prison: '16.4 per cent of all inmates said that they had been involved in international trafficking of drugs, 13.4 per cent for trafficking at a regional/national level and 13.1 per cent said they had been detained for consumption of drugs (in spite of the decriminalization of consumption since 1998).' (Pontón and Torres 2007: 67, my translation)
12. I was never able to find out what these complaints were about. This created an opportunity to ask respondents what I could or should do differently. Their responses were positive (and several offered to smuggle in a tape recorder for me – I declined). After the meeting, one of the women on the committee apologised privately and asked me to please continue to visit.
13. In fact, women also engaged in this physical form of protest, not in the capital Quito, but in Ecuador's second city, Guayaquil, which also housed a large female prison population.
14. This interview took place before Paula was poisoned, so she would have been unaware that her trafficking connections were also still present in prison.
15. Minding mules means travelling with mules to watch over them to make sure they followed the instructions they were given.
16. Stanley and Steedman note that women (and especially poor women) have been required to give a narrative account of themselves ever since the establishment of the burgeoning welfare state in the UK, contrasting starkly with the romantic ideal of self-narratives as artful self-expression (Stanley 2000; Steedman 2000).
17. Tisha would want me to also record here that she did mend her heart. She gained parole, left prison, and finally returned home.
18. Although consumption had been decriminalised since the 1990s, in practice, users were often imprisoned for possession of small quantities (Edwards 2003). Resolución 001 Consep-CD-2013 sets out these quantities: cocaine (1g), cocaine base (2g) heroin (0.1g) and marijuana (10g). According to the Procurator General, Diego García, possession and use are to be considered issues of health, rather than criminal offences (El Telégrafo 2013).
19. Fieldwork is described in more detail elsewhere (Fleetwood 2009).
20. Although I never interviewed anyone waiting for trial, many inmates were engaged in the long legal struggle of appeal. Processes for transfer, deportation, and parole were slow and nerve-wracking. Court dates were constantly moved or delayed, lawyers absconded with money, files got lost, and the constant state of not knowing what was happening was extremely stressful.
21. Note-taking was useful since data could be made anonymous, and 'disutilised' at the source (Lee 1995), and respondents could see what I was and was not recording. I could also gain trust from respondents by showing them the care I was taking to ensure that they could speak freely (for example, using symbols instead of names or places). After transcription, all documents were password protected, and notes were securely destroyed.

4 Who are the 'Traffickers'?

1. Before the interview began, we had a long discussion about confidentiality. Lorenzo insisted that I use his real name, but in the end I persuaded him to use a pseudonym. Lorenzo insisted that his friends stay for the interview.

2. I did not record interviews in the men's prison and relied on note-taking. This quote was recoded verbatim, 'No tenía mafia, no tenía contactos. No debes nada, nadie debes a ti.'
3. Zaitch undertook fieldwork in the Netherlands and Colombia, with Colombian traffickers (2002). He reports that independent traffickers were rare in Colombia since the drug business was dominated by small groups. Lorenzo was one of several independent traffickers that I met; however, none were Colombian. Thus, the prevalence of independent traffickers may vary according to national contexts.
4. Inmates explained that 'the big fish go free'. In fact, several reported that police asked them for bribes shortly after they were arrested to let them go free (in the realm of $125,000 US). It is impossible to validate these claims. Just three respondents claimed to work for people who they counted as bosses or leaders of a hierarchical and long-standing criminal collaboration. All were men from Latin America. It is impossible to rule out the possibility that organised, cartel-type groups coexist with smaller, flexible, less permanent collaborations (Wright 2006).
5. Some researchers exploring these social connections draw on data from surveillance such as phone taps (Natarajan 2000), or data from police crime investigations (Kleemans and de Poot 2008); however, despite mention of female participants, neither explore the significance of gender. Others have argued for the use of social network analysis to study crime (Coles 2001; Chattoe and Hamill 2005) and drug trafficking in particular (Bright et al. 2012). However, Von Lampe criticizes research that seeks to understand 'organised crime' from a rational choice perspective, and in particular this kind of approach to 'social facilitators': people who stimulate crime by encouraging offending (2011).
6. This may not be coincidental since traffickers may actively seek to extend social networks to include contacts or people with particular skills as needed (Dorn et al. 2005; Hobbs 2013: 159).
7. On the same theme, Zhang et al. (2007) demonstrate that norms and values in China, especially *guanxi* (which roughly translates as 'connections', but it is also tied to complex social protocols including favours and responsibilities) and increases in divorce facilitate women's involvement in human trafficking.
8. This is illustrated by the recent case of two British women reported in Peru. Their claims to be coerced were met with skepticism by Spanish police (Collyns 2013), and by the British Press (Malone 2013).
9. Skint means having very little money.
10. Despite not fitting the usual mule stereotype, all three were arrested. Nonetheless, Jensen had worked as a mule many times before he was arrested.
11. Ironically, the opposite seems to be the case. Women were often fearful of speaking to police precisely because they were worried for their children.

5 For Money and Love: Women's Narratives about Becoming Mules

1. It is not possible to include Nan's nationality as it would make her easily identifiable. National backgrounds have only been included with the respondent's explicit permission.

2. Most women involved in prostitution probably do as well. (see Phoenix 2000).
3. In prior research on Nigerian mules, she reported that mules earned an average of £1,100 (£2000 the highest, £300 the lowest) (Green 1991: 39).
4. As mentioned in previous chapters, Howard was approached several times by his contact who wanted him to get involved in trafficking, so he knew what he should have been paid. Despite being threatened, he saw no reason not to be paid and demanded that he be paid in full. Although this was agreed in principle, in practice his contact disappeared after Howard was arrested.
5. Marina attended the interview, helping to translate where Manuela's English was poor. She was a good friend, and Manuela wanted her there for support.

6 Beginning Mule-work

1. Guayaquil is Ecuador's largest city and has Ecuador's only other international airport.
2. Quito also receives international immigrants from all over the world: China, Japan, the Middle East and other parts of Latin America. Foreigners in La Mariscal mostly came from Europe and North America.
3. No respondents had second thoughts at this stage. (Actually, those who had successfully backed out would not have been included in this sample).
4. Bobby was vague about what exactly the 'cartelito' comprised; however, he did work for someone else, undertaking a variety of tasks relating to trafficking.
5. This figure is based on information collated from respondents who trafficked drugs by mule. I am assuming the mule is carrying around 2 kilos of cocaine (an approximate average) costing about $2000 per kilo, plus packaging fees, a fee for the contact in Ecuador, plane tickets, documentation, and any upfront payment for the mule.

7 Mule-work and Gender

1. Unlu and Ekici's research in Turkey found regional differences; for example, they found that two thirds of South Americans had swallowed drugs, but the vast majority of Europeans and Asians carried drugs in luggage (2012: 307).
2. Harper et al. offer percentages based on totals including non-carriers. I have recalculated these figures for carriers only. Men carried drugs in luggage (43%), in clothes or strapped to bodies (32%), and swallowed (25%). Women carried drugs in luggage (52%), in clothes or strapped to bodies (27%), and swallowed (21%) (2000: 107).
3. The exception was Lorenzo, who did not know what he would be carrying or how, until the last day of his trip (see the start of Chapter 4).
4. A report published by the United Nations Commission on Crime Prevention and Criminal Justice in 2001 identified 33 countries in which capital punishment (including the death penalty) were applied as punishment for trafficking drugs. These countries are: Bahrain, Bangladesh, Brunei Darussalam, China, Cuba, Democratic Republic of Congo, Egypt, Guyana, India, Indonesia, Iran, Iraq, Jordan, Kuwait, Libya, Malaysia, Myanmar, Oman, Pakistan, Philippines,

Qatar, South Korea, Saudi Arabia, Singapore, Sri Lanka, Sudan, Syrian Arab Republic, Taiwan, Tajikistan, Thailand, United Arab Emirates, the United States (federal law), Uzbekistan, and Vietnam. (Lines 2007: 17; Gallahue and Lines 2010)

5. See also the film 'Maria Full of Grace' (Marston 2005) which depicts mules pretending to eat then spitting the food into airsickness disposal bags.

8 Backing Out

1. Mules who tried to back out may be over-represented here. They may have been more anxious, and so more likely to be arrested at the airport.
2. Manuela, Donna, and Amanda all thought that their contacts were intermediaries whose only job was to guard them.
3. Howard may be referring to a film called 'Cocaine Cowboys' that was released in 1979 (Lommel 1979).

9 Conclusion: Women's Offending in Global Context

1. It is also notable that political discourse about drug trafficking has long seen women mules as victims of male drug traffickers. At the same time though, this discourse has fuelled laws, policies, and practices that drive women's incarceration. In 1983, the judge in the case of *R v. Aramah* ruled out mitigating circumstances in cases of drug mules (in an English court), claiming that doing so would discourage traffickers from recruiting vulnerable people (Green 1998). His ruling stood for nearly 30 years and resulted in women mules serving sentences of up to 14 years for importing Class A drugs. The point I wish to make here is that understanding women's participation in the international drug trade through the lens of victimisation has not led to lesser or more reasonable punishment on the whole. At the time of writing, the tide seems to be slowly turning with sentence reform for drug offences recently passed in England and Wales (Sentencing Council 2012), and underway in Ecuador (Asamblea Nacional de la República del Ecuador 2013) as well as Brazil, South Africa, and New Zealand (Lai 2012: 2). These reforms have been driven by concerns about disproportionality, rather than the plight of women mules. Of course, questions about proportionality are bound up with the need to take mitigating circumstances, which are of course gendered, into account.

Bibliography

Aas, K. F. (2013) *Globalization and Crime*, 2nd ed. London: Sage.

—— (2012) '"The Earth Is One but the World Is Not": Criminological Theory and Its Geopolitical Divisions', *Theoretical Criminology*, 16(1): 5–20.

—— (2007) 'Analysing a World in Motion: Global Flows Meet 'Criminology of the Other', *Theoretical Criminology*, 11(2): 283–303.

Adkins, L. (2004) 'Introduction: Feminism, Bourdieu and after', in L. Adkins and B. Skeggs (eds), *Feminism after Bourdieu*, Oxford: Blackwell Publishers.

Adler, F. (1976) *Sisters in Crime*, New York: McGraw-Hill.

Adler, P. A. (1993) *Wheeling and Dealing: An Ethnography of an Upper-Level Drug Dealing and Smuggling Community*, 2nd ed., New York: Columbia University Press.

Agnew, R. (2006) 'Storylines as a Neglected Cause of Crime', *Journal of Research in Crime and Delinquency*, 43(2): 119–147.

Agozino, B. (2003) *Counter-colonial Criminology: A Critique of Imperialist Reason*, London: Pluto Press.

——(2000) 'Theorizing Otherness, the War on Drugs and Incarceration', *Theoretical Criminology*, 4(3): 359–376.

Agustín, L. M. (2007) *Sex at the margins: migration, labour markets and the rescue industry*, London: Zed books.

Albrecht, H. -J. (1996) 'Drug Couriers: The Response of the German Criminal Justice System', in P. Green (ed.), *Drug Couriers: A New Perspective*, London: Quartet.

Aliaga, C. C. G. (2001) 'Características que diferencian a mujeres recluidas por tráfico de estupefacientes del resto del población penetenciaria femenina', *Revista de Estudios Criminológicos y Penitenciarios* (Santiago de Chile), 2: 41–64.

Allen, H. (1998) 'Rendering Them Harmless: The Professional Portrayal of Women Charged with Serious Violent Crimes', in K. Daly and L. Maher (eds), *Criminology at the Crossroads: Feminist Readings in Crime and Justice*, New York, Oxford: Oxford University Press.

Allum, F. (2007) 'Doing It for Themselves or Standing in for Their Men? Women in the Neapolitan Cammorra (1950–2003)', in G Fiandaca (ed.), *Women and the Mafia: Female Roles in Organized Crime Structures*, New York, London: Springer.

Anderson, T. L. (2005) 'Dimensions of Women's Power in the Illicit Drug Economy' *Theoretical Criminology*, 9(4):371–400.

Appadurai, A. (2009) 'The Shifting Ground from Which We Speak', in J. Kenway and J. Fahey (eds), *Globalizing the Research Imagination*, London: Routledge.

Asamblea Nacional de la República del Ecuador (2013) *Proyecto de Código Orgánico Integral Penal*, Borrador, Segundo Debate, 28th September, Comisión Especializada Permanente de Justicia y Estructura del Estado, Quito.

Bagley, B. M. (2012) *Drug Trafficking and Organized Crime in the Americas: Major Trends in the Twenty-First Century*, Woodrow Wilson International Center for Scholars, Latin American Program.

Bagley, B. M. and W. Walker (1994) *Drug Trafficking in the Americas*, London: Transaction.

Bailey, C. (2013) 'Exploring Female Motivations for Drug Smuggling on the Island of Barbados: Evidence From Her Majesty's Prison, Barbados', *Feminist Criminology*, 8(2): 117–141.

Baker, V. (17 January 2009) 'Prison Break', *The Guardian*, UK.

Bancroft, A. (2009) *Drugs, Intoxication and Society*, Cambridge: Polity.

Barham, L., Bramley-Harker, E., Hickman, M., Hough, M., and Turnbull, P. J. (2003) 'Research Briefing: Sizing the Market for Powder Cocaine – is a New Approach Needed?', *The Howard Journal of Criminal Justice*, 42(4): 366–373.

Batchelor, S. (2011) 'Beyond Dichotomy: Towards an Explanation of Young Women's Involvement in Street Gangs', in B. Goldson (ed.), *Youth in Crisis? Gangs, Territoriality and Violence*, London: Routledge.

—— (2009) 'Girls, Gangs and Violence: Assessing the Evidence', *Probation Journal*, 56(4): 399–414.

—— (2005) '"Prove Me the Bam!": Victimization and Agency in the Lives of Young Women Who Commit Violent Offences', *Probation Journal*, 52(4): 358–375.

Bauman, Z. (1998) *Globalization: The Human Consequences*, Cambridge: Polity Press.

BBC (13th September 2003) 'Jamaica's Women Drug Mules Fill UK Jails', BBC news online.

Beck, U. (1999) *What Is Globalization?*, Malden, MA: Polity Press.

Benson, C. and R. Matthews (1995) 'Street Prostitution: Ten Facts in Search of a Policy', *International Journal of the Sociology of Law*, 23(4): 395–415.

Bergman, M. and E. Azaola (2007) 'Cárceles en México: Cuadros de una Crisis', *URVIO: Revista Latinoamericana de Seguridad Ciudadana*, 1(May): 74–87.

Bewley-Taylor, D., C. Hallam, and R. Allen (2009) *The Incarceration of Drug Offenders: An Overview*, London: Beckley Foundation/International Centre for Prison Studies, Kings College London.

Birkbeck C. (2011) 'Imprisonment and Internment: Comparing Penal Institutions North and South', *Punishment & Society*, 13(3): 307–332.

Bjerk, D. and C. Mason (2011) 'The Market for Mules: Risk and Compensation of Cross- Border Drug Courier', Social Science Research Network.

Blumer, H. (1969) *Symbolic Interactionism: Perspective and Method*, London: Prentice Hall.

Bohman, J. (1997) 'Reflexivity, Agency and Constraint: The Paradoxes of Bourdieu's Sociology of Knowledge', *Social Epistemology*, 11(2): 171–186.

Boseley, S. and T. Radford (23 September 1992) 'Drugs "Mule" Dies in Tragic Trade with Fatal Pay Off', *The Guardian*.

Bosworth, M. (1999) *Engendering Resistance: Agency and Power in Women's Prisons*, Brookfield, VT: Ashgate.

Bourdieu, P. (1990) *The Logic of Practice*, Stanford University Press.

—— (1986) 'The Forms of Capital', in J. G. Richardson (ed.), *Handbook of Theory and Research for the Sociology of Education*, New York; London: Greenwood Press.

—— (1977) *Outline of a Theory of Practice*, Cambridge: Cambridge University Press.

Bourgois, P. (2003) *In Search of Respect: Selling Crack in El Barrio*, 2nd ed. Cambridge: Cambridge University Press.

—— (1989) 'In Search of Horatio Alger: Culture and Ideology in the Crack Economy', *Contemporary Drug Problems*, 16(4): 619–649.
Bovenkerk, F. (2000) 'Wanted: Mafia Boss' – Essay on the Personology of Organized Crime', *Crime Law and Social Change*, 33(3): 225–242.
Bovenkerk, F., D. Siegel and D. Zaitch, (2003) 'Organized Crime and Ethnic Reputation Manipulation', *Crime Law and Social Change*, 39(1): 23–38.
Box, S. and C. Hale (1983) 'Liberation and Female Criminality in England and Wales', *British Journal of Criminology*, 23(1): 35–49.
Boyd, S. C. (2007) 'Drug Films, Justice, and Nationhood 1', *Contemporary Justice Review*, 10(3): 263–282.
Bravo, D. (12 November, 2013) 'Hasta el 80% de detenidas está por tráfico de drogas', *El Comercio, Ecuador.*
Bright, D. A., C. E. Hughes, and J. Chalmers (2012) 'Illuminating Dark Networks: A Social Network Analysis of an Australian Drug Trafficking Syndicate', *Crime, Law and Social Change*, 57(2): 151–176.
Broidy, L. and R. Agnew (1997) 'Gender and Crime: A General Strain Theory Perspective', *Journal of Research in Crime and Delinquency*, 34(3): 275–306.
Brotherton, D. (1996) ''Smartness', 'Toughness' and 'Autonomy': Drug Use in the Context of Gang Female Delinquency', *Journal of Drug Issues*, 21(6): 261–278.
Brotherton, D. and L. Barrios (2011) *Banished to the Homeland: Dominican Deportees and Their Stories of Exile*, New York: Columbia University Press.
Browne, D., M. Mason, and R. Murphy (2003) 'Drug Supply and Trafficking: An Overview', *The Howard Journal of Criminal Justice*, 42(4): 324–334.
Bruner, J. (1991) 'The Narrative Construction of Reality', *Critical Inquiry*, 18(1): 1–21.
Bucktin, C. (2013) 'Peru Drug Arrests: Gangsters Held Guns to Our Heads and Said Smuggle Cocaine or We Will Kill You, Claim British Girls', *The Mirror*, UK.
Burawoy, M. (2008) 'Rejoinder: For a Subaltern Sociology?', *Current Sociology*, 56(3): 435–444.
—— (2000) 'Introduction: Reaching for the Global', in M. Burawoy (ed.), *Global Ethnography: Forces, Connections, and Imaginations in a Postmodern World*, Berkeley, London: University of California Press.
Burgess-Proctor, A. (2006) 'Intersections of Race, Class, Gender, and Crime: Future Directions for Feminist Criminology', *Feminist Criminology*, 1(1): 27–47.
Burman, M. (2004) 'Breaking the Mould; Patterns of Female Offending', in G. McIvor (ed.), *Women Who Offend*, London: Jessica Kingsley Publishers.
Burman, M. J., S. Batchelor and J Brown (2001) 'Researching Girls and Violence: Facing the Dilemmas of Fieldwork', *British Journal of Criminology*, 41: 443–459.
Bush-Baskette, S. (2004) 'The War on Drugs as a War against Black Women', in M. Chesney-Lind and L. Pasko (eds), *Girls, Women, and Crime: Selected Readings*, London: Sage.
—— (2000) 'The War on Drugs and the Incarceration of Mothers', *Journal of Drug Issues*, 30(4): 919–928.
Butler, J. (1990) *Gender Trouble: Feminism and the Subversion of Identity*, London: Routledge.
Byrne, B. (2006) 'White Lives: The Interplay of "Race", Class and Gender in Everyday Life', London: Routledge.
—— (2003) 'Reciting the Self: Narrative Representations of the Self in Qualitative Interviews', *Feminist Theory*, 4(1): 29–49.

Cain, M. (2000) 'Orientalism, Occidentalism and the Sociology of Crime', *British Journal of Criminology*, 40(2): 239–260.
Cain, M. and A. Howe (2008) *Women, Crime and Social Harm Towards a Criminology for the Global Age*, London: Hart Publishing.
Camacho, M. (2007) *Cuerpos encerrados, cuerpos emancipados: travestis en el ex penal García Moreno*, Quito: Abya-Yala; El Conejo.
Campbell, H. (2009) *Drug War Zone: Voices from the US-Mexico Border*, Austin, Texas: University of Texas Press.
—— (2008) 'Female Drug Smugglers on the U.S.-Mexico Border: Gender, Crime and Empowerment', *Anthropological Quarterly*, 81(1): 233–267.
Carlen, P. (1988) *Women, Crime and Poverty*, Milton Keynes: Open University Press.
—— (1983) *Women's Imprisonment: A Study in Social Control*, London: Routledge.
Carrión, F. (8th June 2013) '¿Fin a la guerra de las drogas?', *Diario Hoy*, Ecuador.
—— (2007) 'Por qué todos los caminos conducen a la miseria del panoptico?', *URVIO: Revista Latinoamericana de Seguridad Cuidana*, 1: 5–9.
Carvel, J. (30 July 1990) 'Foreign Drug Mules Swell Female Jails', *The Guardian*.
Castles, S. and M. J. Miller (2009) *The Age of Migration*, 4th ed. Basingstoke: Palgrave.
Caulkins, J., P. H. Burnett, and E. Leslie (2009) 'How illegal drugs enter an island country: insights from interviews with interviews with incarcerated traffickers', *Global Crime* 10 (1–2): 66–96.
Chambliss, W. (1979) 'On the paucity of research on organised crime', *American Sociologist*, 10(39).
Chattoe, E and H. Hamill, (2005) 'It's Not Who You Know—It's What You Know About People You Don't Know That Counts Extending the Analysis of Crime Groups as Social Networks'. *British Journal of Criminology*, 45(6): 860–876.
Chesney-Lind, M. (2006) 'Patriarchy, Crime, and Justice: Feminist Criminology in an Era of Backlash', *Feminist Criminology*, 1(1): 6–26.
——(2002) 'Imprisoning Women: The Unintended Victims of Mass Imprisonment', in M. Mauer and M. Chesney-Lind (eds), *Invisible Punishment: The Collateral Consequences of Mass Imprisonment*, New York: New Press.
Chesney-Lind, M. and M. Eliason (2006) 'From Invisible to Incorrigible: The Demonization of Marginalized Women and Girls', *Crime, Media, Culture*, 2(1): 29–47.
Chesney-Lind, M. and K. Irwin (2008) *Beyond Bad Girls*, London: Routledge.
Chesney-Lind, M. and J. Pollock (1994) 'Women's Prisons: Equality with a Vengeance', in A. Merlo and J. Pollock (eds), *Women, Law and Social Control*, Boston: Allyn and Bacon.
Chow, E. N. (2003) 'Gender Matters: Studying Globalization and Social Change in the 21st Century', *International Sociology*, 18(3): 443–460.
Christie, N. (1994) *Crime Control As Industry: Towards Gulags, Western Style*, London: Routledge.
Clark, J. (1995) 'The Impact of the Prison Environment on Mothers', *The Prison Journal*, 75(3): 306–329.
Clines, F. (18 July 1993) 'On Sunday; Finding Mercy for Conscripts In Drug War', *The New York Times*.
Cloyd, J. W. (1982) *Drugs and Information Control: The Role of Men and Manipulation in the Control of Drug Trafficking*, Westport, Conn. London: Greenwood.

CNN (26 May 2010) 'Former model arrested in Argentina on drugs charges', *CNN*.

Cohen, S (1988) 'Western Crime Models in the Third World: Benign or Malignant', in Against Criminology New Brunswick New Jersey: Transaction, original paper presented University of Ibadan, Nigeria 1980.

Coles, N. (2001) 'It's Not What You Know – It's Who You Know That Counts: Analysing Serious Crime Groups as Social Networks', *British Journal of Criminology*, 48(4): 580–594.

Collyns, D. (17 August 2013) 'Peru drug arrests: Spanish Cast Doubt on UK Women's Claims', *The Guardian*.

Comack, E. (1999) 'Producing Feminist Knowledge: Lessons from Women in Trouble', *Theoretical Criminology*, 3(3): 287–306.

Connell, R. (2007) *Southern Theory*, London: Polity.

—— (2002) *Gender*, Cambridge: Polity.

—— (1993) 'Introduction', in J. W. Messerschmidt (ed.), *Masculinities and Crime: Critique and Reconceptualisation of Theory*, Maryland, US: Rowman and Littlefield.

—— (1987) *Gender and Power*, Cambridge: Polity.

Contreras, J. (9 October 2007) 'Underworld Queenpin: Sexy Stylish and Female. Meet Mexico's Unlikely Drug Lord', *Newsweek*, US.

Cook, D. (1997) *Poverty, Crime and Punishment*, Child Poverty Action Group.

Coomber, R. (2007) 'Introduction to the Special Issue', *Journal of Drug Issues*, 37(4): 749–753.

—— (2006) *Pusher Myths: Re-Situating the Drug Dealer*, London: Free Association.

Corda, R. A. (2011) 'Imprisonment for Drug Related Offences in Argentina', in P. Metaal and C. Youngers (eds), *Systems Overload: Drug Laws and Prisons in Latin America*, Transnational Institute/Washington Office on Latin America.

Cornish, D. B. and R. Clarke (1986) 'Introduction', in D. Cornish and R. Clarke (eds), *The Reasoning Criminal: Rational Choice Perspectives on Offending*, New York: Springer-Verlag.

Corva, D. (2008) 'Neoliberal Globalization and the War on Drugs: Transnationalizing Illiberal Governance in the Americas', *Political Geography*, 27: 176–193.

Cosslett, T., C. Lury, and P. Summerfield (2000) 'Introduction', in T. Cosslett, C. Lury, and P. Summerfield (eds), *Feminism and Autobiography: Texts, Theories, Methods*, London: Routledge.

Costa, A. M. (9 March 2008) 'Every Line of Cocaine Means a Little Part of Africa Dies', *The Observer*, London.

Craig, G., A. Corden and P. Thornton (2000) 'Safety Issues in Social Research', Social Research Update, 20, http://sru.soc.surrey.ac.uk/SRU29.html (accessed September 2013).

Crewe, B. (2006) 'Prison Drug Dealing and the Ethnographic Lens', *The Howard Journal* 45(4): 347–368.

Cunneen, C. (2011) 'Postcolonial Perspectives for Criminology', in M. Bosworth and C. Hoyle (eds), *What Is Criminology?*, Oxford: Oxford University Press.

Daly, K. (1997) 'Different Ways of Conceptualising Sex/Gender in Feminist Theory and Their Implications for Criminology', *Theoretical Criminology*, 1(1): 25–51.

Daly, K. and L. Maher (1998) 'Crossroads and Intersections: Building from Feminist Critique', in K. Daly and L. Maher (eds), *Criminology at the Crossroads: Feminist Readings in Crime and Justice*, Oxford: Oxford University Press.

Davies, P. A. (2003) 'Is Economic Crime a Man's Game', *Feminist Theory*, 4(3): 283–303.

De Sousa Santos, B. (ed.) (2008) *Another Knowledge Is Possible: Beyond Northern Epistemologies*, London: Verso Books.

Dean, G., I. Fahsing, and P. Gottshalk (2010) *Organized Crime: Policing Illegal Business Entrepreneurialism*, Oxford: Oxford University Press.

Decker, S. H. and M. Chapman (2008) *Drug Smugglers On Drug Smuggling: Lessons from the Inside*, Philadelphia: Temple University Press.

Deitel, M. and A. Syed (1973) 'Intestinal Obstruction by an Unusual Foreign Body', *Canadian Medical Association Journal*, 109: 211–212.

del Olmo, R. (1986) 'Female Criminality and Drug Trafficking in Latin America: Preliminary Findings', in E. Morales (ed.), *Drugs in Latin America*, Williamsburg, VA.: Dept. of Anthropology, College of William and Mary.

—— (1996) 'Discourses, Perceptions and Policies', in P. Green (ed.), *Drug Couriers: A New Perspective*, London: Quartet.

—— (1993) 'The Geopolitics of Narco-Trafficking in Latin America (Globalization and Economic Crisis)', *Social Justice*, 20(3–4): 1–23.

—— (1990) 'The Economic-Crisis and the Criminalization of Latin-American Women', *Social Justice-a Journal of Crime Conflict and World Order*, 17(2): 40–53.

Denton, B. (2001) *Dealing: Women in the Drug Economy*, Sydney, Australia: University of New South Wales Press.

Denton, B. and P. O'Malley (1999) 'Gender, Trust and Business: Women Dealers in the Illicit Economy', *British Journal of Criminology*, 39(4): 513–530.

Desroches, F. J. (2007) 'Research on Upper Level Drug Trafficking: A Review', *Journal of Drug Issues*, 37(4): 827–844.

—— (2005) *The Crime That Pays: Drug Trafficking and Organized Crime in Canada*, Toronto: Canadian Scholars' Press.

Diaz-Cotto, J. (2005) 'Latinas and the War on Drugs', in J. Sudbury (Oparah), *Global Lockdown: Race, Gender, and the Prison-Industrial Complex*, New York, N.Y.; London, Routledge.

Dirección Nacional de Estupefacientes (DNE) (2002) *Las "Mulas" del Eje Cafetero: Una aproximación multidisciplinaria al fenómeno de los correos humanosinternacionales del narcotráfico*, Dirección Nacional de Estupefacientes, Colombia: Programa de las Naciones Unidas para la Fiscalización Internacional de Drogas.

Dirección Nacional de Rehabilitación Social (DNRS) (2005) 'El sistema penitenciario Ecuatoriano en cifras', unpublished bulletin.

Dorado, M.-C. (2005) 'Desventajas del castigo penal 'exclusivo' a las colombianas, mensajeras de drogas en Europa, in M. T. Martín Palomo, M. J. Miranda López, and C. Vega Solís (eds), *Delitos y Fronteras: Mujeres extranjeras en prisión*, Madrid: Editorial Complutense.

Dorado, M. C. (1996) 'A Comparative Study of Columbian Women Prisoners in the UK, the Netherlands, Germany and Spain', European Conference on Drug Couriers, Männendorf, Switzerland: Conference Permanente Europeende la Probation, Hertogenbosch, Netherlands.

Dorn, N., K. Murji and N. South (1992) *Traffickers: Drug Markets and Law Enforcement*, London, Routledge.

Dorn, N., Levi, M. and L. King (2005) *Literature Review on Upper Level Drug Trafficking*, London: Home Office.

Dorn, T., M. Ceelan, M. Buster, K. Keijzer, and C. Das (2008) 'Prevalence of Drug Body Packing in Amsterdam, the Netherlands', Poster presented at the European Conference of Criminology, Edinburgh.

Dunlap, E., Johnson, B. and Manwar, A. (1994) 'A Successful Female Crack Dealer: Case Study of a Deviant Career', *Deviant Behavior*, 15(1): 1–25.

Eakin, P. J. (1999) *How Our Lives Become Stories: Making Selves*, Ithaca, NY: Cornell University Press.

Edwards, A. and P. Gill (2002) 'Crime as Enterprise? The Case of "Transnational Organised Crime"', *Crime Law and Social Change*, 37(3): 203–223.

Edwards, S. G. (2011) 'A Short History of Ecuador's Drug Legislation and the Impact on Its Prison Population', in P. Metaal and C. Youngers (eds), *Systems Overload: Drug Laws and Prisons in Latin America*, Amsterdam/Washington: Trans National Institute/Washington Office on Latin America.

—— (2003) *Illicit Drug Control Policies and Prisons: The Human Cost*, Washington: Washington Office on Latin America.

El Comercio (17 October 2013) 'Baltasar Garzón pide que el hacinamiento en la cárcel de mujeres se resuelva', El Comercio.

—— (2 September2006) 'Una guía fue baleada ayer en la puerta de la cárcel de mujeres', no author, http://www.elcomercio.com/politica/baleada-ayer-puerta-carcel-mujeres_0_131389467.html.

El Telégrafo, (2013) 'La nueva tabla para consumo de drogas es una guía para jueces', *El telegrafo*, Ecuador.

European Monitoring Centre for Drugs and Drug Addiction (EMCCDA) (2012) *A Definition of "Drug Mules" for Use in a European Context*, Lisbon: European Monitoring Centre for Drugs and Drug Addiction.

—— (2010) *Cocaine: A European Union Perspective in the Global Context*, Lisbon: European Monitoring Centre for Drugs and Drug Addiction.

Emirbayer, M. and A. Mische (1998) 'What is agency?', *American Journal of Sociology*, 103(4): 962–1023.

England, P. (1989) 'A Feminist Critique of Rational Choice Theories', *The American Sociologist*, 20(10): 14–28.

Eschle, C. (2010) 'Feminist Studies of Globalisation: Beyond Gender, Beyond Economism?', *Global Society*, 18(2): 98–125.

Erel, U. (2010) 'Migrating Cultural Capital: Bourdieu in Migration Studies', *Sociology*, 44(4): 642–660.

Evans, R. and G. Couzens (12 August 2013) 'Are Ibiza Gangs Targeting Britons as Drug Mules? Girls Face 25 Years in Jail "for Smuggling £1.5 Million of Cocaine"', *Mail Online*.

Fagan, J. (1994) 'Women and Drugs Revisited: Female Participation in the Cocaine Economy', *The Journal of Drug Issues*, 24 (Winter/Spring).

Ferber, M. A. and J. A. Nelson (1993) *Beyond Economic Man: Feminist Theory and Economics*, Chicago; London: The University of Chicago Press.

Ferrell, J. (2006) 'The Aesthetics of Cultural Criminology', in B. A. Arrigo and C. R. Williams (eds), *Philosophy, Crime, and Criminology*, Urbana, Ill.: University of Illinois Press: Chesham.

Fiandaca, G. (2007a) 'Introduction', in G. Fiandaca (ed.), *Women and the Mafia: Female Roles in Organized Crime Structures*, New York, London: Springer.

Fiandaca, G. (ed.) (2007b) *Women and the Mafia: Female Roles in Organized Crime Structures*, New York, London: Springer.

Findlay, M. (1999) *The Globalisation of Crime: Understanding Transitional Relationships in Context*, Cambridge: Cambridge University Press.
Firestone, S. (1972) *The Dialectic of Sex*, London: Paladin.
Fleetwood, J. (2014) 'Keeping Out of Trouble: Women Crack Cocaine Dealers in England' *European Journal of Criminology*, 11(1).
—— (2011) 'Five Kilos: Penalties and Practice in the International Cocaine Trade', *British Journal of Criminology*, 51(2): 375–393.
—— (2009) 'Emotional Work: Ethnographic Fieldwork in Prisons in Ecuador', *E-Sharp*, Special Issue: Researching Hidden Communities: 28–50.
Fleetwood, J. and A. Torres (2011) 'Mothers and Children of the International Drug War', in D. Barrett (ed.), *Children of the Drug War*, International Harm Reduction Association/idebate.
Fleetwood, J. and N. Urquiza Haas (2011) 'Gendering the Agenda: Women Drug Mules in Resolution 52/1 of the Commission of Narcotic Drugs at the United Nations', *Drugs and Alcohol Today*, 11(4): 194–203.
Flores Aguirre, X. A. (2007) 'La detención en firme: Crítica de un continuo fraude de la Constitución y la Ley de la República del Ecuador', *URVIO: revista Latinoamericana de Seguridad Cuidana*, 1: 23–30.
Fortson, R. (2012) *Misuse of Drugs and Drug Trafficking Offences*, 4th ed. London: Sweet & Maxwell.
Foucault, M. (1981) *The History of Sexuality. Vol. 1: An Introduction*, Harmondsworth: Penguin.
—— (1972) *The Archaeology of Knowledge and the Discourse on Language*, New York: Pantheon.
Fox, K. J. (1999) 'Changing Violent Minds: Discursive Correction and Resistance in the Cognitive Treatment of Violent Offenders in Prison', *Social Problems*, 46(1): 88–103.
Francis, B., L. Humphreys, S. Kirby, and K. Soothill (2013) *Understanding Criminal Careers in Organised Crime*, Research Report 74, London: Home Office.
Francis, D. (27 August 2008) 'The Young Women Targeted as Mules by Cocaine Smugglers', *The Guardian*.
Fraser, A. (2013b). 'Street Habitus: Gangs, Territorialism and Social Change in Glasgow', *Journal of Youth Studies*, (ahead-of-print), 1–16.
—— (2013a) 'Ethnography at the Periphery: Redrawing the Borders of Criminology's World-Map', *Theoretical Criminology*, 17(2): 251–260.
Fraser, H. (2005) 'Women, Love and Intimacy 'Gone Wrong': Fire, Wind and Ice', *Affilia*, 20(1): 10–20.
—— (2003) 'Narrating Love and Abuse in Intimate Relationships', *British Journal of Social Work*, 33(3): 273–290.
Fraser, N. (1995) "From redistribution to recognition? Dilemmas of justice in a 'post socialist' age", *New Left Review*, 212: 68–94.
Fukumi, S. (2008) *Cocaine Trafficking in Latin America: EU and US Policy Responses*, London: Ashgate.
Gallahue, P. and R. Lines (2010) *The Death Penalty for Drug Offences: Global Overview 2010*, London: Harm Reduction International.
Gallardo, C. and J. Nuñez (2006) Una lectura cuantativa del sistema de cárceles en Ecuador. Quito, Programa de estudios de la cuidad, FLACSO.
Galloway, R. (16 August 2013) 'Are you kidding?', *The Sun* (England).

Garces, C. (2010) 'The Cross Politics of Ecuador's Penal State', *Cultural Anthropology*, 25(3): 459–496.

Gaskins, S. (2004) 'Women of Circumstance – The Effects of Mandatory Minimum Sentencing on Women Minimally Involved in Drug Crimes', *American Criminal Law Review*, 41(1533).

Gelsthorpe, L. (2004) 'Female Offending: A Theoretical Overview', in G. McIvor (ed.), *Women Who Offend*, London: Jessica Kingsley Publishers.

—— (1990) 'Feminist Methodologies in Criminology: A New Approach or Old Wine in New Bottles?', in L. Gelsthorpe and A. Morris (eds), *Feminist Perspectives in Criminology*, Milton Keynes: Open University Press.

—— (1989) *Sexism and the Female Offender*, Aldershot: Ashgate.

Gelsthorpe, L. and A. Morris (2002) 'Women's Imprisonment in England and Wales: A Penal Paradox', *Criminology and Criminal Justice*, 2(3): 277–301.

Gergen, K. J. and Gergen, M. M. (1988) 'Narrative and the Self as Relationship', *Advances in Experimental Social Psychology*, 21(1): 17–56.

Giacomello, C. (2013b) *Mujeres, Delitos de Drogas y Sistemas Penitenciarios en América Latina*, London: International Drug Policy Consortium.

—— (2013a) *Género, Drogas y Prisión: Experiencia de Mujeres Privadas de su Libertad en México*, D.F. Mexico: Tirant lo blanch.

Gillan, A. (1 October 2003) 'Struggle for Everyday Survival That Forces Women to Risk the Dangers of the Drug Run', *The Guardian*.

Gilligan, C. (1982) *In a Different Voice: Psychological Theory and Women's Development*, London: Harvard University Press.

Gootenberg, P. (1999) 'Introduction: Cocaine: The Hidden Histories', *Cocaine: Global Histories*, London: Routledge.

Goffman, E. (1968) *Stigma: Notes on the Management of Spoiled Identity*, London: Penguin.

Gottwald, M. (2006) 'Asylum Claims and Drug Offences: The Seriousness Threshold of Article 1F(B) of the 1951 Convention Relating to the Status of Refugees and the UN Drug Conventions', *International Journal of Refugee Law*, 16: 81–117.

Green, P. (1998) *Drugs, Trafficking and Criminal Policy: The Scapegoat Strategy*, Winchester: Waterside Press.

—— (1996) 'Introduction', in P. Green (ed.), *Drug Couriers: A New Perspective*, London: Waterside Press.

—— (1991) *Drug Couriers*, London: Howard League.

Green, P., C. Mills, and T. Read (1994) 'The Characteristics and Sentencing of Illegal Drug Importers', *British Journal of Criminology*, 34(4): 479–486.

Gregory, S. and M. Tierney (2002) *Forget You Had a Daughter: Doing Time in the 'Bangkok Hilton' – Sandra Gregory's Story*, London: Vision.

Grundetjern, H. and S. Sandberg (2012) 'Dealing with a Gendered Economy: Female Drug Dealers and Street Capital', *European Journal of Criminology*, 9(6): 621–635.

Gubrium, J. F. and J. A. Holstein (2008) 'Narrative Ethnography', in S. N. Hesse-Biber and P. Leavy (eds), *Handbook of Emergent Methods*, New York: The Guidford Press, 241–264.

—— (1998) 'Narrative Practice and the Coherence of Personal Stories', *The Sociological Quarterly*, 39(1): 163–187.

Guo, J.-y. (2012) '"Anyone in My Shoes Will End Up Like Me": Female Inmates' Discourse of Responsibility for Crime', *Discourse & Society*, 23(1): 34–46.

Hallsworth, S. and T. Young (2008) 'Crime and Silence: "Death and Life Are in the Power of the Tongue" (Proverbs 18:21)', *Theoretical Criminology*, 12(2): 131–152.

Hardie-Bick, J., J. Sheptycki, and A. Wardak (2005) 'Introduction: Transnational and Comparative Criminology in a Global Perspective', in J. Sheptycki and A. Wardak (eds), *Transnational and Comparative Criminology*. London: Glasshouse.

Harding, S. G. (1987) *Feminism and Methodology: Social Science Issues*, Bloomington: Indiana University Press.

Harris, G. (2011) *Expert Seminar on Proportionality of Sentencing for Drug Offences, London 20th May 2011, proceedings*, International Drug Policy Consortium, Transnational Institute and Sentencing Council.

Harper, R., G. C. Harper, and J. E. Stockdale (2000) 'The Role and Sentencing of Women in Drug Trafficking Crime', *Legal and Criminological Psychology*, 7(1): 101–114.

Haywood, C. and M. Mac an Ghaill (2003) *Men and Masculinities: Theory, Research and Social Practice*, Buckingham: Open University Press.

Heaven, O. (1996) 'Hibiscus: Working with Nigerian Women', in P. Green (ed.), *Drug Couriers: A New Perspective*, London: Quartet.

Heidensohn, F. (2006) 'New perspectives and established views', in F. Heidensohn (ed.), *Gender and Justice: New Concepts and Approaches*, Cullompton, Devon, Portland, OR: Willan.

—— (1968) 'The Deviance of Women: A Critique and an Enquiry', *The British Journal of Sociology*, 19(2): 160–175.

Heinemann, A., S. Miyaishi, S. Iwersen, A. Schmoldt, and K. Püschel (1998) 'Body-packing as cause of unexpected sudden death', *Forensic Science International*, 92(1): 1–10.

Henne, K. and E. Troshynski (2013) 'Mapping the Margins of Intersectionality: Criminological Possibilities in a Transnational World', *Theoretical Criminology*, 17(4): 455–473.

Her Majesty's Government (2011) *Local to Global: Reducing the Risk from Organised Crime*, London: Home Office.

Herrera, M. (2005) *El Comité: La Toma del Penal Garcia Moreno* (film), Ecuador: FLACSO.

Heyl, B. S. (2001) 'Ethnographic Interviews', in P. Atkinson, A. Coffey, S. Delamont, J. Lofland and L. H. Lofland (eds), *Handbook of Ethnography*, London: SAGE.

Hobbs, D. (2013) *Lush Life: Constructing Organized Crime in the UK*, Oxford: Clarendon.

—— (2001) 'The Firm: Organizational Logic and Criminal Culture on a Shifting Terrain', *British Journal of Criminology*, 41(4): 549–560.

—— (1998) 'Going Down the Glocal: The Local Context of Organised Crime', *The Howard Journal*, 37(4): 407–422.

—— (1995) *Bad Business: Professional Crime in Great Britain*, Oxford: Oxford University Press.

Hochschild, A. R. (1979) 'Emotion Work, Feeling Rules, and Social-Structure', *American Journal of Sociology*, 85(3): 551–575.

Hoefinger, H. (2013) *Sex, Love and Money in Cambodia: Professional Girlfriends and Transactional Relationships*, London: Routledge.

Holstein, J. A. and J. F. Gubrium (2000) *The Self We Live By: Narrative Identity in a Post Modern World*, Oxford: Oxford University Press.

Home Office (2011) *Future Directions for Organised Crime Research*, London: Home Office.

hooks, b. (1984) *Feminist theory: From Margin to Centre*, Boston: South End Press.

—— (1982) *Ain't I A Woman: Black Women and Feminism*, London: Pluto.

Huling, T. (1996) 'Prisoners of War: Drug couriers in the United States', in P. Green (ed.), *Drug Couriers: A New Perspective*, London: Quartet.

—— (1995) 'Women Drug Couriers: Sentencing Reform Needed for Prisoners of War', *Criminal Justice*, 9: 15–19.

Ianni, F. and I. Reus-Ianni (1972) *A Family Business: Kinship and Social Control in Organised Crime*, London: Routledge and Kegan Paul.

Ianni, F. A. (1974) 'Form and Social Organisation in an Organised Crime "Family": A Case Study', *University of Florida Law Review*, 24: 31–41.

Iakobishvili, E. (2012) *Cause for Alarm: The Incarceration of Women for Drug Offences in Europe, Central Asia and the Need for Legislative and Sentencing Reform*, London: Harm Reduction International.

Ilan, J. (2013) 'Street Social Capital in the Liquid City', *Ethnography*, 14(1): 3–24.

Illouz, E. (1997) *Consuming the Romantic Utopia*, Berkeley: University of California Press.

Irwin, K., (2006) 'Into the Dark Heart of Ethnography: The Lived Ethics and Inequality of Intimate Field Relationships', *Qualitative Sociology*, 29(2): 155–175.

Jackson, M. (2002) *The Politics of Storytelling: Violence, Transgression and Intersubjectivity*, Copenhagen: Museum Tusculanum Press (University of Copenhagen).

Jackson, S. (2001) 'Why a Materialist Feminism Is (Still) Possible – and Necessary', *Women's Studies International Forum*, 24(3–4): 289–293.

——(1998) 'Telling Stories: Memory, Narrative and Experience in Feminist Research and Theory', in K. Henwood, C. Griffin, and A. Phoenix (eds), *Standpoints and Differences : Essays in the Practice of Feminist Psychology*, London: Sage.

—— (1993) 'Even Sociologists Fall in Love: An Exploration in the Sociology of Emotions', *Sociology*, 27: 201–220.

Jacobs, B. A. (2006) 'The case for dangerous fieldwork', in D. Hobbs and R. Wright (eds), *The Sage Handbook of Fieldwork*, London: SAGE.

Jacobs, B. A. and J. Miller (1998) 'Crack Dealing, Gender, and Arrest Avoidance', *Social Problems*, 45(4): 550–569.

Jamieson, L. (1998) *Intimacy: Personal Relationships in Modern Societies*, Cambridge: Polity.

Jeavans, C. (3 October 2005) 'Sunshine Island's Deadly Trade', *BBC News Online*.

Jewkes, Y. (2012) 'Autoethnography and Emotion as Intellectual Resources: Doing Prison Research Differently', *Qualitative Inquiry*, 18(1): 63–75.

—— (2009) *Media and Crime*, 2nd ed. London: Sage.

Joe, K. A. and M. Chesney-Lind (1995) 'Just Every Mothers Angel – an Analysis of Gender and Ethnic Variations in Youth Gang Membership', *Gender & Society*, 9(4): 408–431.

Joseph, J. (2006) 'Drug Offences, Gender, Ethnicity, and Nationality – Women in Prison in England and Wales', *Prison Journal*, 86(1): 140–157.

Katz, J. (1988) *Seductions of Crime: The Moral and Sensual Attractions of Doing Evil*, New York: Basic Books.

Kalunta-Crumpton, A. (1998) 'Drug Trafficking and Criminal Justice', *International Journal of the Sociology of Law*, 26(3): 321–338.

Kane, S. (1998) 'Reversing the Ethnographic Gaze: Experiments', in J. Ferrell and M. S. Hamm (eds), *Cultural Criminology. Ethnography at the Edge: Crime, Deviance, And Field Research*, Boston: Northeastern University Press.

Kelly, J., Corrigan, M., Cahill, R., and Redmond, H. (2007) 'Contemporary Management of Drug-Packers', *World Journal of Emergency Surgery*, 2(1): 9–14.

Kenney, M. (2007) 'The Architecture of Drug Trafficking: Network Forms of Organisation in the Colombian Cocaine Trade', *Global Crime*, 8(3): 233–259.

Kenway, J. and J. Fahey (2009) 'Imagining Research Otherwise', in J. Kenway and J. Fahey (eds), *Globalizing the Research Imagination*, London: Routledge.

Kleemans, E. R. and C. J. de Poot. (2008) 'Criminal Careers in Organized Crime and Social Opportunity Structure', *European Journal of Criminology*, 5(1): 69–98.

Kleemans, E. R. and H. van de Bunt (1999) 'The Social Embeddedness of Organized Crime', *Transnational Organized Crime*, 5(1): 19–36.

Klein, A. (2009) 'Mules or Couriers: The Role of Nigerian Drug Couriers in the International Drug Trade', in M. Childs and T. Falola (eds), *The Changing Worlds of Atlantic Africa : Essays in Honor of Robin Law*, Durham, North Carolina: Carolina Academic Press, 411–429.

—— (2008) *Drugs and the World*, London: Reaktion Books.

Klein, D. (1995) 'The Etiology of Female Crime', in J. Muncie and E. McLoughlin (eds), *Criminological Perspective: Reader*, London: Sage.

Kohn, M. (1992) *Dope Girls: The Birth of the British Drug Underground*, London: Lawrence & Wishart.

Krais, B. (2006) 'Gender, Sociological Theory and Bourdieu's Sociology of Practice', *Theory, Culture & Society*, 23(6): 119–134.

Krebs, C. P., M. T. Costelloe, and D. Jenks (2000) 'Black Powder Drugs: An Innovative Response to Drug Control Policy', *International Journal of Drug Policy*, 11: 351–356.

Laidler, K. J. and G. Hunt (2001) 'Accomplishing Femininity Among the Girls in the Gang', *British Journal of Criminology*, 41(4): 656–678.

Lawrence, S. N. and T. Williams (2006) 'Swallowed Up: Drug Couriers at the Borders of Canadian Sentencing', *University of Toronto Law Journal*, 56(4): 285–332.

Lee, R. (1995) *Dangerous Fieldwork*, London: Sage.

Leonard, E. B. (1982) *Women, Crime and Society: A Critique of Criminological Theory*, London: Longman.

Levi, M. (2007) 'Organized Crime and Terrorism', in M. Maguire, R. Morgan, and R. Reiner (eds), *The Oxford Handbook of Criminology*, 4th ed. Oxford: Oxford University Press.

Lines, R. (2007) 'The Ultimate Price', *Druglink*, (July), Drugscope, UK.

Lloyd, A. (1995) *Doubly Deviant, Doubly Damned: Society's Treatment of Violent Women*, London: Penguin.

Lommel, U. (1979) *Cocaine Cowboys* (film), US.

Lovell, T. (2000) 'Thinking Feminism with and against Bourdieu', *Feminist Theory*, 1(1): 11–32.

Lumsden, K. (2009) '"Don't Ask a Woman to Do Another Woman's Job": Gendered Interactions and the Emotional Ethnographer', *Sociology*, 43(3): 497–513.

Madsen, F. G. (2009) *Transnational Organised Crime*, London: Routledge.

Mac an Ghaill, M. and C. Haywood (2007) *Gender, Culture and Society: Contemporary Femininities and Masculinities*, Basingstoke: Palgrave MacMillan.

Maher, L. (1997) *Sexed Work: Gender, Race, and Resistance in a Brooklyn Drug Market*, Oxford: Clarendon Press.

Malone, C. (18 August 2013) 'Are Drug Girls Really Victims?', *Daily Mirror.*

Marez, C. (2004) *Drug Wars: The Political Economy of Narcotics*, Minneapolis: University of Minnesota Press.

Marshall, E. and Moreton, K. (2011) *Drug 'Mules': Twelve Case Studies*, London: Sentencing Council.

Marston, J. (2005) *Maria Full of Grace* (film), US.

Martel, S. (2013) 'The Recruitment of Female "Mules" by Transnational Criminal Organizations Securitization of Drug Trafficking in the Philippines and Beyond', *Social Transformations*, 1(2): 13–41.

Maruna, S. (2001) *Making Good: How Ex-Convicts Reform and Rebuild Their Lives*, Washington, D.C.: American Psychological Association Press.

Maruna, S., L. Wilson, and K. Curran (2006) 'Why God Is Often Found Behind Bars: Prison Conversions and the Crisis of Self-Narrative', *Research in Human Development*, 3(2): 161–184.

Maton, K. (2008) 'Habitus', in M. Grenfell (ed.), *Pierre Bourdieu: Key Concepts*, Durham: Acumen.

Matrix Knowledge Group (2007) *The Illicit Drug Trade in the United Kingdom*, London: LSE/Home Office.

Matthews, R. (2009) 'Beyond "So What?" Criminology: Rediscovering Realism', *Theoretical Criminology*, 13(3): 341–362.

—— (1997) *Prostitution in London: An Audit*, Faculty of Social Science, Middlesex University.

McGuire, D. M. (2011) 'Doing the Life: An Exploration of the Connection between the Inmate Code and Violence Among Female Inmates', *Journal of the Institute of Justice & International Studies*, 11: 145–158.

Mcivor, G. and M. Burman (2011) *Understanding the Drivers of Female Imprisonment in Scotland*, Glasgow: SCCJR.

McKendy, J. P. (2006) '"I'm Very Careful about That": Narrative and Agency of Men in Prison', *Discourse & Society*, 17(4): 473–502.

McKinley (Jr). J. C. (11 October 2010) 'In Mexico, a Fugitive's Arrest Captivates the Cameras', *The New York Times.*

McMahon, V. and E. McMenamy (11 August 2013) '"Someone Must Have Taken Advantage of Michaella, She's Only 20 Years Old" Family's Horror after Irish Girl Is Held in Peru Drug Bust', *Daily Mirror*, UK.

McNay, L. (2004) 'Agency and Experience: Gender as a Lived Relation', *The Sociological Review*, 52 (Supplemental Issue): 173–190.

—— (2000) *Gender and Agency: Reconfiguring the Subject in Feminist and Social Theory*, Cambridge: Polity Press.

—— (1999) 'Gender, Habitus and the Field: Pierre Bourdieu and the Limits of Reflexivity', *Theory, Culture & Society*, 16(1): 95–117.

Measham, F. (2002) '"Doing Gender"—"Doing Drugs": Conceptualizing the Gendering of Drugs Cultures', *Contemporary Drug Problems*, 29(2).

Measham, F., K. Moore, and J. Østergaard (2011) 'Mephedrone, "Bubble" and Unidentified White Powders: The Contested Identities of Synthetic "Legal Highs"', *Drugs and Alcohol Today*, 11(3): 137–146.
Merton, R. (1968) *Social Theory And Social Structure*, London: Collier-Macmillan.
—— (1938) 'Social Structure and Anomie', *American Sociological Review*, 3: 672–682.
Messerschmidt, J. (2005) 'Men, Masculinities and Crime', in M. S. Kimmel, J. Hearn, and R. Connell (eds), *Handbook of Studies on Men & Masculinities*, Thousand Oaks, CA: Sage Publications.
—— (1997) *Crime as Structured Action: Gender, Race, Class and Crime in the Making*, London: Sage.
—— (1995) 'From Patriarchy to Gender: Feminist Theory, Criminology and the Challenge of Diversity', in N. H. Rapter and F. Heidensohn (eds), *International Feminist Perspectives in Criminology: Engendering a Discipline*, Buckingham: Open University Press.
—— (1993) *Masculinities and Crime: Critique and Reconceptualisation of Theory*, Lanham, Md.: Rowman & Littlefield.
Metaal, P. and S. Edwards (2009) 'Pardon for Mules in Ecuador, a Sound Proposal', *Series on Legislative Reform of Drug Policies*, Washington: Washington Office on Latin America.
Miller, J. (2002) 'The Strengths and Limits of "Doing Gender" for Understanding Street Crime', *Theoretical Criminology*, 6(4): 433–460.
—— (2001) *One of the Guys: Girls, Gangs, and Gender*, Oxford: Oxford University Press.
—— (1998) 'Up It Up: Gender and the Accomplishment of Street Robbery', *Criminology*, 36(1): 37–66.
Ministry of Justice (2012) *Offender Management Statistics Quarterly Bulletin, October to December 2011*, London: Ministry of Justice.
Moi, T. (1991) 'Appropriating Bourdieu: Feminist Theory and Pierre Bourdieu's Sociology of Culture', *New Literary History*, 22(4): 1017–1049.
Mohanty, C. T. (2003) *Feminism Without Borders: Decolonizing Theory, Practicing Solidarity*, Durham: Duke University Press.
Mohanty, C. T. (1991) 'Under Western Eyes: Feminist Scholarship and Colonial Discourses', in C. T. Mohanty, A. Russo, and L. Torres (eds), *Third World Women and the Politics of Feminism*, Bloomington and Indianapolis, IN: Indiana University Press.
Moir, J. (15 August 2013) 'Yes, Their Story Might Be True. but Those Silly Girls Were Their Own Worst Enemies', *Mail Online*.
Morgan, P. and K. Joe (1996) 'Citizens and Outlaws: The Private Lives and Public Lifestyles of Women in the Illicit Drug Economy', *Journal of Drug Issues*, 26(1): 125–142.
Morris, S. (10 December 2007) 'Detection System Criticised after "Drug Mule" Death', *The Guardian*.
Morselli, C. (2001) 'Structuring Mr. Nice: Entrepreneurial Opportunities and Brokerage Positing in the Cannabis Trade', *Crime, Law and Social Change*, 35: 203–244.
Mujeres de Frente (ed.) (2006) *Sitiadas: Un trabajo de mujeres hartas de su situación*, Quito: Mujeres de frente: externas e internas en la cárcel de mujeres de Quito.
Mulchandani, R. and T. Hand (2010) *Seizures of Drugs in England and Wales, 2009/10*, London: Home Office.

Mullins, C. W. (2006) *Holding Your Square: Masculinities, Streetlife, and Violence*, Cullompton, England: Willan.
Mullins, C. W. and Wright, R. (2003) 'Gender, Social Networks and Residential Burglary', *Criminology*, 41(3): 813–840.
Murji, K. (2007) 'Hierarchies, Markets and Networks: Ethnicity/Race and Drug Distribution', *Journal of Drug Issues*, 37(4): 781–804.
Natarajan, M. (2000) 'Understanding the Structure of a Drug Trafficking Organization: A Conversational Analysis', *Crime Prevention Studies*, 11: 273–298.
—— (1998) 'Varieties of Drug Trafficking Organizations: A Typology of Cases Prosecuted in New York City', *Journal of Drug Issues*, 28(4).
Newburn, T. (2002) 'Atlantic Crossings: "Policy Transfer" and Crime Control in the USA and Britain', *Punishment & Society*, 4: 165–194.
Norton-Hawk, M. (2010) 'Exporting Gender Injustice: The Impact of the U.S. War on Drugs on Ecuadorian Women', *Critical Criminology*, 18(2): 132–146.
Norrie, A. (1986) 'Practical reasoning and criminal responsibility: A jurisprudential approach', in D. B. Cornish and R. V. G. Clarke (eds), *The Reasoning Criminal: Rational Choice Perspectives on Offending*, New York: Springer-Verlag.
Nuñez, J. (2007) 'Las cárceles en la epoca del narcotráfico: una mirada etnográfica', *Nueva Sociedad*, 208 (Marzo-Abril).
—— (2006b) 'La crisis del sistema penitenciario en Ecuador', *Ciudad Segura (Boletín)*. Programa de Estudios de la Ciudad, Quito: FLACSO sede Ecuador: 4–9.
—— (2006a) *Cacería de brujos: drogas 'illegales' y sistema de cárceles en el Ecuador*, Quito, Ecuador: FLACSO, Ecuador; Abya-yala.
O'Brien, K. (forthcoming) *Gender, Drugs and Street Life: An Ethnography of a British Housing Estate*, London: Routledge.
—— (2009) 'Inside Doorwork: Gendering the Security Gaze', in R. Ryan-Floor and R. Gill (eds), *Silence and Secrecy in the Research Process: Feminist Reflections*, London: Routledge.
O'Neill, M. and L. Seal (2012) *Transgressive Imaginations: Crime, Deviance and Culture*, Basingstoke: Palgrave Macmillan.
Oakley, A. (1996) *Own or Other Culture*, London: Routledge.
—— (1981) 'Interviewing Women: A Contradiction in Terms?', in Helen Roberts (ed.), *Doing Feminist Research*, London: Routledge.
Okin, S. M. (1979) *Women in Western Political Thought*, Princeton, NJ, Guildford: Princeton University Press.
Oliss, P. (1994) 'Mandatory Minimum Sentencing: Discretion, the Safety Valve and the Sentencing Guidelines', *University of Cincinnati Law Review*, 63: 1851–1892.
Palma Campos, C. (2011) 'Delito y sobrevivencia: Las mujeres que ingresan a la cárcel el buen pastor en Costa Rica por tráfico de drogas', *Anuario de Estudios Centroamericanos de Costa Rica*, 37: 245–270.
Paoli, L. (2005) 'Italian Organised Crime: Mafia Associations and Criminal Enterprises', in M. Galeotti (ed.), *Global Crime Today*, London: Routledge.
—— (2002b) 'The Paradoxes of Organized Crime', *Crime, Law and Social Change*, 37: 51–97.
—— (2002a) 'Flexible Hierarchies and Dynamic Disorder: The Drug Distribution System in Frankfurt and Milan', *Drugs-Education Prevention and Policy*, 9(2): 143–151.

—— (2001) 'Drug Trafficking in Russia: A Form of Organized Crime?', *Journal of Drug Issues*, 31(4): 1007–1037.
Paternoster, R. and Bushway, S. (2009) 'Desistance and the "Feared Self": Toward an Identity Theory of Criminal Desistance', *The Journal of Criminal Law and Criminology*, 99(4): 1103–1156.
Pearson, G. and D. Hobbs (2003) 'King Pin? A Case Study of a Middle Market Drug Broker', *The Howard Journal of Criminal Justice*, 42(4): 335–347.
—— (2001) *Middle Market Drug Distribution*, London: Home Office Research, Development and Statistics Directorate.
Phoenix, J. (2000) 'Prostitute Identities – Men, Money and Violence', *British Journal of Criminology*, 40(1): 37–55.
Piacentini, L. (2004) *Surviving Russian Prisons: Punishment, Economy and Politics in Transition*, Cullompton: Willan.
Pickering, S. and C. Lambert (eds) (2004) *Global Issues: Women and Justice*, Syndney: Sydney Institute of Criminology.
Platell, A. (18 August 2013) 'Spare Your Pity for the Drug Girl's Poor Dad', *Mail Online*.
Plummer, K. (2000) 'A World in the Making: Symbolic Interactionism in the Twentieth Century', in Bryan S. Turner (ed.), *The Blackwell Companion to Sociology*, 2nd ed. Oxford: Blackwell, 193–222.
Polsky, N. (1985) *Hustlers, Beats, and Others*, Chicago and London: The University of Chicago Press.
Pontón, J. (2013) 'Presentacion', *URVIO: Revista Latinoamericana de Seguridad Cuidadana*, 13: 7–10.
—— (2008) 'Mujeres, cuerpo y encierro: acomodo y resistencias al sistema penitenciario', in K. Aruajo and M. Prieto (eds), *Estudios sobre sexualidades en America Latina*, Quito, Ecuador: FLACSO, Ecuador, 309–330.
—— (2005) 'Mujeres que cruzaron la linea: Vida cotidiana en el encierro' (report), Estudios de la Cuidad, Quito: FLACSO.
Pontón, J. and A. Torres (2007) 'Cárceles del Ecuador: los efectos de la criminalización por drogas', *URVIO: Revista Latinoamericana de Seguridad Cuidadana*, 1: 55–73.
Power, N. (2009) *One dimensional woman*, Winchester, UK: O Books.
Presser, L. (2012) 'Getting on Top through Mass Murder: Narrative, Metaphor, and Violence', *Crime, Media, Culture*, 8(1): 3–21.
—— (2010) 'Collecting and Analyzing the Stories of Offenders', *Journal of Criminal Justice Education*, 21(4): 431–446.
—— (2009) 'The Narratives of Offenders', *Theoretical Criminology*, 13(2): 177–200.
—— (2008) *Been a Heavy Life: Stories of Violent Men*, Urbana, IL: University of Illinois Press.
—— (2005) 'Negotiating Power and Narrative in Research: Implications for Feminist Methodology', *Signs: Journal of Women in Culture and Society*, 30(4): 2067–2090.
Presser, L. and Sandberg, S. (eds) (forthcoming) 'Narrative Criminology: What's the Story', in L. Presser and S. Sandberg (eds), *Crime as Story: An Introduction to Narrative Criminology*, New York: New York University Press.
Radford, L. and K. Tsutsumi (2004) 'Globalization and Violence against Women's Inequalities in Risks, Responsibilities and Blame in the UK and Japan', *Women's Studies International Forum*, 27(1): 1–12.

Raeder, M. S. (1993) 'Gender Issues in the Federal Sentencing Guidelines and Mandatory Minimum Sentences', *Criminal Justice*, 8(20).

Ray, L. (2007) *Globalization and Everyday Life*, London: Routledge.

Reissman, C. K. (2008) *Narrative Methods for the Human Sciences*, London: Sage.

—— (1993) *Narrative Analysis*, London: Sage.

Renzetti, C. (2013) *Feminist Criminology*, London: Routledge.

Reuter, P. (1983) *Disorganized Crime: The Economics of the Visible Hand*, Cambridge, MA, London: MIT Press.

Reuter, P. and Haaga, J. (1989) 'The Organization of High-Level Drug Markets: An Exploratory Study', The National Institute of Justice, US Department of Justice.

Reydburd, P. (1994) 'Who Are the Bad Guys? Literary Images of Narcotraffickers', in B. M. Bagley and W. O. Walker (eds), *Drug Trafficking in the Americas*, New Brunswick, NJ, London: Transaction.

Reyes, G. and G. Guillen (28 March 2010) 'Women Break through Glass Ceiling of Drug-Dealing Underworld', *The Miami Herald*.

Reynolds, M. (2008) 'The War on Drugs, Prison Building, and Globalization: Catalysts for the Global Incarceration of Women', *NWSA Journal*, 20(2): 72–95.

Richie, B. (1996) *Compelled to Crime: The Gender Entrapment of Battered Black Women*, New York: Routledge.

Riley, E. (26 August 2013) 'Peru Drug Mules Brag about "Big Wonga"', *Daily Star*, UK.

Ritter, A. (2006) 'Studying Illicit Drug Markets: Disciplinary Contributions', *International Journal of Drug Policy*, 17: 453–463.

Rivera, V. F. (2005) 'Ecuador: Untangling the Drug War', in C. Youngers and E. Rosin (eds), *Drugs and Democracy in Latin America: The Impact of U.S. Policy*, Boulder, CO, London: L. Rienner.

Rossi, A. (2007) 'Women in Organised Crime in Argentina', in G. Fiandaca (ed.), *Women and the Mafia: Female Roles in Organized Crime Structures*, London: Springer.

Ruggiero, V. and N. South (1995) *Eurodrugs: Drug use, Markets and Trafficking in Europe*. London, UCL Press.

Sampson, H. and M. Thomas (2003) 'Lone Researchers at Sea: Gender, Risk and Responsibility', *Qualitative Research*, 3(2): 165–189.

Sandberg, S. (2011) 'Is Cannabis Use Normalized, Celebrated or Neutralized? Analysing Talk as Action', *Addiction Research & Theory*, (1): 1–10.

—— (2010) 'What can "Lies" Tell Us about Life? Notes towards a Framework of Narrative Criminology', *Journal of Criminal Justice Education*, 21(4): 447–465.

—— (2009) 'A Narrative Search for Respect', *Deviant Behavior*, 30(6): 487–510.

—— (2008b) 'Street Capital Ethnicity and Violence on the Streets of Oslo', *Theoretical Criminology*, 12(2): 153–171.

—— (2008a) 'Black Drug Dealers in a White Welfare State: Cannabis Dealing and Street Capital in Norway', *British Journal of Criminology*, 48(5): 604–619.

Sandberg, S. and W. Pederson (2009) *Street Capital: Black Cannabis Dealers in a White Welfare State*, Bristol: The Policy Press.

Sassen, S. (2007) 'Introduction: Deciphering the Global', in S. Sassen (ed.), *Deciphering the Global: Its Scales, Spaces, and Subjects*, London: Routledge.

Schemenauer, E. (2012) 'Victims and Vamps, Madonnas and Whores: The Construction of Female Drug Couriers and the Practices of the US Security State', *International Feminist Journal of Politics*, 14(1): 83–102.

Scheper-Hughes, N. (1995) 'The Primacy of the Ethical – Propositions for a Militant Anthropology', *Current Anthropology*, 36(3): 409–440.

Scott, J. (1992) 'Experience', in J. Butler and J. Scott (eds), *Feminists Theorize the Political*, London: Routledge.

Scott, M. B. and S. M. Lyman (1968) 'Accounts', *American Sociological Review*, 33(1): 46–62.

Seal, L. (2010) *Women, Murder and Femininity: Gender Representations of Women Who Kill*, Basingstoke: Palgrave Macmillan.

Seddon, T. (2008) 'Women, Harm Reduction and History: Gender Perspectives on the Emergence of the "British System" of Drug Control', *International Journal of Drug Policy*, 19(2): 99–105.

Sentencing Council (2012) *Drug Offences: Definitive Guideline*, London: Sentencing Council of England and Wales.

Sentencing Council (2011b) 'Sentencing for Drugs Offences – Public Consultation Launched on New Guideline for Judges', 28 March, http://sentencingcouncil.judiciary.gov.uk/media/571.html (accessed 18/11/2013).

Sentencing Council (2011a) 'Drugs Offences, Analysis and Research Bulletins', London.

Sevigny, E. L. and J. P. Caulkins (2004) 'Kingpins or Mules: An Analysis of Drug Offenders Incarcerated in Federal and State Prisons', *Criminology and Public Policy*, 3(3): 401–434.

Siebert, R. (2007) 'Mafia Women: The Affirmation of a Female Pseudo Subject. the Case of the Ndrangheta', in G. Fiandaca (ed.), *Women and the Mafia : Female Roles in Organized Crime Structures*, New York, London: Springer.

Skeggs, B. (2004) 'Exchange, value and affect: Bourdieu and the "self"', in L. Adkins and B. Skeggs (eds), *Feminism After Bourdieu*, Oxford: Blackwell Publishers.

—— (2001) 'The toilet paper: Femininity, class and misrecognition', *Women's Studies International Forum*, 24(3–4): 295–307.

—— (1997) *Formations of Class and Gender: Becoming Respectable*, London: SAGE.

—— (1995) 'Theorising, Ethics and Representation in Feminist Ethnography', in B. Skeggs (ed.), *Feminist Cultural Theory: Process and Production*, Manchester: Manchester University Press.

—— (1994) 'Situating the Production of Feminist Ethnography', in M. Maynard and J. Purvis (eds), *Researching Women's Lives from a Feminist Perspective*, London: Taylor and Francis.

Sluka, J. A. (1995) 'Reflections on Managing Danger in Fieldwork: Dangerous Anthropology in Belfast', in C. Nordstrom and A. C. M. Robben (eds), *Fieldwork Under Fire: Contemporary Studies of Violence and Survival*, London: University of California Press.

Smart, C. (1989) *Feminism and the Power of Law*, London: Routledge.

—— (1979) 'New Female Criminal – Reality or Myth', *British Journal of Criminology*, 19(1): 50–59.

—— (1977) *Women, Crime and Criminology: A Feminist Critique*, London: Routledge and Kegan Paul.

Smith, C. and E. Wincup (2000) 'Breaking in: Researching Criminal Justice Institutions for Women', in R. D. King and E. Wincup (eds), *Doing Research on Crime and Justice*, Oxford: Oxford University Press.

Smith, D. C. (1994) 'Illicit Enterprise. an Organized Crime Paradigm for the Nineties', in R. J. Kelly, K. Chin, and R. Schatzberg (eds), *Handbook of Crime in the United States*, Westport: Greenwood Publishing Group.

Snider, L. (2003) 'Constituting the Punishable Woman: Atavistic Man Incarcerates Postmodern Woman', *British Journal of Criminology*, 43(2): 354–378.

Soberón Garrido, R. (2013) 'Los intentos de reforma de las políticas sobre drogas en América Latina', *URVIO: Revista Latinoamericana de Seguridad Cuidadana*, 13: 27–39.

—— (2011) 'Drugs Legislation and Prison Population in Peru', in P. Metaal and C. Youngers (eds), *Systems Overload: Drug Laws and Prisons in Latin America*, Transnational Institute/Washington Office on Latin America.

Somers, M. R. (1994) 'The Narrative Construction of Identity: A Relational and Network Approach', *Theory and Society*, 23: 605–649.

Stanley, L. (2000) 'From "Self-Made Women" to "Women's Made-Selves": Audit Selves, Simulation and Surveillance in the Rise of the Public Woman', in T. Cosslett, C. Lury, and P. Summerfield (eds), *Feminism and Autobiography: Texts, Theories, Methods*, London: Routledge.

Stanley, L. and S. Wise (1993) *Breaking Out Again: Feminist Ontology and Epistemology*, 2nd ed. London: Routledge.

Steedman, C. (2000) 'Enforced Narratives: Stories of Another Self', in T. Cosslett, C. Lury, and P. Summerfield (eds), *Feminism and Autobiography: Texts, Theories, Methods*, London: Routledge.

Steffensmeier, D. (1983) 'Organization Properties and Sex-Segregation in the Underworld – Building a Sociological Theory of Sex-Differences in Crime', *Social Forces*, 61(4): 1010–1032.

Steffensmeier, D. and E. Allen (1996) 'Gender and Crime: Towards a Gendered Theory of Female Offending', *Annual Review of Sociology*, 22: 459–487.

Stewart, A., N. D. Heaton, and B. Hogbin (1990) 'Body Packing: A Case Report and Review of the Literature', *Postgraduate Medical Journal*, 66(778): 659–661.

Strange, H. (13 August 2013) 'British Women Accused of Cocaine Smuggling in Peru Protest Innocence', *The Telegraph*.

Strober, M. H. (2003) 'The Application of Mainstream Economic Constructs to Education: A Feminist Analysis', in M. A. Ferber and J. A. Nelson (eds), *Feminist Economics Today: Beyond Economic Man*, Chicago, London: University of Chicago Press.

Stuart, H. (13 November 2003) 'Briton Who Ate 121 Bags of Cocaine Dies', *The Guardian*.

Sturcke, J. (12 July 2007) 'British Teenagers in Ghana Charged Over Drugs', *The Guardian*.

Sudbury (Oparah), J. (2005b) '" Mules", "Yardies" and other folk devils: Mapping cross border imprisonment in Britain', in J. Sudbury (ed.), *Global Lockdown: Race, Gender, and the Prison-Industrial Complex*, New York, London: Routledge.

—— (2005a) 'Introduction: Feminist critiques, transnational landscapes, abolitionist visions', in J. Sudbury (Oparah) (ed.), *Global Lockdown: Race, Gender, and the Prison-Industrial Complex*, New York, London: Routledge.

—— (2004) 'A World without Prisons: Resisting Militarism, Globalized Punishment and Empire', *Social Justice*, 31(1/2): 9–30.

—— (2002) 'Celling Black Bodies: Black Women in the Global Prison Industrial Complex', *Feminist Review*, 70: 57–74.

Swanstrom, N. (2007) 'The Narcotics Trade: A Threat to Security? National and Transnational Implications', *Global Crime*, 8(1): 1–25.

Sweeney, J. (25 September 2013) 'Why No Tears Will Be Shed Over Jailing of Drug Mules', *Belfast Telegraph*.

Sykes, G. (2007) *The Society of Captives: A Study of a Maximum Security Prison*, Princeton: Princeton University Press.

Taylor, A. (1993) *Women Drug Users: An Ethnography of the Female Injecting Community*, Oxford: Clarendon.

Thompson, T. (23 May 2010) 'Britain's Girl Gangsters Are Getting Ready to Fight Their Way to the Top', *The Observer*.

Thoumi, F. E. (2005) 'The Numbers Game: Let's All Guess the Size of the Illegal Drug Industry!', *Journal of Drug Issues*, 35(1): 185–200.

—— (2002) 'Can the United Nations Support "Objective" and Unhampered Illicit Drug Policy Research? a Testimony of a UN Funded Researcher', *Crime, Law and Social Change*, 38(2): 161–183.

Torres, A. (2008) *Drogas, Cárcel y Género en Ecuador: la Experiencia de Mujeres Mulas*, Quito, Ecuador: FLACSO/Abya Yala.

—— (2006) 'El encierro femenino en Ecuador: La persistencia del modelo conventual en un contexto de debilidad institucional' (report), Quito: FLACSO.

Townsend, P. (1979) *Poverty in the United Kingdom: A Survey of Household Resources and Standards of Living*, Harmondsworth: Penguin.

Traub, S. J., R. S. Hoffman, and L. S. Nelson (2003) 'Body Packing: The Internal Concealment of Illicit Drugs', *New England Journal of Medicine*, 349(26): 2519–2526.

Tuckman, J. (6 October 2007) 'Queen of the Pacific Has Mexico Hooked as She Faces Drug Charges', *The Guardian*.

Ugelvik, T. (2012) 'Prisoners and Their Victims: Techniques of Neutralization, Techniques of the Self', *Ethnography*, 13(3): 259–277.

United Nations (2010) *United Nations Rules for the Treatment of Women Prisoners and Non-custodial Measures for Women Offenders (the Bangkok Rules)*, Vienna: United Nations.

—— (1955) *Standard Minimum Rules for the Treatment of Prisoners*, Vienna: United Nations.

United Nations Commission on Narcotic Drugs (UNCND) (2011), 'Promoting International Cooperation in Addressing the Involvement of Women and Girls in Drug Trafficking, Especially as Couriers', Report of the Executive Director, UN doc. E/CN7/2011/7.

—— (2009) 'Promoting International Cooperation in Addressing the Involvement of Women and Girls in Drug Trafficking, Especially as Couriers', Draft Resolution L.7, UN Doc. E/CN.7/2009/L.7/Rev.1, 17 March 2009.

United Nations Office on Drugs and Crime (UNODC) (2013) 'World Drug Report', Vienna: United Nations Office on Drugs and Crime.

—— (2012) 'World Drug Report', Vienna: United Nations Office on Drugs and Crime.

—— (2008) 'World Drug Report', Vienna: United Nations Office on Drugs and Crime.

—— (2005) 'World Drug Report', Vienna: United Nations Office on Drugs and Crime.

United States Drug Enforcement Agency (2013) 'Federal Trafficking Penalties for Schedules I, II, III, IV, and V (except Marijuana)', http://www.justice.gov/dea/druginfo/ftp3.shtml.

Unlu A. and U. Evcin (2011) 'Uyuşturucu Kurye Profiline Madde Türünün Etkisi Ve Önleme Politikalarına Yansımaları', in OÖ Demir, Sever M. (ed.), Örgütlü Suçlar ve Yeni Trendler. Polis Akademisi Yayınları, Ankara, 3–28.

Unlu, A. and B. Ekici (2012) 'The Extent to Which Demographic Characteristics Determine International Drug Couriers' Profiles: A Cross-Sectional Study in Istanbul', *Trends in Organized Crime*, 15(4): 296–312.

Urry, J. (2003) *Global Complexity*, Cambridge: Polity.

—— (2000) 'Mobile Sociology', *British Journal of Sociology*, 51(1): 185–203.

US Department of State (2007) *International Narcotics and Law Enforcement: FY 2008 Program and Budget Guide, September 2007*, Bureau of International Narcotics and Law Enforcement Affairs.

Vale, E. and P. Kennedy (2004) 'Adolescent Drug Trafficking Trends in the United Kingdom: A 10-Year Retrospective Analysis', *Journal of Adolescence*, 27: 749–754.

Van San, M. (2011) 'The Appeal of "Dangerous" Men: On the Role of Women in Organized Crime', *Trends in Organized Crime*, 14(4): 281–297.

van Wormer, K. (2009) 'Anti-Feminist Backlash and Violence against Women Worldwide', *Social Work & Society*, 6(2): 324–337.

Veyrie, N., S. Servajean, A. Aissat, N. Corigliano, C. Angelakovand, and J. Bouillot (2008) 'Value of a Systematic Operative Protocol for Cocaine Body Packers', *World Journal of Surgery*, 32(7): 1432–1437.

Von Lampe, K. (2011) 'The Application of the Framework of Situational Crime Prevention to "Organized Crime"', *Criminology and Criminal Justice*, 11(2): 145–163.

Wacquant, L. (2002) 'The Curious Eclipse of Prison Ethnography in the Age of Mass Incarceration', *Ethnography*, 3(4): 371–397.

—— (1999) 'How Penal Common Sense Comes to Europeans: Notes on the Transatlantic Diffusion of the Neoliberal Doxa', *European Societies-London*, 1(3): 319–335.

Walby, S. (2009) *Globalization and Inequalities: Complexity and Contested Modernities*, London: Sage.

Ward, C. (3 September 2008) 'My Little Girl Was a Drug Mule – Don't Let Your Daughter Be Next', *The Daily Mirror*, London.

Weatherall, A. (2002) *Gender, Language and Discourse*, London: Routledge.

West, C. and D. H. Zimmerman (1987) 'Doing Gender', *Gender and Society*, 1(2): 125–151.

West, C. and S. Festernmaker (1995) 'Doing Difference', *Gender and Society*, 9: 8–37.

Widdicombe, A. (21 August 2013) 'Remember the Real Victims of the Drug Trade', *The Express*.

Williams, T., E. Dunlap, B. D. Johnson, and A. Hamid (1992) 'Personal Safety in Dangerous Places', *Journal of Contemporary Ethnography*, 21(3): 343–374.

Wilson, L. and A. Stevens (2008) *Understanding Drug Markets and How to Influence Them*, London Beckley Foundation.

Winlow, S. (2001) *Badfellas: Crime, Tradition and New Masculinities*, Oxford: Berg.

Woodiwiss, M. and D. Hobbs (2009) 'Organized Evil and the Atlantic Alliance: Moral Panics and the Rhetoric of Organized Crime Policing in America and Britain', *British Journal of Criminology*, 49(1): 106–128.

Wright Mills, C. (1940) 'Situated Actions and Vocabularies of Motive', *American Sociological Review*, 5(6): 904–913.

Wright, A. (2006) *Organised Crime*, Cullompton: Willan Publishing.

Wurtzel, E. (1998) *Bitch: In Praise of Difficult Women*, London: Quartet Books.

Young, A. (1996) *Imagining Crime: Textual Outlaws and Criminal Conversations*, London: Sage.

Young, J. (2007) *The Vertigo of Late Modernity*, Los Angeles, London: Sage.

—— (2003) 'Merton with Energy, Katz with Structure: The Sociology of Vindictiveness and the Criminology of Transgression', *Theoretical Criminology*, 7: 388–414.

—— (1999) *The Exclusive Society: Social Exclusion, Crime and Difference in Late Modernity*, London: Sage.

Young, R. and T. McFadden (2003) *Marching Powder: A True Story of Friendship, Cocaine and South America's Strangest Jail*, Sydney, NSW: Macmillan.

Youngers, C. (2013) 'El debate sobre políticas de drogas en América Latina', *URVIO: Revista Latinoamericana de Seguridad Cuidadana*, 13: 13–25.

Youngers, C. and E. Rosin (2005) 'The US "War on Drugs": Its impact in Latin America and the Caribbean', in C. Youngers and E. Rosin (eds), *Drugs and Democracy in Latin America: The impact of U.S. Policy*, London: L. Rienner.

Zaitch, D. (2005) 'The Ambiguity of Violence, Secrecy, and Trust Among Colombian Drug Entrepreneurs', *Journal of Drug Issues*, 35: 201–228.

—— (2003) 'Recent Trends in Cocaine Trafficking in the Netherlands and Spain', in D. Siegel, H. van de Bunt, and D. Zaitch (eds), *Global Organized Crime: Trends and Developments*, London: Kluwer Law International.

—— (2002) *Trafficking Cocaine: Colombian Drug Entrepreneurs in the Netherlands*, The Hague, London: Kluwer Law International.

Zhang, S. X., C. -L. Chin, and J. Miller (2007) 'Women's Participation in Chinese Transnational Human Smuggling: A Gendered Market Perspective', *Criminology*, 45(3): 699–733.

Index

Entries in **bold** are the most significant.

Printed and bound by CPI Group (UK) Ltd, Croydon, CR0 4YY